COMPUTING FOR SENIORS

QuickSteps™

MARTY MATTHEWS

CAROLE BOGGS MATTHEWS

GARY DAVID BOUTON

BOBBI SANDBERG

McGraw Hill

New York Chicago San Francisco
Lisbon London Madrid Mexico City
Milan New Delhi San Juan
Seoul Singapore Sydney Toronto

The McGraw-Hill Companies

Library of Congress Cataloging-in-Publication Data

Computing for seniors QuickSteps / Marty Matthews ... [et al.].

    p. cm.

  Includes index.

  ISBN-13: 978-0-07-174035-7 (alk. paper)

  ISBN-10: 0-07-174035-X (alk. paper)

  1. Computers and older people—Handbooks, manuals, etc.

  2. Microcomputers—Handbooks, manuals, etc. 3. Computer

literacy—Handbooks, manuals, etc. I. Matthews, Martin S.

  QA76.5.C61726 2011

  004.084'6—dc23

                 2011014721

COMPUTING FOR SENIORS QUICKSTEPS™

34567890   QDB QDB   10987654321

ISBN   978-0-07-174035-7

MHID   0-07-174035-X

SPONSORING EDITOR / Roger Stewart

EDITORIAL SUPERVISOR / Jody McKenzie

PROJECT MANAGER / Vasundhara Sawhney (Glyph International)

ACQUISITIONS COORDINATOR / Joya Anthony

COPY EDITOR / Lisa McCoy

PROOFREADER / Paul Tyler

INDEXER / Valerie Perry

PRODUCTION SUPERVISOR / Jean Bodeaux

COMPOSITION / Glyph International

ILLUSTRATION / Glyph International

ART DIRECTOR, COVER / Jeff Weeks

COVER DESIGNER / Pattie Lee

SERIES CREATORS / Marty and Carole Matthews

SERIES DESIGN / Bailey Cunningham

To all the seniors who have contributed time and
effort to place a part of themselves in this book.
They make this book more readable and
authentic—and enjoyable.
Thanks to all of you!

Acknowledgments

We are, as always, indebted to the editing, layout, proofreading, indexing, and project management expertise of a number of people, only some of whom we know. We thank all of them and, in particular, acknowledge:

Roger Stewart, editorial director and sponsoring editor of this book and the *QuickSteps*™ series

Jody McKenzie, editorial supervisor

Jean Bodeaux, production supervisor

Vasundhara Sawhney, project manager

Joya Anthony, acquisitions coordinator

Valerie Perry, indexer

Lisa McCoy, copy editor

Paul Tyler, proofreader

Glyph International, layout and production

About the Authors

  **Marty and Carole Matthews** have been programmers, system analysts, managers, executives, and entrepreneurs in the software business for many years. For the last 25 years, they have authored, co-authored, or managed the writing and production of more than 100 books. They live on an island in Puget Sound in Washington State.

 **Gary David Bouton** has been illustrating and producing videos for more than 30 years; the co-author, with a background in advertising, has been teaching through books for the past 18 years. His titles include *Adobe Photoshop CS4 QuickSteps™*, *The CorelDraw Official Guide*, and *Xara Xtreme: The Official Guide*, for McGraw-Hill; for Joseph Wiley, *Photoshop Elements for Dummies*. With his wife Barbara, the Boutons support Gary's books through theboutons.com, a lively discussion forum dedicated to digital graphics, free typefaces and other media to download, and shameless plugs of his books. Currently, Gary works on post-production and CG effects in films and commercials for Australian-based Monkey Pants Media.

 **Bobbi Sandberg** has long been involved with computers, accounting, and writing. She is a retired accountant currently filling her time as a trainer, technical writer, and small-business consultant. As a Quicken user and teacher since its inception, she knows the questions users ask and gives easy-to-understand explanations of each step within the program. She teaches at several venues, offering step-by-step instruction in a variety of computer applications. Her extensive background, coupled with her ability to explain complex concepts in plain language, has made her a popular instructor, consultant, and speaker. She has authored and co-authored more than a dozen computer books, including *Quicken 2011: The Official Guide* and *Quicken 2011 Quicksteps™*, both for McGraw-Hill.

Contents at a Glance

1
2
3
4
5
6
7
8
9
10

Contents

3

4

Chapter 5 **Socializing and Communicating Online** 123

Chapter 6 **Using Applications** 153

10

Introduction

We four authors were delighted to write this book. Being "seniors" and each being involved with computers for a long time, we know how much our lives have changed because of computers. Take genealogy for instance: we no longer have to trudge to Salt Lake City to find detailed records or seek out librarians who might remember something about our parents. Now we just click a few buttons, and archives that were unimagined not so long ago open.

As seniors we have more time, supposedly—and less money, for sure. So in addition to the vast improvements in how we do things, we can now take the time to learn how to do tasks that we once thought we couldn't do, and at less cost. Imagine trying to learn how to create a digital photo album with three kids tugging at your side. Or did you ever think you could plan that big anniversary trip without a travel agent? Now's the time to learn how to do all this and more.

Computing for Seniors QuickSteps™ describes in one book some of the most common ways seniors use computers, for work and pleasure. It not only covers core programs, such as Windows, Word, Excel, and Quicken, but also more fun activities, such as genealogy, dating online, managing and enhancing photos, and accessing digital media including music and videos.

QuickSteps™ books are recipe books for computer users. They answer the question "How do I…" by providing a quick set of steps to accomplish the most common tasks for a particular situation. These sets of steps are the central focus of the book. QuickSteps sidebars show how to quickly perform many small functions or tasks that support the primary functions. QuickFacts sidebars supply information that you need to know about a subject. QuickQuotes, contributed by senior friends and acquaintances, tell how topics are being used by real people. Notes, Tips, and Cautions augment the steps and are presented in a separate column so that they do not interrupt the flow of the steps. The introductions are minimal rather than narrative, and numerous illustrations and figures, many with callouts, support the steps.

Conventions Used in This Book

Computing for Seniors QuickSteps™ uses several conventions designed to make the book easier for you to follow:

- A ⊙ in the How To list in each chapter references a QuickSteps sidebar in the chapter and a ⊘ references a QuickFacts sidebar.

- **Bold** type is used for words or objects on the screen that you are to do something with—for example, "Click **Start** and click **Computer**."

- ***Bold italic*** type is used for a word or phrase that is being defined.

- *Italic* type is used for a word or phrase that deserves special emphasis or is a title, as for a book.

- <u>Underlined</u> type is used for text that you are to type from the keyboard.

- SMALL CAPITAL LETTERS are used for keys on the keyboard, such as ENTER and SHIFT.

- When you are expected to enter a command, you are told to press the key(s). If you are to enter text or numbers, you are told to type them.

How to...

Chapter 1

Getting Started

Computing extends your ability to do many things, including your ability to:

- **Communicate** using email, instant messaging, and Internet telephone.

- **Find out what is going on** in the world through Internet news sites, blogs of all types, emailed newsletters, and syndicated news feeds.

- **Learn** through a myriad of Internet information sources, from online encyclopedias such as Wikipedia to online universities.

- **Find information** using many search sites such as Google and Microsoft Bing.

- **Shop** thousands of online stores from major retailers such as Sears and Macy's, to large online or mail-order-only

NOTE

This chapter has a lot of information that will seem like a drink from a fire hose. You should not feel you have to absorb it all at once. Use it to get started with your computer. As you go through the book and get experience using your computer, things will become more clear.

outlets such as Lands End and L.L. Bean, to small specialty purveyors of hard-to-find items.

- **Manage your finances** using online banking, online bill paying, online investing, and financial management programs.

- **Explore your creative abilities** in writing, drawing, photography, poetry, and music using many online resources as well as programs that run on your computer.

- **Connect with others** and join online communities through social networking sites.

- **Start and run a business**, either online or offline, with websites, programs, and tools for running and managing a business.

- **Enjoy music, still pictures, and video** through many sources such as iTunes and YouTube.

- **Find out about your ancestors** and explore genealogy through many sites such as Ancestry.com and Familysearch.org, and programs such as Legacy and Family Tree Maker.

There are, of course, many other reasons to use a computer, and it may be that you simply want to "play" with it and see what you can do. Whatever your reason, you will need to have a computer available to you with an operating system such as Windows and the necessary programs to do the things you want to do.

This chapter explores your computer and explains how to get started using it. It then looks at how to start and use the Windows 7 operating system, including its screens, windows, menus, and dialog boxes, and how to shut both it and your computer down. You will also learn how to get help and discover some ways to have fun with Windows, as well as how to create, use, and manage files and folders. Other chapters will look at how you accomplish the many other things you can do with a computer.

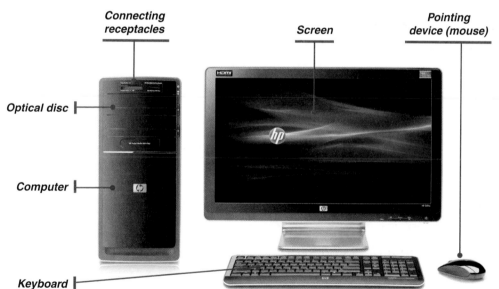

Figure 1-1: *Desktop computers are larger and heavier, and are not meant to be moved very often. (Courtesy of HP © 1994–2011 Hewlett-Packard Company. All Rights Reserved.)*

Explore Your Computer

The computer you are using can be:

- A **desktop** computer, because it requires a larger stationary surface such as a table or desk, as shown in Figure 1-1.

- A **laptop** computer that is relatively mobile, with all the components in one slim case that can be used from your lap or other temporary surface, as shown in Figure 1-2.

- An **integrated** computer that combines the screen and the computer in a single case with the optical drive and the connecting receptacles. The keyboard and mouse are still separate, as you see in Figure 1-3.

Screen

Keyboard

Computer

Pointing device

Connecting receptacles

Optical disc

Figure 1-2: Laptop computers are meant to be portable and easily (more or less) carried from place to place. (Courtesy of HP © 1994–2011 Hewlett-Packard Company. All Rights Reserved.)

Identify the Parts of Your Computer

Whether you have a desktop, integrated, or laptop computer, all have the same set of six primary external components.

- The actual **computer** processes what is entered on the keyboard, pointed to by the mouse, or read from a disc and then displayed on the screen.

- The **screen** displays information from the computer.

- The **keyboard** transmits typed information from you to the computer.

- The **pointing device**, such as a mouse, allows you to point to and select objects on the screen.

- The **optical disc drive** reads information, music, or videos contained on either a CD (compact disc) or a DVD (digital video disc) into the computer.

- **Connecting receptacles** allow you to connect other devices to a computer, such as a printer, a camera, an external hard drive, a sound system, or a TV.

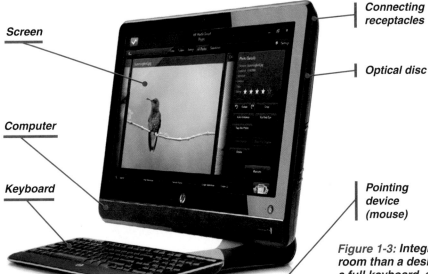

Connecting receptacles

Screen

Optical disc

Computer

Keyboard

Pointing device (mouse)

Figure 1-3: Integrated computers take up less room than a desktop computer, but still give you a full keyboard, a larger screen, and a separate mouse. (Courtesy of HP © 1994–2011 Hewlett-Packard Company. All Rights Reserved.)

QUICK QUOTES

PAGE PICKS AND CHOOSES WHAT SHE NEEDS TO LEARN

In truth, there is far more about my computer that I don't know than what I know, but I get along pretty well and can do what I want to do. I started out with the idea that I had to learn all about my computer, but quickly found that was a tall order, and so changed my objective to learning just what I needed to know to do writing, emailing, online banking, a small amount of shopping, surfing the Internet, and managing my pictures. It works well and is a great asset…and I'm always curious about what I don't know and want to know more.

Page G. B., 68, Washington

TIP

You don't need to know much about the internal components, just that they are there performing their stated functions.

In addition, all computers have four major internal components and many other minor components.

- The **central processing unit**, or CPU, does all the real work of the computer, and the technology behind its intelligence is the reason that the huge computers we knew "back in the day," which took the square footage of half a football field, now can fit in a small space on your desk.

- **Memory** is used to temporarily store information that the computer is using while it is turned on. When you turn the computer off, the contents of the memory disappear.

- The **hard disk** is a rotating magnetic disk within your computer that is used to store both programs and information on your computer that you want stored for longer periods. The information on a hard disk remains intact when you turn your computer off. It is used to store information you write, pictures you take, your email address list, your financial records, and many other pieces of information you don't want to lose.

- The **motherboard** is used to plug in the CPU and memory and to connect to the hard disk and various external components. It is the central connecting device joining all of the computer's components.

Use Your Computer

The exact way that a computer is used depends on the computer. Determining this requires that you refer to the information that came with the computer. Here are some general rules of thumb for using a computer:

- **Start the computer** by quickly pressing and releasing a power button, one of which is shown in Figure 1-4, and most of which have a symbol similar to the one shown.

- **Stop the computer** by indicating to the operating system that you want to do so, as explained in the next section. In a real emergency, you often can stop the computer by pressing and holding down the

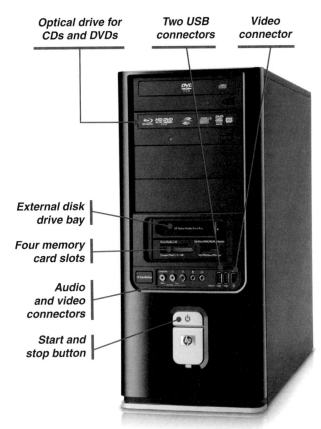

Optical drive for CDs and DVDs

Two USB connectors

Video connector

External disk drive bay

Four memory card slots

Audio and video connectors

Start and stop button

Figure 1-4: A computer may have a few or many connectors into which you can plug external devices such as printers, cameras, and other devices. (Courtesy of HP © 1994–2011 Hewlett-Packard Company. All Rights Reserved.)

power button. This can be dangerous, however, since if you have not saved the information that is in memory, you will lose it. If you use the operating system to shut down, you will be reminded to save information in memory.

- **Insert a disc in an optical drive**, which requires that you open the drive. There is normally a button or area that you press to do this. The button is often located on the drive, either to its right or below the drive. When the drive is open, handle a disc only by its edges or center and place it in the tray that has opened. Then press the button again or gently press the front of the open tray to close it. After a minute or two, you should see some instructions appear on the screen telling you what to do next, as described in the following section.

- **Connect a printer** or other device to the computer. Most printers and many other devices connect to a computer using a Universal Serial Bus (USB) connector, shown in Figure 1-4, into which a cable from the printer or other device is inserted. In addition to USB connectors, your computer may have slots for memory cards used in cameras and other devices, as well as connectors for audio, video, and external hard disks. These connecting receptacles can be on the front, back, and/or sides of a computer. Your computer instructions will describe these to you.

Use Windows

In addition to the physical hardware of a computer, you must have an operating system for it to be functional. Windows 7, as an *operating system*, performs *the* central role in managing what a computer does and how it is done. An operating system provides the interface between you and the computer hardware: It lets you store a file, print a document, connect to the Internet, or retrieve information from a CD without you knowing anything about how the hardware works.

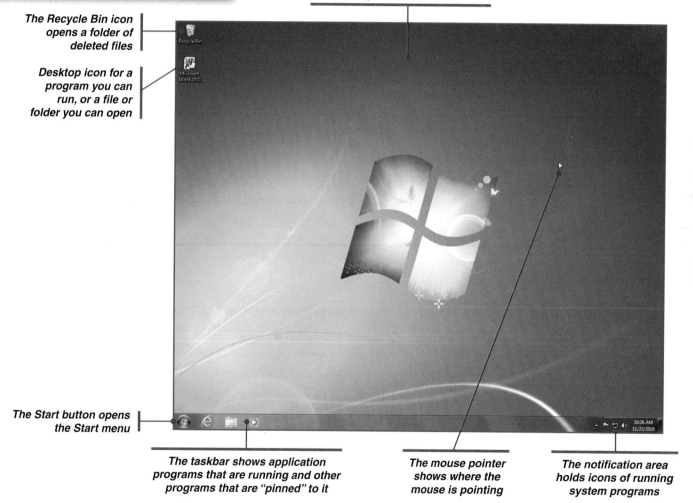

NOTE

The desktop image on your screen may be different from the standard Windows one shown in Figure 1-5. Computer manufacturers can have their own image, and you can select a different one for yourself.

Start and Explore Windows

To start Windows, you only need to turn on the computer. When you do, you'll see a screen similar to Figure 1-5.

The desktop is used for windows, dialog boxes, and icons

The Recycle Bin icon opens a folder of deleted files

Desktop icon for a program you can run, or a file or folder you can open

The Start button opens the Start menu

The taskbar shows application programs that are running and other programs that are "pinned" to it

The mouse pointer shows where the mouse is pointing

The notification area holds icons of running system programs

Figure 1-5: When you have started Windows 7, your screen should look something like this.

TIP

If you're left handed, you may want to switch mouse buttons by clicking **Start**, clicking **Control Panel**, selecting **Category** in the upper-right area, clicking **Hardware And Sound**, clicking **Mouse** under Devices And Printers, clicking **Switch Primary And Secondary Buttons**, and finally clicking **OK** and closing the Control Panel. Later sections in this chapter will help you do this.

QUICKSTEPS

USING THE MOUSE

- **Highlight an *object*** (a button, an icon, a border, etc.) on the screen by pointing to it. *Point* at an object on the screen by moving the mouse until the tip of the pointer is on top of the object.

- **Select an object on the screen** by clicking it. *Click* means to point at an object you want to select and quickly press and release the left mouse button.

- **Open an object or start a program** by double-clicking it. *Double-click* means to point at an object you want to select and press and release the mouse button twice in rapid succession. If nothing happens, you may have waited too long between clicks and need to click twice more quickly.

- **Open a context menu**, which allows you to do things specific to an object, by right-clicking it. *Right-click* means to point at an object you want to select and quickly press and release the right mouse button.

Continued . . .

USE THE MOUSE

In this book, for simplicity, we'll call any pointing device—including a touch pad, trackballs, pointing sticks, and graphic tablets—with two or more buttons a *mouse*. (We also assume you are using a two-button mouse.) Moving the mouse moves the pointer on the screen. You *select* an object on the screen by moving the pointer so that it is on top of the object and then pressing the left button on the mouse.

You can control the mouse with either your left or right hand; therefore, the buttons may be switched. This book assumes you are using your right hand to control the mose and that the left mouse button is "the mouse button." The right button is always called the "right mouse button." If you switch the buttons, you must change your interpretation of these phrases.

USE THE SCREEN

The Windows 7 screen can hold windows and other objects. In its simplest form, shown in Figure 1-5, you see a background scene, a bar at the bottom with a button on the left and the time and date on the right, and some icons in the upper-left area.

The parts of a screen are:

- The **desktop**, which takes up most of the screen.
- The **Start button** in the lower-left corner, which opens the Start menu.
- The **taskbar** across the bottom, which identifies programs that are running or "pinned" to it.
- The **notification area** in the lower-right corner, which holds icons of running system programs.

    - **Desktop icons**, which can be in any number and anywhere on the desktop, are in the upper-left corner of Figure 1-5. Desktop icons are used to start programs or open files or folders.

    - The **mouse pointer**, which can be anywhere on the screen.

USING THE MOUSE *(Continued)*

- **Move an object on the screen** by dragging it. *Drag* means to point at an object you want to move, then press and hold the mouse button while moving the mouse. You will drag the object as you move the mouse. When the object is where you want it, release the mouse button.

USING THE NOTIFICATION AREA

The *notification area* on the right of the taskbar contains the icons of special programs and system features, as well as the time and date.

- **Show hidden icons** by clicking the up arrow to see the icons of hidden programs and then click any you wish to open.

- **Open a system feature** by clicking one of the icons in the middle to open a system feature.

  Set the time and date by clicking the time and date area to see a calendar and an analog clock, and then click **Change Date And Time Settings**.

- **Show the desktop** by clicking the far-right area of the taskbar in an unmarked rectangular area, which, if you click in it, will minimize all open windows and dialog boxes and display the desktop.

USE THE DESKTOP

The *desktop* is the entire screen, except for the bar at the bottom. Windows, dialog boxes, and icons, such as the Recycle Bin, are displayed on the desktop. You can store *shortcuts*, which are icons to load your favorite programs, on the desktop. You can drag windows, dialog boxes, files, and icons around the desktop. Double-click an icon on the desktop to open it.

USE THE TASKBAR

The *taskbar* at the bottom of the screen contains the active *tasks*, which are icons and titles of the programs that are available or running on the computer, or folders that are open. The taskbar also holds the Start button on the left and the notification area on the right. Click a program on the taskbar to open it.

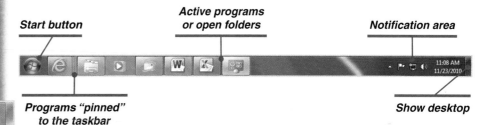

USE A DESKTOP ICON

A *desktop icon* represents a program or folder that can be started or opened and moved about the screen. For example, the Recycle Bin is a desktop icon for a folder that contains all of the files that have been deleted since the Recycle Bin was last emptied. Double-click a desktop icon to open or start what it refers to.

USE THE MOUSE POINTER

The *mouse pointer*, or simply the *pointer* or *mouse*, shows where the mouse is pointing. Move the mouse to move the pointer.

NOTE

The icons you have in the notification area will depend on the programs and processes you have running and the system features you have available. The icons shown here include system messages, which opens the Action Center ▣, Network, which opens the Network and Sharing Center ▦, and Speakers, which allows you to control the sound from your computer ◀). In a laptop or notebook computer, you probably have two additional icons: Power ▣ and Wireless ▦.

NOTE

The two steps describing how to open the Start menu can be replaced with the two words "click Start." You can also open the Start menu by pressing the Windows flag key ⊞ on your keyboard, if you have that key, or by pressing both the CTRL and ESC keys together (CTRL+ESC). In the rest of this book, you will see the phrase "click Start." This means open the Start menu using any technique you wish.

Use the Start Menu

The *Start button*, located on the left of the taskbar, also called just "Start," opens the Start menu when clicked. This provides you with primary access to the programs, utilities, and settings that are available in Windows. To open the Start menu:

1. Point at the **Start** button by moving the pointer so that it is over the Start button. You will see that the button changes color. When this happens, the button is said to be selected or *highlighted*.

2. Press and release the left mouse button while the pointer is on the Start button. The Start menu will open, as you can see in Figure 1-6.

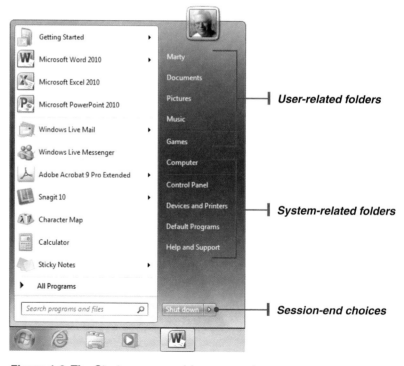

Figure 1-6: **The Start menu provides access to the programs, utilities, and settings in Windows.**

2

3

4

5

6

7

8

9

10

GENE DEPENDS ON HIS COMPUTER

When there is a disaster, the Federal Emergency Management Agency (FEMA) may call me in to help communities recover from the event. I can be sent anywhere in the country, and I go with my own laptop computer and am issued another one by FEMA. I wouldn't and couldn't be without those computers. I use them many times a day to keep in contact with my colleagues at the agency, with the congressional staffs with which I'm working, and with my family and friends back home.

Gene L., "over 65," Washington

NOTE

Depending on the edition of Windows 7 you have (Starter, Home Basic, Home Premium, Professional, Enterprise, or Ultimate), your Start menu may be slightly different from the one shown here for Windows 7 Ultimate edition.

EXPLORE THE START MENU

The left column of the Start menu contains named icons for programs and folders, as well as access to control functions and other menus, as shown in Figure 1-6. The most important menu item is All Programs, which opens a submenu within the Start menu of all your programs. The buttons in the lower-right area—Shut Down and session-ending choices—are important control functions discussed later in this chapter. The Search text box in the lower-left corner allows you to enter criteria and search the files and folders on the computer or the Internet for those that contain a match. All other options on the menu open folders or start programs, or both. The seven lower icons on the left change to reflect the programs you have used most recently, which are probably different from those shown here. In most cases, these are the programs that Windows 7 initially displays.

The remaining items in the right column of the Start menu fall into two categories: user-related folders and system-related folders, programs, and options.

OPEN USER-RELATED FOLDERS

The top five options on the right in Figure 1-6 (including the user's name at the top) are used to access folders related to the user who is logged on. These options start the Windows Explorer program and display the folder identified. Clicking the user's name opens a folder containing the user's libraries displaying four subsidiary folders, as shown next. Windows Explorer will be discussed later in this chapter and again in Chapter 3.

OPEN SYSTEM-RELATED FOLDERS

The remaining five choices in the bottom-right corner of the Start menu (see Figure 1-7) help you manage your computer and its resources or get help. The function of each is as follows:

- **Computer** starts the Windows Explorer program and displays disk storage devices on the computer. From this point, you can open any disk, folder, and file that is available to you on your computer and the network to which you are connected.

- **Control Panel** provides access to many of the settings that govern how Windows and the computer operate. This allows you to customize much of Windows and to locate and solve problems.

QUICKSTEPS

STARTING A PROGRAM

The method for starting a program depends on where the program icon is located. Here are the alternatives:

- **On the desktop** Double-click the program icon, or "shortcut," on the desktop.

- **On the Start menu** Click the program icon on the Start menu.

- **On the taskbar or notification area** Click the program icon in the notification area.

- **On the All Programs menu**:

  1. Click **Start**.
  2. Click **All Programs**.
  3. Click the relevant folder or folders.
  4. Click the program icon, as shown in Figure 1-7.

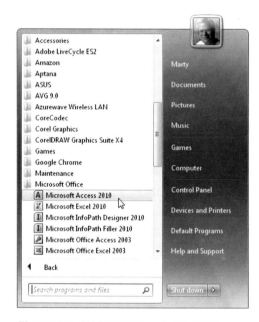

Figure 1-7: All Programs on the Start menu may lead you through several folders before you find the program you want.

- **Devices And Printers** allows you to check the status of and change the settings on the hardware devices and printers in or connected to your computer.

- **Default Programs** allows you to associate a program with a file type and automatically start that program when you double-click that type of file.

- **Help And Support** opens a window from which you can search for information on how to use Windows 7. It includes a tutorial and a troubleshooting guide. Help is discussed in more detail later in this chapter.

Your computer's manufacturer may have added an icon that connects you to the manufacturer's Internet Help center.

Use a Window

When you start a program or open a folder, the program or folder appears in a "window" on your screen, as shown with the Windows Explorer window in Figure 1-8.

The window in Figure 1-8 has a number of features that are referred to in the remainder of this book. Not all windows have all of the features shown in the figure, and some windows have features unique to them.

- The **title bar** is used to drag the window around the screen, and may contain the name of the program or folder in the window (the Windows Explorer window in Windows 7 does not contain a name in the title bar).

- The **address bar** displays the complete address of what is being displayed in the subject pane. In Figure 1-8, this is (from right to left) the Ch01 folder, in the Senior Computing, QuickSteps, Anew folders, on drive O of the Win7 computer in the local network.

- The **toolbar** contains tools related to the contents of the window. Click a tool to use it. The toolbar is always displayed.

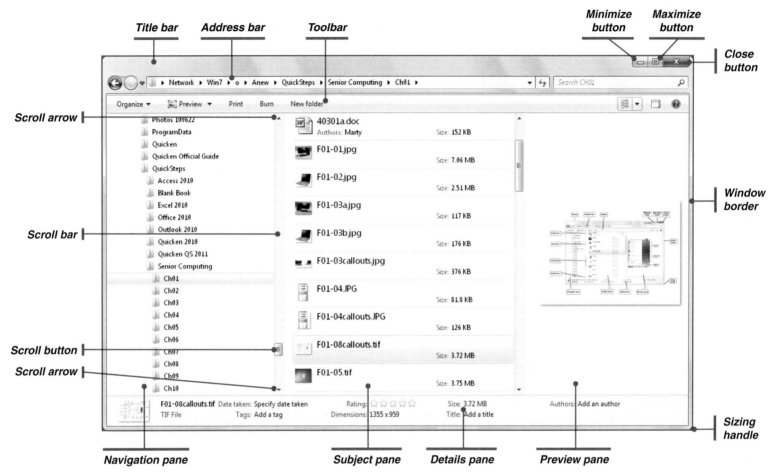

Figure 1-8: The Windows Explorer window has a number of different features that allow you to perform many tasks.

- The **Minimize button** decreases the size of the window so that you see it only as a task on the taskbar.

- The **Maximize button** increases the size of the window so that it fills the screen. When the screen is maximized, this button becomes the **Restore button**, which, when clicked, returns the screen to its previous size.

TIP

Double-clicking a window's title bar toggles between maximizing and restoring a window to its previous size. This may be easier than clicking the Maximize and Restore buttons.

NOTE

All windows have a title bar with the Minimize, Maximize, and Close buttons. The title bars of program windows also have a control menu icon on the left of the title bar and the program name in the middle of the title bar. All windows also have a border and sizing handle, both of which can be used to change the size of the window. *Almost* all windows have a menu bar. Other features are optional.

- The **Close button** shuts down and closes the program, folder, or file in the window.

- The **window border** separates the window from the desktop, and can be used to size the window horizontally or vertically by dragging the horizontal or vertical border, respectively.

- The **sizing handle** in each corner of the window allows it to be sized diagonally, increasing or decreasing the window's height and width when you drag a handle.

- The **preview pane** displays the object selected in the subject pane. For example, in Figure 1-8, the navigation pane points to a particular folder whose files of screenshots are shown in the subject pane, where one particular file is selected and displayed in the preview pane. By default, the preview pane is turned off.

- The **details pane** displays detailed information about the object that is selected in the subject pane. The preview pane is turned on by default.

- The **subject pane** displays the principal subject of the window, such as files, folders, programs, documents, or images. The subject pane is always on.

- The **navigation pane** provides links to the most commonly used folders related to the user who is logged on, as well as an optional hierarchical list of disks and folders on the computer. The navigation pane is turned on by default.

- **Scroll arrows** move the window contents in small increments in the direction of the arrow.

- The **scroll button** can be dragged in either direction to move the contents accordingly.

- The **scroll bar** allows you to move the contents of the pane within the window so that you can see information that wasn't displayed. Clicking the scroll bar itself moves the contents in larger increments.

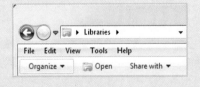
Use a Menu

A *menu* provides a way of selecting an action, such as turning on the preview pane, as shown in Figure 1-9. To use a menu in an open window:

1. Click the menu name on the menu bar.
2. Move the pointer to the option you want.
3. Click the option you want.

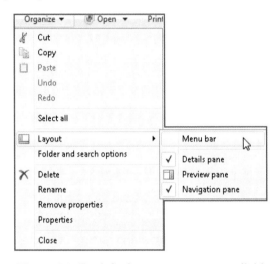

*Figure 1-9: **By default, menus are not available in Windows Explorer, but you can turn them on if you wish.***

Use a Dialog Box

Dialog boxes gather information. A *dialog box* uses a common set of controls to accomplish its purpose. Figures 1-10 and 1-11 show two frequently used dialog boxes with many of the controls often seen.

Title bar   **Preview area**   **Close button**

Tab   **Command button**

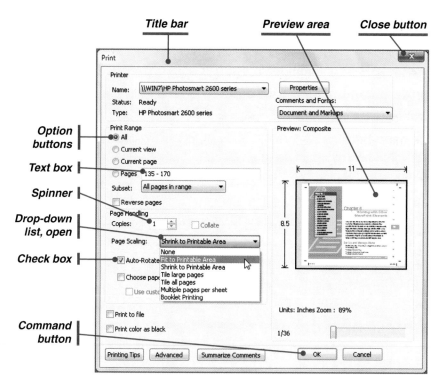

Option buttons

Text box

Spinner

Drop-down list, open

Check box

Command button

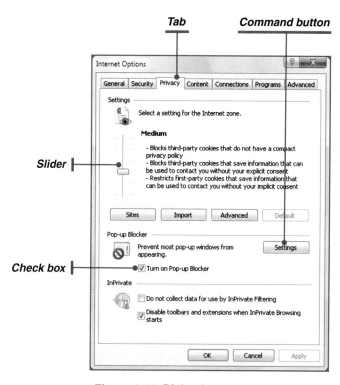

Slider

Check box

Figure 1-10: **This dialog box demonstrates some of the standard controls you'll find in dialog boxes.**

Figure 1-11: **Dialog boxes come in many different sizes and with different controls.**

The common controls in dialog boxes are used in these ways:

- The **title bar** contains the name of the dialog box and is used to drag the box around the desktop.

- **Tabs** let you select from among several pages in a dialog box.

- A **drop-down list box** displays a list from which you can choose one item that will be displayed when the list is closed.

- A **list box** (not shown) lets you select one or more items from a list; it may include a scroll bar.

TIP

Figure 1-12 shows you an example of personalizing the desktop and, with it, the taskbar and windows borders. To do this, right-click the desktop, click **Personalize**, click a new theme, and click **Close**.

- **Option buttons**, also called *radio buttons*, let you select only one of several options.
- **Check boxes** let you turn features on or off.
- A **preview area** shows you the effect of the changes you make.
- A **text box** lets you enter and edit text.
- **Command buttons** perform functions such as closing the dialog box and accepting any changes (the OK button), or closing the dialog box and ignoring the changes (the Cancel button).
- A **spinner** lets you select from a sequential series of numbers.
- A **slider** lets you select from several values.

You will have a great many opportunities to use dialog boxes. For the most part, you can try dialog boxes and see what happens; if you don't like the outcome, you can come back and reverse the setting.

Navigate the Windows Desktop

When multiple windows are open, and possibly a dialog box or two, navigating among them and displaying the one(s) you want could be difficult. Figure 1-12, for example, shows such a situation. Earlier versions of Windows tried to address this, but Windows 7 has added a number of features to handle it elegantly, including (see the following sections on how to find and use these features):

- **Aero Peek** to see what's hidden on the desktop
- **Aero Shake** to minimize other open windows
- **Aero Snap** to resize and position windows
- **Jump lists** to see recent files and program options
- **Taskbar previews** to see what is open in a program

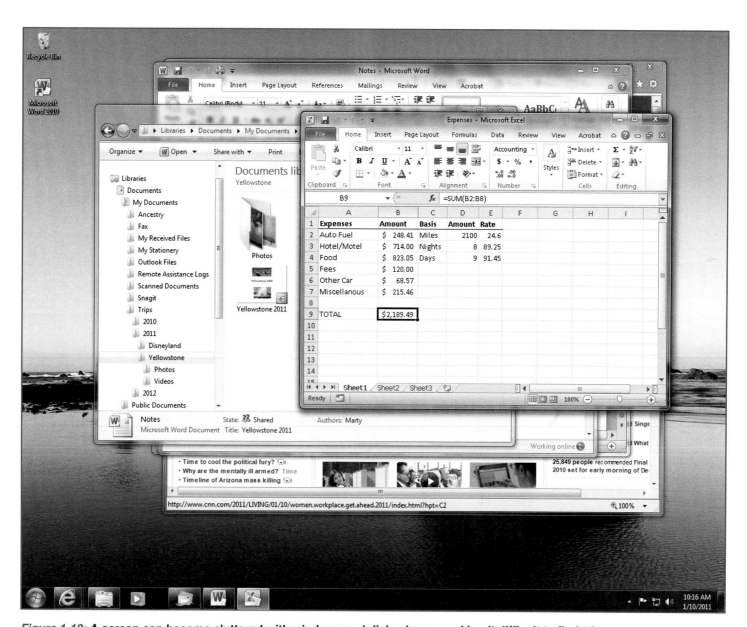

Figure 1-12: **A screen can become cluttered with windows and dialog boxes, making it difficult to find what you want.**

BOBBI FINDS PROGRAMS AND FOLDERS

I often have several programs and folders open on my computer, and until Windows 7, I would have difficulty finding something that I was working on or getting to an icon on my desktop. Now with Aero Peek I can immediately see what's on my desktop, and using taskbar previews I can easily see and choose from among the several documents I might have open in Word or several Internet sites I have open in Internet Explorer. I think these new features are a real asset.

Bobbi S., 69, Washington

USE AERO PEEK

Aero Peek allows you to see what's hidden on the desktop behind all the open windows. You can do this on a temporary (or "peek") basis or a more long-lasting one.

- **Temporarily peek** at the desktop:

  When you have a screen full of windows, like Figure 1-12, move the mouse pointer to ("mouse over") the Show Desktop area on the far right of the taskbar. All the open windows will become transparent ("glass") frames, so you can see anything on the desktop such as the two email messages and folder in Figure 1-13.

- **Return** to the original desktop after a temporary peek:

  Move the mouse pointer away from the Show Desktop area. All the open windows will reappear, as shown in Figure 1-12.

- **Hide** all open windows so you can see and work on the desktop:

  Click in the **Show Desktop** area on the far right of the taskbar. All the open windows will be hidden, and you can move the mouse around the entire desktop.

- **Unhide** all open windows and return to the original desktop:

  Click in the **Show Desktop** area on the far right of the taskbar. All the open windows will be returned to their original positions.

USE AERO SHAKE

Aero Shake allows you to minimize all open windows except for the one you are "shaking." To "shake" a window:

Point to the title bar of the window you want to remain open. Press and hold the mouse button while moving the mouse rapidly to the left and then to the right, as if you were shaking it.

–Or–

Press and hold the **WINDOWS FLAG** key while pressing **HOME**.

To return the minimized windows to their original size and position, repeat the same steps.

Figure 1-13: **With Aero Peek, all open windows become transparent.**

USE AERO SNAP

Aero Snap "snaps" a window to various parts of the screen, a function similar to the Maximize/Restore button (which can still be used) on the title bar of a selected floating (not already maximized) window, with some useful additions.

- **Maximize** a floating window:

  Point within the title bar or the window, not on its edge, and drag it to the top of the screen. The window will be maximized to fill the screen.

  –Or–

  Press and hold the **WINDOWS FLAG** key while pressing **UP ARROW**.

- **Restore** a maximized window (regardless of how it was maximized):

  Double-click the title bar.

  –Or–

  Press and hold the **WINDOWS FLAG** key while pressing **DOWN ARROW**.

- **Vertically maximize** a floating window while not spreading it out horizontally:

  Point to the top or bottom edge of a window, and drag it to the corresponding edge of the screen. The window will be vertically maximized.

  –Or–

  Press and hold the **WINDOWS FLAG** key while pressing **SHIFT+UP ARROW**.

- **Left-align** a floating window and have it occupy 50 percent of the screen:

  Point to the title bar of a window, and drag it to the left edge of the screen. When the mouse pointer (not the edge of the window) reaches the edge of the screen, the window will fill the left 50 percent of the screen.

  –Or–

  Press and hold the **WINDOWS FLAG** key while pressing **LEFT ARROW**.

- **Right-align** a floating window and have it occupy 50 percent of the screen:

  Point at the title bar of a window, and drag it to the right edge of the screen. When the mouse pointer (not the edge of the window) reaches the edge of the screen, the window will fill the right 50 percent of the screen.

  –Or–

  Press and hold the **WINDOWS FLAG** key while pressing **RIGHT ARROW**.

- **Restore** a window that is filling 50 percent of the screen:

  Double-click the title bar twice.

  –Or–

  Press and hold the **WINDOWS FLAG** key while pressing the key opposite the one used to enlarge it.

  –Or–

  Point at the title bar of a window, and drag it down and away from the window edge it was aligned with.

USE JUMP LISTS

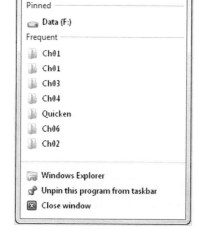

Jump lists are a context or pop-up menu for application icons on the taskbar or the Start menu. When you right-click a program icon on either the Start menu or taskbar, a menu will appear containing a list of recent files or webpages, as well as options to close the application, pin or unpin it from the Start menu or taskbar, and open the application with a blank file or webpage. (This is different than simply pointing at an open taskbar program, which shows the taskbar previews; see the next section.)

USE TASKBAR PREVIEWS

Taskbar previews are a miniature image, or thumbnail, of an open window attached to a taskbar icon. When you mouse over or point at an icon on the taskbar, a thumbnail of the open window or windows

2

3

4

5

6

7

8

9

10

NOTE

If you see an exclamation mark in a shield on the Shut Down button, you are being told that when you click **Shut Down**, Microsoft will automatically download and install updates to your operating system and then the computer will be shut down.

related to that icon will temporarily appear, as shown next. If you then move the mouse to the thumbnail, a temporary full-sized image will appear. When you move the mouse off the thumbnail or the icon, the corresponding image will disappear. Open a window by clicking its thumbnail. Close a window by clicking the **Close** button on the thumbnail.

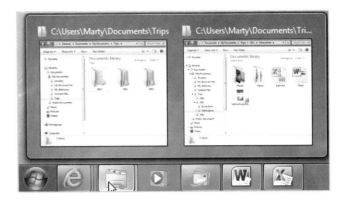

End Your Windows Session

You can end your Windows session in several ways, depending on what you want to do. All of these can be found on the Start menu.

1. Click **Start**. Note in the lower-right corner of the Start menu there is a button marked Shut Down and a right-pointing arrow to open several options in addition to Shut Down.

2. Click either **Shut Down** or the right-arrow, and then click the option you want.

The meanings of the various options are as follows:

- **Shut Down** closes all active programs and network connections and logs off all users so that no information is lost, and then turns off the computer (if it is done automatically) or tells you when it is safe for you to turn it off. When you start up the computer, you must reload your programs and data and reestablish your network connection to get back to where you were when you shut down.

- **Switch User** leaves all active programs, network connections, and your user account active but hidden while you let another person use the computer.

- **Log Off** closes all active programs, network connections, and your user account but leaves Windows 7 and the computer running so another person can log on.

- **Lock** leaves all active programs, network connections, and your user account active but displays the Welcome screen, where you must click your user icon and potentially enter a password, if you have established one, to resume using the computer.

- **Restart** closes all active programs, network connections, and logs off all users so that no information is lost. Windows is then shut down and restarted. This is usually done when there is a problem that restarting Windows will fix or to complete setting up some programs.

- **Sleep** leaves all active programs, network connections, and your user account active and in memory, but also saves the state of everything on disk. Your computer is then put into a low-power state that allows you to quickly resume working exactly where you were when you left. In a desktop computer, it is left running in this low-power state for as long as you wish. In a mobile computer (laptops, notebooks, netbooks, and tablet PCs), after three hours or if the battery is low, your session is again saved to disk and the computer is turned off.

RESUME FROM SLEEP

There are several ways to resume operation after a computer has been put into Sleep mode, which depend on your type of computer, how it

---

TIP

There are two distinct schools of thought on whether you should use Sleep or Shut Down when you leave the computer for any length of time. There are two primary considerations: security and power usage. Older computers used less power running in sleep mode than the power consumed during shutting down and starting up. New computers have reduced the power consumed during these events, so it is now a toss-up. From a security standpoint, there is no security like having your computer completely turned off. A computer is also pretty secure in sleep mode, but it is theoretically possible for a hacker to awaken it. The choice becomes a matter of preference.

NOTE

To read about Windows 7 in more detail, we recommend *Windows 7 for Seniors QuickSteps* (McGraw-Hill, 2011) by Marty Matthews.

was put to sleep, and how long it has been sleeping. A computer can be put into Sleep mode by your action on the Start menu, by shutting the cover of a laptop, or as the result of the computer not being used for a given period. The ways to resume include the following:

- Press any key on your keyboard. This works with most desktop computers and mobile computers that have only been asleep a short time.
- Quickly press the power button on your computer. This works with most recent computers of all types. Holding down the computer's power button will, in most cases, either fully turn off the computer or cause it to restart (shut fully down and then restart).
- Open the top. This works with most laptop computers.

Get Help

Windows 7 Help provides both built-in documentation and online assistance that you can use to learn how to work with Windows 7. For example, to use Help to start a program:

1. Click **Start** and click **Help And Support**. The Windows Help And Support Center window, like the one shown in Figure 1-14, opens.

2. In the Search Help text box type start a program. A number of options related to starting a program will be displayed.

3. Click the **Close** button to close the Help And Support Center.

Work with Information

The information on your computer—documents, email, photographs, music, and programs—is stored in *files*. So that your files are organized and more easily found, they are kept in *folders*, and folders can be placed in other folders for further organization. For example, a folder labeled "Trips," which is contained in the My Documents

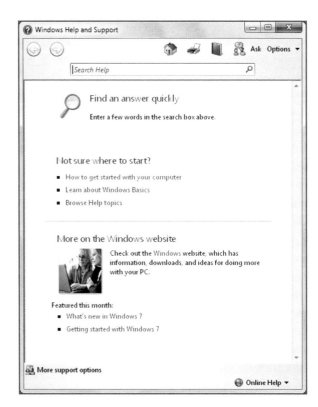

Figure 1-14: The Windows 7 Help And Support Center window provides you with several options for getting help.

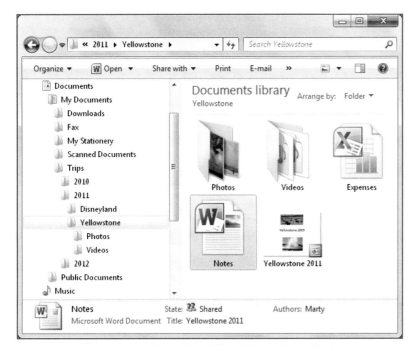

Figure 1-15: **Windows stores files in folders, which can be within other folders.**

folder, contains separate folders for the years 2010, 2011, and 2012. The 2011 folder contains folders for Disneyland and Yellowstone. The Yellowstone folder contains folders of photos and videos, as well as files for notes and expenses. Such a set of files and folders is shown in the My Documents folder in Figure 1-15. The term "objects" is used to refer to any mix of files, folders, and disk drives.

Use Windows Explorer

The tool that Windows 7 provides to locate and work with files and folders is *Windows Explorer* (often called "Explorer," not to be confused with Internet Explorer discussed in Chapter 2). Windows Explorer has a number of components and features, most of which are shown in Figure 1-16 and described in Table 1-1. Much of this chapter is spent exploring these items and how they are used.

When you open Windows Explorer, you can choose what you want it to initially display from among the choices on the upper-right corner of the Start menu. These choices give you access to the following (from top to bottom):

- Your personal folder, which contains your documents, pictures, music, and games
- Your documents
- Your pictures
- Your music
- Your games
- The computer on which you are working

TIP

Windows 7 has a number of games that are available through the Games menu, which you can open by clicking **Start**, clicking **All Programs**, and clicking **Games**.

Games
- Chess Titans
- FreeCell
- Games Explorer
- Hearts
- Internet Backgammon
- Internet Checkers
- Internet Spades
- Mahjong Titans
- Minesweeper
- More Games from Microsoft
- Purble Place
- Solitaire
- Spider Solitaire

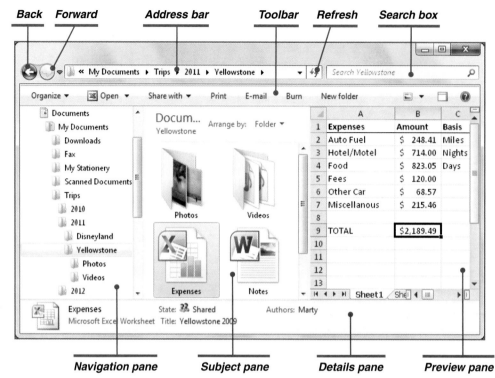

Figure 1-16: *Windows Explorer provides the means to access files, folders, disks, and memory devices on your computer.*

AREA	FUNCTION
Back and Forward buttons	Displays an object previously shown.
Address bar	Displays the location of what is being shown in the subject pane.
Toolbar	Contains tools to work with objects in the subject pane.
Refresh	Updates or refreshes the window specified in the address bar.
Search box	Allows you to search a folder or disk for specific text. Type the text you want to search for.
Preview pane	Displays the contents of the object selected in the subject pane.
Details pane	Provides information about the object selected in the subject pane.
Subject pane	Displays the objects stored at the address shown in the address bar.
Navigation pane	Facilitates moving around among the objects you have available.

Table 1-1: Windows Explorer Components

JOANN'S FAVORITE IS FREECELL

I have to admit that FreeCell is my favorite computer game. It is entertaining, can be quickly played in spare moments, and is enjoyable. In addition, it challenges me to concentrate and think in a creative way to solve a variety of problems. If I see that I am losing a game, I use the Undo command (**CTRL+Z**) to replay the same game until I eventually win. In that way, it keeps my mind active, alert, and skillful.

Joann A., 76, Washington

*Figure 1-17: **Windows 7 starts with a number of standard folders that are part of the personal folder.***

OPEN WINDOWS EXPLORER

To open Windows Explorer:

1. Start your computer, if it's not running.

2. Click **Start**. The Start menu will open, and you'll see the Windows Explorer choices on the right of the menu.

3. Click your personal folder (the one with your name on it). Explorer will open and display in the subject pane the files and folders that either come standard with Windows 7 or that have been placed there by you or somebody else, as shown in Figure 1-17. You can:

Click an object in the subject pane to *select* it and get information about it in the details pane, preview it in the preview pane, or use the toolbar tools with that object.

–Or–

Double-click an object in the subject pane to *open* it so that you can see and work with its contents.

CUSTOMIZE WINDOWS EXPLORER

You can customize how Windows Explorer looks and which features are available with the toolbar.

1. If Windows Explorer is not already open, click **Start** and click your personal folder.

2. Click **Pictures** in the navigation pane, and then double-click **Sample Pictures** in the subject pane. Windows 7's sample pictures should open, and the Explorer's toolbar will change to handle working with pictures, as you can see in Figure 1-18.

3. Click one of the pictures. The toolbar changes to reflect this choice, as shown here.

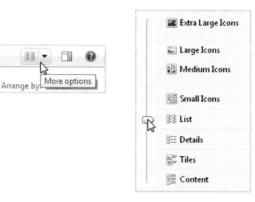

These toolbar options are specific to a picture. The selection of other types of files would have generated different options.

4. Click **Organize** to open the Organize menu. Here you can perform operations on the object you have selected using menu options such as Cut, Copy, Paste, Delete, and Rename, and perform folder-related operations with menu options such as Layout, Folder And Search Options, and Close.

5. Click the **Change Your Views** down arrow (not the button itself, which gives you another view of your folder) on the right of the toolbar, as shown below. Drag the slider up and down to change first the size of the objects in your folder and, as you continue downward, the arrangement of the objects.

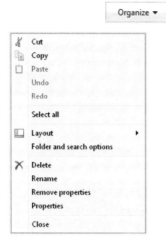

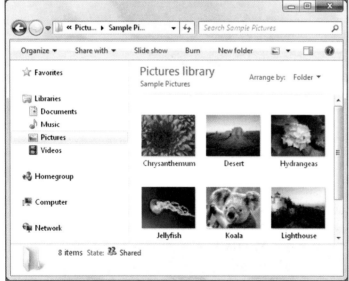

Figure 1-18: Windows Explorer's toolbar changes to provide commands for what is selected in the subject pane.

6. Click the **Change Your Views** down arrow, and click **Details**, which is shown in Figure 1-19.

7. Click **Name** at the top of the left column in the subject pane. The contents of the subject pane will be sorted alphanumerically by name. Click **Name** again, and the contents will be sorted by name in the opposite direction.

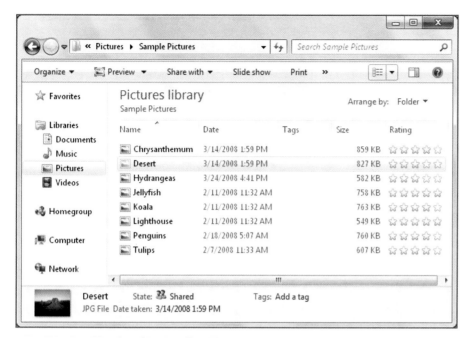

8. Click one of the other column headings, and then click the same column heading again to see the contents sorted that way, first in one direction, and then in the other.

9. Click the **Close** button in the upper-right corner of the Explorer window to close it.

Locate and Use Files and Folders

The purpose of a file system, of course, is to locate and use the files and folders on your computer. Within your computer, there is a storage hierarchy that starts with storage devices, such as disk drives, which are divided into areas called folders, each of which may be divided again into subareas called subfolders. Each of these contains files, which can be documents, pictures, music, and other data.

Figure 1-19: Folder Details view gives you further information about the objects in a folder.

Figure 1-15 showed folders containing subfolders and eventually containing files with information in them. Figure 1-20 shows a computer containing disk drives, which in turn contain folders. Windows Explorer contains a number of tools for locating, opening, and using disk drives, folders, and files.

IDENTIFY STORAGE DEVICES

Files and folders are stored on various physical storage devices, including disk drives, CD and DVD drives, memory cards and sticks, and Universal Serial Bus (USB) flash memory. You will have some, but not necessarily all, of the following:

- Primary floppy disk, labeled "A:"
- Primary hard disk, labeled "C:"

Figure 1-20: Your computer stores information in a hierarchy of disk drives and folders.

- CD or DVD drive, labeled "D:"
- Other storage devices, labeled "E:" and then "F:" and so on

Your primary floppy drive is always labeled "A:" (given that you still have one—most new computers don't). Your primary hard disk is always labeled "C:." Other drives have flexible labeling. Often, the CD or DVD drive will be drive "D:," but if you have a second hard disk drive, it may be labeled "D," as you can see in Figure 1-20.

SELECT AND OPEN DRIVES AND FOLDERS

When you open Windows Explorer and display the items in Computer, you see the disk drives and other storage devices on your computer, as well as several folders, including Program Files, Users, and Windows, as you saw in Figure 1-20. To work with these drives and folders, you must select them; to see and work with their contents, you must open them.

1. Click **Start** and click **Computer** to open Windows Explorer and display the local disk drives.

2. In the subject pane (right pane), click disk **(C:)**. Disk (C:) will be highlighted and its characteristics will be displayed in the details pane (bottom pane).

3. Double-click disk **(C:)** in any pane. Disk (C:) will open and its folders will be displayed in the subject pane.

4. Scroll down and double-click **Users** to open that folder and display your personal folder (the folder with your name on it) along with a Public folder.

5. Double-click your personal folder. The subject pane displays the files and folders in your folder. This will include Contacts, Desktop, My Documents, My Music, and others, as shown in Figure 1-21.

6. Keep double-clicking each folder to open it until you see the contents you are looking for.

BOB FINDS SIMPLE IS EASIER

After being president of a succession of banks, I came into my retirement with little hands-on experience with computers, although I had overseen their introduction and use in our banks. Luckily, I had a number of friends and associates who helped me get set up and started using a personal computer. In this process, I picked up several pointers, primary among them, which I had known from other areas, was the K.I.S.S. principle of keeping it simple. I only have on my computers the programs I want to frequently use, and I have found that the simpler the set of folders I use, the easier it is to find what I need. It is easier to search through a number of files in a single folder then it is to search through a number of folders.

Bob O., 74, Washington

Figure 1-21: *Double-clicking a drive or folder will open it in the subject pane.*

Navigate Folders and Disks

Opening Windows Explorer and navigating through several folders—beginning with your hard disk—to find a file you want is fine. However, if you want to quickly go to another folder or file, you won't want to have to start with your hard disk every single time. The Windows 7 Explorer gives you three ways to do this: through the Libraries folder in the navigation pane, by using the folder tree in the navigation pane, or by using the address bar.

NAVIGATE USING LIBRARIES

The Windows 7 suggested way to navigate is through the Libraries folder, which contains links to the folders within your personal

Libraries

Open a library to see your files a...

Documents Library

Music Library

Pictures Library

Videos Library

4 items

folder (called a "library" in this case, as shown in the illustration to the left). By clicking a library in the navigation pane and then double-clicking folders within the subject pane, you can move around the folders and files within your personal folder. For example, given the folder structure shown in Figure 1-15, here are the steps to open the Yellowstone folder:

1. Click **Start** and click **Documents**, which opens the Documents library within your personal Libraries folder.

2. In the navigation pane, click the right-pointing triangle or arrow opposite the Documents library to open it.

3. Still in the navigation page, click the right-pointing arrow opposite My Documents to open it.

4. Repeat step 3 to open the Trips and 2011 folders, and then click the **Yellowstone** folder to open it in the subject pane.

NAVIGATE USING FOLDERS

The portion of the navigation pane starting with Computer is a folder tree that contains all the disk drives, folders, and files on your computer in a tree, or hierarchical, structure. To open the same folder structure shown in Figure 1-15 through Computer:

1. Click **Start** and click **Computer**, which opens Computer in the navigation pane, as you saw in Figure 1-21.

2. In the navigation pane, click the right-pointing arrow opposite (C:) disk drive to open it.

3. Still in the navigation pane, click the right-pointing arrow opposite Users to open it.

4. Repeat step 3 to open your personal folder and then the My Documents, Trips, and 2011 folders.

5. Click the **Yellowstone** folder to open it in the subject pane.

TIP

It is easy to get confused with the various folders in the navigation pane. Both Favorites and Libraries are folders with *shortcuts*, or links to folders and files on your computer. The shortcuts in Libraries are links to the actual folders in the C:/Users/*Personal Folder*/My Documents, as you see in "Navigate Using Folders."

TIP

The small down arrow between the Forward button and the address bar displays a list of disks and folders that you recently displayed.

QUICKSTEPS

RENAMING AND DELETING FILES AND FOLDERS

Sometimes, a file or folder needs to be renamed or deleted, whether it was created by you or by an application, because you may no longer need it or for any number of reasons.

RENAME A FILE OR FOLDER

With the file or folder in view but not selected, to rename it:

In the subject pane, slowly click the name twice (don't double-click), type the new name, and press **ENTER**.

–Or–

In either the navigation or subject pane, right-click the name, click **Rename**, type the new name, and press **ENTER**.

DELETE A FILE OR FOLDER TO THE RECYCLE BIN

With the file or folder in view in either the navigation or subject pane, to delete it:

Click the icon for the file or folder to select it, press **DELETE**, and click **Yes** to confirm the deletion.

–Or–

Right-click the icon, click **Delete**, and click **Yes** to confirm the deletion.

Continued . . .

You can see that Libraries saves a couple of steps, but at the cost of possible confusion.

NAVIGATE USING THE ADDRESS BAR

Windows 7 gives you another way to quickly navigate through your drives and folders by clicking segments of a folder address in the address bar:

> Computer ▸ Asus (C:) ▸ Users ▸ Marty ▸ My Documents ▸ Trips ▸ 2011 ▸ Yellowstone ▸

If you click any segment of the address, you will open that level in the subject pane. If you click the arrow to the right of the segment, it displays a drop-down list of subfolders that you can jump to. By successively clicking segments and their subordinate folders, you can

easily move throughout the storage space on your computer and beyond to any network you are connected to.

RENAMING AND DELETING FILES AND FOLDERS *(Continued)*

RECOVER A DELETED FILE OR FOLDER

To recover a file or folder that has been deleted:

Click the **Organize** menu, and click **Undo**. This only works if you perform the undo operation immediately after the deletion.

–Or–

Double-click the **Recycle Bin** on the desktop to display the Recycle Bin. Right-click the file or folder icon, and choose **Restore**.

PERMANENTLY DELETE A FILE OR FOLDER

If you're sure you want to permanently delete a file or folder:

Click the icon to select it, press and hold **SHIFT** while pressing **DELETE**, and click **Yes** to confirm the permanent deletion.

–Or–

Right-click the icon, press and hold **SHIFT** while clicking **Delete**, and click **Yes** to confirm the permanent deletion.

CREATE NEW FOLDERS

While you could store all your files within one of the ready-made folders in Windows 7—such as Documents, Music, or Pictures—you will probably want to make your files easier to find by creating several subfolders.

For example, to create the Trips folder discussed earlier:

1. Click **Start** and click **Documents**. Make sure nothing is selected.

2. Click **New Folder** on the toolbar. A new folder will appear in the Documents folder with its name highlighted.

3. Type the name of the folder, such as <u>Trips</u>, and press **ENTER**. Double-click your new folder to open it (you will see it's empty).

As an alternative to clicking New Folder on the toolbar, right-click the open area in the subject pane of Windows Explorer, click **New**, and click **Folder**. Type a name for the folder, and press **ENTER**.

Chapter 2
Using the Internet

The Internet provides a major means for worldwide communication between both individuals and organizations, as well as a major means for locating and sharing information. For many, having access to the Internet is the primary reason for having a computer. To use the Internet, you must have a connection to it using one of the many means that are now available. You then can send and receive email; access the World Wide Web; watch movies; and participate in blogs, forums, and newsgroups, among many other things.

Connect to the Internet

You can connect to the Internet using a telephone line, a cable TV connection, a satellite link, or a land-based wireless link. Across these various types of connections there are a myriad of speeds, degrees of reliability, and costs. The most important factor is what is available to you at the location where you want to use it. In an urban area, you have a number of alternatives, from landline phone companies, cell phone companies, and cable TV companies, all with varying degrees of speed, reliability, and cost. As you move farther and farther away from the urban area, your options will decrease until you have only a telephone dial-up connection and/or a satellite link available. With a telephone line, you can connect with a *dial-up* connection, a *DSL* (digital subscriber line) connection, or other high-speed connections of various types. DSL, cable, satellite, and some wireless connections are called **broadband** connections and offer higher speeds and are always on—you don't have to turn them on and off. You must have access to at least one of these forms of communication in order to connect to the Internet, and the Internet connection itself may need to be set up.

Research the types of connections available to you and their cost. Start by talking to your friends and neighbors, see what they use and how happy they are with their service. Then call your phone company and your cable TV company and ask them about their Internet offerings. If you have to use a dial-up connection, which you should avoid if possible because of its very slow speed, your phone company can lead you through the process of getting set up and becoming familiar with its use. You may need to get a *modem*, a device to connect your computer to a phone line, or one may be built into your computer; your phone company will be able to tell.

With most forms of Internet connections, you have a choice of speed and ancillary services, such as the number of free email accounts and possibly a personal website. Also, depending on the type of connection, you may need dedicated equipment, such as a modem, DSL router, or satellite receiving equipment, which may or may not be included in the monthly cost. Also, make sure you know not only what your Internet service will initially cost, but also what it will cost after the introductory period.

NOTE

For the sake of writing convenience, and because Windows 7 comes with Internet Explorer, this book assumes you are using Internet Explorer to access the Internet. Other browsers, such as Mozilla Firefox (mozilla.com) and Google Chrome (google.com), also work fine.

Set Up an Internet Connection

Broadband Internet services, including DSL, TV cable, satellite, and high-speed wireless, provide an Internet link with a device called a *router* that connects your computer to the service. Normally, your Internet service provider (ISP) will provide the router and physically install it. With a router in place, your computer is connected to a broadband service and you are connected to the Internet at all times.

There may be nothing else you need to do to connect to a broadband service. The easiest way to check if you are connected to the Internet is to try it out by clicking the **Internet Explorer** icon normally pinned to the left of the taskbar.

If a webpage is displayed, like the MSN page shown in Figure 2-1, then you are connected and you need do no more. If you did not connect to the Internet, then you need to run through the following steps:

1. Have you, or someone for you, contacted an ISP (such as your phone or cable company) and contracted to have Internet service connected to your computer? If so, go to the next question. If not, you need to locate an ISP and contract for the service. To find a good ISP, in addition to asking friends and neighbors who are using the Internet, ask the store where you bought your computer.

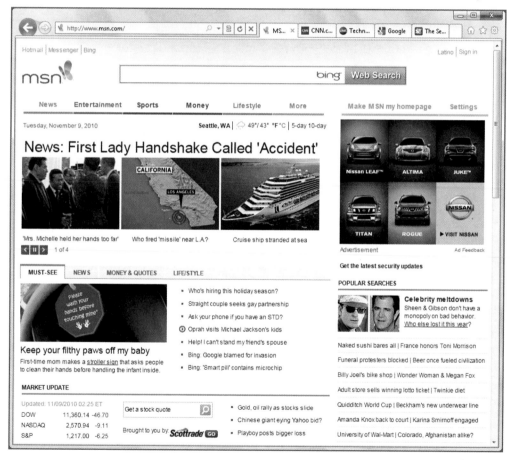

Figure 2-1: The easiest way to see if you have an Internet connection is to try to connect to the Internet.

⏱ QUICKSTEPS

BROWSING THE INTERNET

Browsing the Internet (also called "surfing" the Internet) refers to using a browser, like Internet Explorer, to go from one website to another to see the sites' contents. You can browse to a site by directly entering a site address, by navigating to a site from another site, or by using the browser controls. First, of course, you have to start the browser.

START A BROWSER

To start your default browser (assumed to be Internet Explorer), click the **Internet Explorer** icon on the left of the taskbar.

ENTER A SITE DIRECTLY

To go directly to a site:

1. Start your browser and click the existing address, or URL (Uniform Resource Locator), in the address bar to select it.

2. Type the address of the site you want to open, as shown next, and either click **Go To** (the right-pointing arrow) next to the address bar or press **ENTER**.

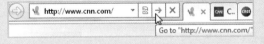

USE SITE NAVIGATION

Site navigation is using a combination of links and menus on a webpage to locate and open another webpage, either in the same site or in another site.

Continued . . .

2. If you know that you have contracted for an Internet service, then is your computer connected to it? Can you physically see the connection? If you can answer yes to both of those questions, go to the next question. If not, contact your ISP and ask them about connecting your computer. They will either send someone out to do it or lead you through the steps to do it yourself.

3. If you have a service and your computer is connected to it and you still cannot connect to the Internet, then you probably need to change some settings on your computer. Contact your ISP and have them lead you through the changes you need to make. This is their job. They need to make sure your connection is working properly.

Use the World Wide Web

The *World Wide Web* (or just the *Web*) is the sum of all the websites in the world—examples of which are CNN, Google, and MSN (which was shown in Figure 2-1). The World Wide Web is what you can access with a *web browser*, such as Internet Explorer, which comes with Windows 7.

Search the Internet

You can search the Internet in two ways: by using the search capability built into Internet Explorer and by using a search facility built into a website.

SEARCH FROM INTERNET EXPLORER

To use Internet Explorer's Search box:

1. Click the **Internet Explorer** icon on the taskbar to open it.

2. In IE 8, click in the **Search** box on the right of the address bar, or in IE 9, click in the address bar. In either case, begin typing what you want to search for. (The first time you search in IE 9, click **Turn On Search Suggestions**.) Click one of the suggestions below the Search box, click **Search** (the magnifying glass in IE 8) on the right end of the Search box, or click **Go To** (IE 9), or press **ENTER**. By default, the Bing

UICKSTEPS

BROWSING THE INTERNET (Continued)

- **Links** are words, phrases, sentences, or graphics that always have an open hand displayed when the mouse pointer is moved over them and, when clicked, take you to another location. They are often underlined—if not initially, then when you move the mouse pointer to them.

Live: Follow all the college football action
TCU faces Utah in a clash of unbeatens, 'Bama takes on LSU

- **Menus** contain one or a few words in a horizontal list, vertical list, or both that always have an open hand displayed when the mouse pointer is moved over them and, when clicked, take you to another location.

| Home | Local | Nation/World | Business/Tech | Sports | Entertainment |

Quick links: Traffic | Movies | Restaurants | Toda   Home

Saturday, November 6, 2010 - Page updated at 01:19 p   High School

Washington 0, #1 Oregon 3 13:26 2nd | NCAAF score   Mariners
California 0, WashSt 0 12:00 1st | NCAAF scoreboar   Seahawks

USE BROWSER NAVIGATION

Browser navigation is using the controls within your browser to go to another location. Internet Explorer has two controls not discussed elsewhere that are used for navigation.

- **Back** and **Forward** buttons take you to the next or previous page in the stack of pages you have viewed most recently.

Continued . . .

search site will open with the results of the search, as you can see in Figure 2-2.

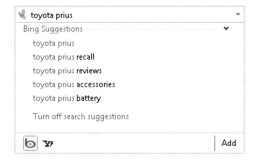

3. Click the link of your choice to go to that site.

Figure 2-2: The results of a search using Internet Explorer's Search box.

BROWSING THE INTERNET *(Continued)*

Moving your mouse over these buttons will display a tooltip showing you the name of the page the button will take you to. Right-clicking these buttons will open a drop-down menu of recent pages you have visited going in the direction of the button (forward or back).

• **The Pages recently entered** button displays a drop-down list of webpages that you have recently entered into the address bar, as well as a list of sites you recently visited (in IE 9).

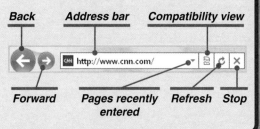

Back   Address bar   Compatibility view

Forward   Pages recently entered   Refresh   Stop

NOTE

Older webpages are shown in Compatibility View as indicated with the icon of a torn page at the right end of the address bar.

SEARCH FROM AN INTERNET SITE

There are many independent Internet search sites. The most popular is Google.

1. In Internet Explorer, click the current address in the address bar, type google.com, and either click **Go To** (the blue arrow) or press **ENTER**.

2. In the text box, type what you want to search for. As you type, Google will display some guesses based upon what you have typed, with the resulting websites for those guesses shown in a full webpage, as illustrated in Figure 2-3.

3. Click the link of your choice to go to that site.

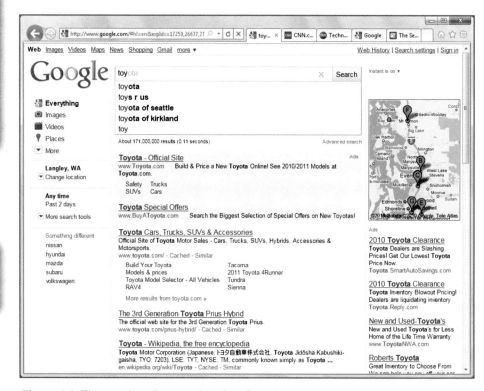

Figure 2-3: **The results of a search using Google**

BOB DOES MEDICAL RESEARCH ON THE INTERNET

The personal computer and the Internet were not things that I immediately embraced, but now, after several years, I find that the Internet is essential to my research from the National Library of Medicine. I use it every day.

Bob A., MD, 78, Washington

NOTE

By default, Internet Explorer uses Microsoft's Bing search engine. You can change this by clicking the down arrow on the right of the Search box and clicking **Find More Providers** in IE 8, or in IE 9, clicking the down arrow on the right of the address bar and clicking **Add**. In either case, the Add-Ons Gallery will open and allow you to add another search provider by clicking **Add To Internet Explorer** under the provider you want.

Save a Favorite Site

Sometimes, you visit a site that you would like to return to quickly or often. Internet Explorer has a memory bank called Favorites to which you can save sites for easy retrieval.

ADD A FAVORITE SITE

To add a site to Favorites:

1. In Internet Explorer, open the webpage you want to add to your Favorites list, and make sure its correct address (URL) is in the address bar.

2. In IE 8, click **Favorites** in or above the tab row. In IE 9, click the **Favorites** icon on the right of the tab row.

3. In either case, click **Add To Favorites**. The Add A Favorite dialog box appears. Adjust the name as needed in the text box (you may want to type a name you will readily associate with that site), and click **Add**.

OPEN A FAVORITE SITE

To open a favorite site you have saved:

- In Internet Explorer 8, click **Favorites** above the tab row. In IE 9, click the **Favorites** icon on the right of the tab row. In either case, click the site you want to open.

QUICKSTEPS

CHANGING YOUR HOME PAGE

When you first start Internet Explorer, a webpage is automatically displayed. This page is called your *home page*. When you go to other webpages, you can return to this page by clicking the **Home** icon on the tab row. When IE starts, you can have IE open several pages in addition to the home page, with the additional pages displayed as tabs (see "Use Tabs" in this chapter), which will also be opened when you click the Home Page icon. To change your home page and the other pages initially opened:

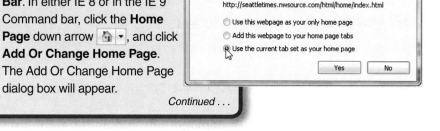

1. In Internet Explorer, directly enter or browse to the site you want as your home page. If you want additional pages, open them in separate tabs.

2. In IE 9, right-click the **Home Page** icon, and click **Command Bar**. In either IE 8 or in the IE 9 Command bar, click the **Home Page** down arrow, and click **Add Or Change Home Page**. The Add Or Change Home Page dialog box will appear.

Continued . . .

Use Tabs

Internet Explorer 8 and 9 allow you to have several webpages open at one time and easily switch between them by clicking the tab associated with the page. The tabs reside on the *tab row*, immediately above the displayed webpage, which also has the address bar in IE 9, as shown in Figure 2-4. Originally, only one page was open at a time in versions of Internet Explorer before IE 7. If you opened a second page, it replaced the first page. IE 7 and on, however, give you the ability to open multiple pages as separate tabs that you can switch among by clicking their tabs.

OPEN PAGES IN A NEW TAB

To open a page in a new tab instead of opening the page in an existing tab:

1. Open Internet Explorer with at least one webpage displayed.

2. Click **New Tab** on the right end of the tab row, or press **CTRL+T**, and open another webpage in any of the ways described earlier in this chapter.

   –Or–

   Hold down **CTRL** while clicking a link in an open page. (If you just click the link, you'll open a page in the same tab.) Then click the new tab to open the page.

Figure 2-4: *Tabs allow you to quickly switch among several websites.*

QUICKSTEPS

CHANGING YOUR HOME PAGE

(Continued)

3. Click:

- **Use This Webpage As Your Only Home Page** if you wish to have only a single home page.

- **Add This Webpage To Your Home Page Tabs** if you wish to have several home pages on different tabs.

- **Use The Current Tab Set As Your Home Page** if you want all the current tabs to appear when you start Internet Explorer or click the Home Page icon (this option is only available if you have two or more tabs open).

4. Click **Yes** to complete your home page selection and close the dialog box.

You can also change the home page by clicking the **Tools** menu in IE 8 or the **Tools** icon in IE 9, clicking **Internet Options** in either case, and making the desired changes at the top of the General tab.

TIP

You can open the home page in its own tab instead of replacing the current tab by holding **CTRL** while clicking the **Home Page** icon.

SWITCH AMONG TABS

To switch among open tabs:

Click the tab of the page you want to open.

–Or–

Press **CTRL+TAB** to switch to the next tab to the right, or press **CTRL+SHIFT+TAB** to switch to the next tab to the left.

–Or–

Press **CTRL+***n*, where *n* is a number from 1 to 8 to switch to one of the first eight tabs, numbered from the left in the order they were opened. You can also press **CTRL+9** to switch to the last tab that was opened, shown on the right of the tab row. (Use a number key on the top of the main keyboard, *not* on the numeric keypad on the right.)

CLOSE TABS

To close one or more tabs:

Right-click the tab for the page you want to close, and click **Close Tab** on the context menu; or click **Close Other Tabs** to close all of the pages except the one you clicked.

–Or–

Press **CTRL+W** to close the current page.

Access Web History

Internet Explorer keeps a history of the websites you visit, and you can use that history to return to a site. You can set the length of time to keep sites in that history, and you can clear your history.

USE WEB HISTORY

To use the Web History feature:

1. Click **Favorites** or its icon, and click the **History** tab; or press **CTRL+H** to open the History pane.

QUICK QUOTES

JIM FINDS LOTS OF INFORMATION

I use my computer for a lot of things, including email, banking, and working with my photos, including organizing them, putting them on CDs, and printing them. Probably most valuable, though, is the access to the Internet, which I use quite often. While I'm now retired, I often go on Web MD to look up drug interactions and other information. I also find the Internet very useful in looking up random information. For example, we had a house guest from France and got to talking about bridges. I mentioned a bridge in France I knew about that he did not. We looked it up on the Internet and, sure enough, found the bridge I had remembered. I think this capability is truly amazing to have in your home. Before the Internet, you might have been able to go to a library and find it, but even there, it would have been much more difficult.

Jim T., DDS, 76, Missouri

2. Click the down arrow on the History tab bar to select how you want the history sorted. Depending on what you select, you will be able to further specify the type of history you want to view. For example, if you click View By Date, you can then click the day, website, and webpage you want to open, as shown in Figure 2-5.

DELETE AND SET HISTORY

You can set the length of time to keep your Internet history, and you can clear this history.

1. In Internet Explorer, click **Tools** or its icon at the right end of the tab row, and click **Internet Options**.

2. In the General tab, under Browsing History, click **Delete** to open the Delete Browsing History dialog box. If needed, select the check box opposite **History** to delete it. Select any other check box to delete that information, although you should keep the **Preserve Favorites Website Data** check box selected to *keep* that information (it is a confusing dialog box). Click **Delete**.

   –Or–

   In the General tab of the Internet Options dialog box, under Browsing History, click **Settings**. Under History, at the bottom of the dialog box, use the **Days** spinner to set the number of days to keep your browsing history. Click **OK**.

3. Click **OK** again to close the Internet Options dialog box.

Figure 2-5: **The Web History feature allows you to find a site that you visited in the recent past.**

ORGANIZING FAVORITE SITES

After a while, you will probably find that you have a number of favorite sites and it is becoming hard to find the one you want. Internet Explorer provides two places to store your favorite sites, a Favorites list, which is presented to you in the form of a menu you can open, and a Favorites bar, which can be displayed at all times. There are several ways to organize your favorite sites.

REARRANGE THE FAVORITES LIST

The items on your Favorites list are displayed in the order you added them, unless you drag them to a new location.

- In Internet Explorer, click **Favorites** or the icon, locate the site you want to reposition, and drag it to the location in the list where you want it.

CREATE NEW FOLDERS

Internet Explorer (both 8 and 9) comes with several default folders added by Microsoft or by the computer's manufacturer. You can also add your own folders within the Favorites list.

1. In Internet Explorer, click **Favorites** or the icon, click the **Add To Favorites** down arrow, and click **Organize Favorites** to open the Organize Favorites dialog box, shown in Figure 2-6.
2. Click **New Folder**, type the name for the folder, and press **ENTER**.
3. Drag the desired site links to the new folder, drag the folder to where you want it on the list, and then click **Close**.

Continued . . .

Figure 2-6: As with files, organizing your favorite websites helps you find easily what you want.

Copy Internet Information

You may occasionally find something on the Internet that you want to copy—a picture, some text, or a webpage.

COPY A PICTURE FROM THE INTERNET

To copy a picture from a webpage to a folder on your hard disk:

1. Open Internet Explorer and locate the webpage containing the picture you want.

ORGANIZING FAVORITE SITES (Continued)

PUT FAVORITES IN FOLDERS

You can put a site in either your own folders (see "Create New Folders") or the default ones when you initially add it to your Favorites list.

1. Open the webpage you want in your Favorites list, and make sure its correct address or URL is in the address bar.

2. Click **Favorites** or the icon, click **Add To Favorites**, adjust the name as needed in the text box, click the **Create In** down arrow, select the folder to use, and click **Add**.

ADD A SITE TO THE FAVORITES BAR

In IE 8, by default, a Favorites bar is displayed on the same row with and to the right of the Favorites menu. In IE 9, you can turn on the Favorites bar by right-clicking any of the three icons (Home, Favorites, and Tools) on the right of the tab row and clicking **Favorites Bar**. By default, the Favorites bar has two sites on it, but you can add others.

Open the site you want to add to the Favorites bar. In either IE 8 or IE 9, if the Favorites bar is open, click the **Add To Favorites Bar** button on the left of the Favorites bar
–Or–

In either IE 8 or 9, click **Favorites**, click the **Add To Favorites** down arrow, and click **Add To Favorites Bar**.

2. Right-click the picture and click **Save Picture As**. Locate the folder in which you want to save the picture, enter the file name you want to use, as well as the file type if it is something other than the default .jpg, and click **Save**.

3. Close Internet Explorer if you are done.

COPY TEXT FROM THE INTERNET TO WORD OR EMAIL

To copy text from a webpage to a Microsoft Word document or email message:

1. Open Internet Explorer and locate the webpage containing the text you want.

2. Drag across to highlight the text, right-click the selection, and click **Copy**.

3. Open a Microsoft Word document or an email message in which you want to paste the text. Right-click where you want the text, and click **Paste**.

4. Save the Word document and close Internet Explorer, Microsoft Word, or your email program if you are done with them.

COPY A WEBPAGE FROM THE INTERNET

To make a copy of a webpage and store it on your hard disk:

1. Open Internet Explorer and locate the webpage you want to copy.

2. In IE 8, click **Page** on the tab row and click **Save As**. In IE 9, click the **Tools** icon, click **File**, and click **Save As**.

3. In the Save Webpage dialog box, select the folder in which to save the page, enter the file name you want to use, and click **Save**.

4. Close Internet Explorer if you are done.

TIP

To delete a favorite site from either the Favorites list or the Favorites bar, right-click it and click **Delete**.

Play Internet Audio and Video Files

You can play audio and video files on the Internet with Internet Explorer directly from a link on a webpage. Many webpages have links to audio and video files, such as the one shown in Figure 2-7. To play these files, simply click the links. If you have several audio players installed (for example, Windows Media Player and Real Player), you will be asked which one you want to use. Make that choice, and the player will open to play the requested piece. To truly enjoy audio and video files from the Internet, you should have a broadband connection.

Figure 2-7: Play an audio or video file on a webpage by clicking the link.

CAUTION

Material you copy from the Internet is normally protected by copyright; therefore, what you can do with it is limited. Basically, you can store it on your hard disk and refer to it. You cannot put it on your own website, sell it, copy it for distribution, or use it for a commercial purpose without the permission of the owner.

TIP

Search sites such as Google and Bing provide the ability to search the entire Internet. Search boxes on other sites, such as CNN and Amazon, are used to search those sites, not the Internet.

Use the Internet

The Internet is a major way in which you can connect with the world that provides information, shopping, contact with government agencies, getting directions and maps, and planning and purchasing travel, to name only a fraction of what you can do. In later chapters of this book we'll look at using the Internet for email, social networking, digital photography, music and video, personal finance, and genealogy. For the rest of this chapter, we'll look at using the Internet in a number of other, possibly more general, ways.

Get Information

The start of many things you do on the Internet is through a search. As you have seen earlier in this chapter, searching the Internet is easy through either Internet Explorer's Search box, which by default is the Microsoft Bing search engine, or a search website like Google.com. Although there are a number of other search sites, for example Ask.com, I've found that Google and Bing are as good as any and handle all that I want to do.

You can search for almost anything and in most cases find it. Sometimes, you need to be more diligent than other times, but often, you can find what you are looking for. Several examples of searches follow.

MARY TUDOR VS. MARY QUEEN OF SCOTS

In the last several years there have been movies and television programs on England's King Henry VIII and Queen Elizabeth I, his daughter. In these, two historical figures named Mary come up: Mary Tudor and Mary Queen of Scots. Let's say you are curious and want to know more about these two people and how they are related.

Searches on the Internet are seldom the same, as it is a dynamic and changing environment. New pages, re-ordered pages, and obsolete pages are constantly changing and creating new results for searches.

1. In Internet Explorer's address bar, highlight the current contents and type google.com.

2. In Google's text box, type Mary Tudor and Mary Queen of Scots and press **ENTER**. The Google page similar to that shown in Figure 2-8 will open.

3. Review the first several entries, and click the first one you want to see. A page similar to the one shown in Figure 2-9 will open.

4. If the results of the first entry do not satisfy your curiosity, click **Previous** in Internet Explorer's address bar to return to the list of search results and click another entry.

WHITE BEAN SOUP

The Internet is a tremendous resource for recipes. All you have to do is search. Here is an example with white bean soup.

1. In the Internet Explorer Search box (in IE 8) or in the address bar (in IE 9), type white bean soup. By default, the Bing search engine is used and, as you are typing, search suggestions will appear below the Search box.

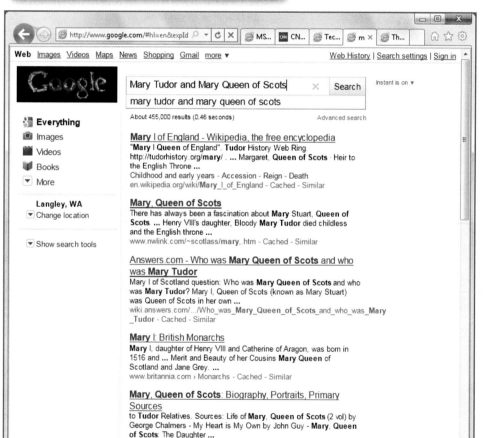

Figure 2-8: A search can be a question, a statement, a word, or a phrase. Often, a question can be truncated, as it is here, where "who were" has been left off.

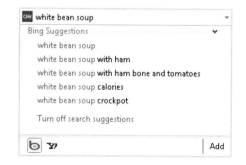

Figure 2-9: Sometimes, a search can quickly lead you to the answer you want.

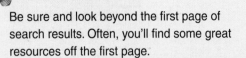

TIP

Be sure and look beyond the first page of search results. Often, you'll find some great resources off the first page.

2. If you want one of the suggestions, click it. Otherwise, press **ENTER**. A list of sites with a recipe for this dish appears similar to what you see in Figure 2-10.

Figure 2-10: If you like to cook, the Internet is a great resource for you.

Get the News

With the Internet's almost immediate communication, it is a great vehicle for getting news of all types, including local and national newspapers, general and specialized magazines, and newsletters of all types. Several examples follow.

READ ONLINE NEWSPAPERS

Most newspapers have been online for some time. Generally, you can go right to their site by putting their name directly into the address bar followed by ".com" without searching for them. For example, the following URLs all work:

- ajc.com (*Atlanta Journal Constitution*)
- bostonherald.com
- chicagotribune.com
- denverpost.com
- kcstar.com (*Kansas City Star*)
- latimes.com (*Los Angeles Times*)
- miamiherald.com
- times.com (*New York Times*)
- philly.com (*Philadelphia Inquirer*)
- seattletimes.com
- wsj.com (*Wall Street Journal*)
- washingtonpost.com

READ ONLINE MAGAZINES

Many magazines that once had paper editions are now only online, while others are now charging for their online editions. For example *Consumer Reports* (consumerreports.org, .com also works) and *Cooks Illustrated* (cooksillustrated.com), which give you their home page for free, ask you to pay when you want to see the detail, as you can see in Figure 2-11. For the most part, you can directly use the magazine title with ".com" in the Internet Explorer's address box.

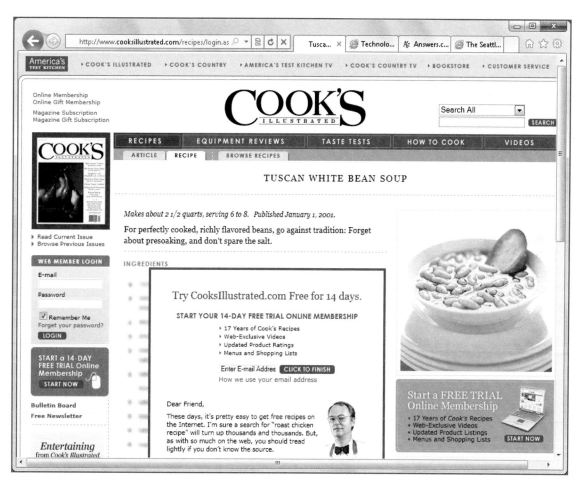

Figure 2-11: While the majority of Internet news and information content is free, an increasing number of sites are beginning to charge for it.

READ NEWSLETTERS

There are a great many newsletters on the Internet. Practically every organization that has an Internet presence has a newsletter, either as a part of their site or one that is emailed to you. If you belong or are otherwise a part of an organization, inquire about looking at their newsletter online or receiving it by email.

DICK SEARCHES FOR TRAVEL DEALS

My wife and I find that we use the Internet quite a bit. We use email to communicate with our friends and family. We do a lot of shopping online, as well as much of our banking activity, including bill paying. We find we can easily set up and manage the paying of both recurring and one-time bills so that we don't have to worry about their payment. We also have found that we can easily make donations to our favorite charities online. Probably as much as anything else, we use the Internet to research things we are considering buying, like going to Edmunds.com before buying a car, or looking at the costs of airfare, hotels, and rental cars on any of the travel sites like Orbitz. com, Hotwire.com, and Priceline.com. We do a fair amount of travel both within the United States and abroad, including to India, Turkey, and Viet Nam, and we have found we can plan and book a fairly complex trip as well as save quite a bit of money using the resources on the Internet.

Dick W., 77, Washington

Contact Government Agencies

Most government agencies from the local to the federal level have an online presence that can be quite useful in finding out about government programs, learning about public officials, and getting the results of elections. Three examples are the Social Security Administration, researching the position of a congressperson, and looking at the results of a statewide election.

SOCIAL SECURITY ADMINISTRATION

Probably the fastest way of locating a website is to search the name of the entity, and similarly, the fastest way to find what you want in a site is to do an intrasite search. Let's say you want to find the current eligibility requirements for Social Security.

1. In the Internet Explorer Search box (in IE 8) or in the address bar (IE 9), type <u>social security</u> and press **ENTER**. One of the entries that appears is titled "Social Security Online—The Official Website..."

2. In the search box under "Search within www.ssa.gov," type <u>eligibility requirements</u> and click **Search**.

3. Review the search results, and click the entry that is most likely to give you the information you need.

4. Follow any additional links that you need to get your information.

washington state congressional districts ☒ | Search

About 9,010,000 results (0.23 seconds)   Advanced search

▶ Statewide Map of **Washington** Legislative **Districts**
History of the **State** Legislature ... You may use the information below to find your
legislative district and **congressional district**. ...
apps.leg.**wa**.gov/**District**Finder/ - Cached

Washington's Representatives - Congressional District
Maps (WA ...
The two senators from **Washington** are Sen. Cantwell, Maria [D-**WA**] and Sen.
... The map to the right shows the **congressional districts** in this **state**. ...
www.govtrack.us › Congress › Members of Congress - Cached - Similar

Washington State Legislature
Congress - the Other **Washington** ... Legislator Information, Find Your **District**,
Bill Search ... (List of legislators, their committees, **districts**, ...
Bill Information - Find Your Legislator - RCW
www.leg.**wa**.gov/ - Cached - Similar

Washington Elections Information
Ballot, voter registration, current initiative, and general information for **elections** as
reported through the **Washington** Secretary of **State's** office.
www.secstate.wa.gov/elections · Cached page

RESEARCH A CONGRESSPERSON

If you would like to determine the views of your congressperson and you don't remember her or his name or the district number he or she represents, you can find all that online.

1. In the Internet Explorer address bar, type google.com.
2. In the Google search box, type your state name and congressional districts, and press **ENTER**. Your results should look something like the illustration.
3. Click the entry with "Congressional District Maps" in its title with the URL govtrack.us. The result should look similar to Figure 2-12, except for your state.
4. Note your district, scroll down to locate your congressperson, and click his or her name. A page about her or him should open. From here, you can see a brief or official biography, track his or her voting record, find out who donated to her or his campaign, and the bills that he or she alone sponsored.
5. Follow any of the links that interest you.

FOLLOW STATEWIDE ELECTIONS

Most government jurisdictions (cities, counties, and states) maintain a page with the most recent election results. To find the results for a statewide race:

1. In Internet Explorer's Search box (IE 8) or address bar (IE 9), type the name of your state and the words state election results, and press **ENTER**. A list of related topics should appear.
2. Click the entry that looks most promising to you. A related detail page will open. Review that page and determine if you need to go further or if the information you want is available there.

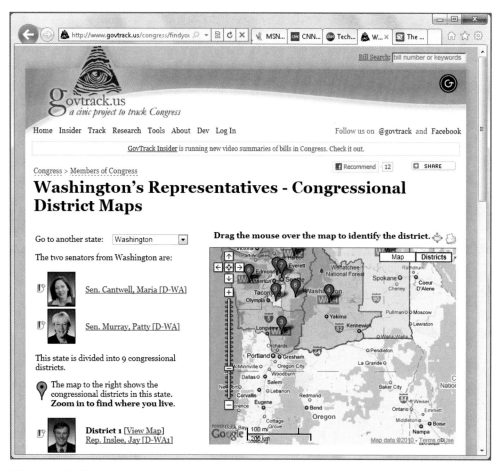

Figure 2-12: *The Internet has a number of resources to help you understand and work with local, state, and federal governments.*

Get Maps and Directions

Google and Microsoft, as well as others, have excellent, detailed maps and driving directions. Here how each works.

MICROSOFT MAPS

1. In Internet Explorer's Search box (IE 8) or address bar (IE 9), type an address or location you want to see on a map, and press **ENTER**. Among the search results is a small map.

2. Click **View Large Map** to see a full-sized map of the location or address you entered, as shown in Figure 2-13.

3. On this map you can:

   - Zoom in for more detail or zoom out for area references by clicking or dragging in the scale on the upper left of the map.

   - Drag the map around to see areas not currently in view by moving the mouse onto the map and dragging it in the direction you want it moved.

   - View the map as a road map or as an aerial photograph in either straight down aerial view or the slightly angled bird's-eye view using the option on the top right.

   - Get driving directions from another location by clicking the auto icon on the bottom left of the page.

   - Locate restaurants, businesses, malls, and hotels by clicking the options on the left side of the page.

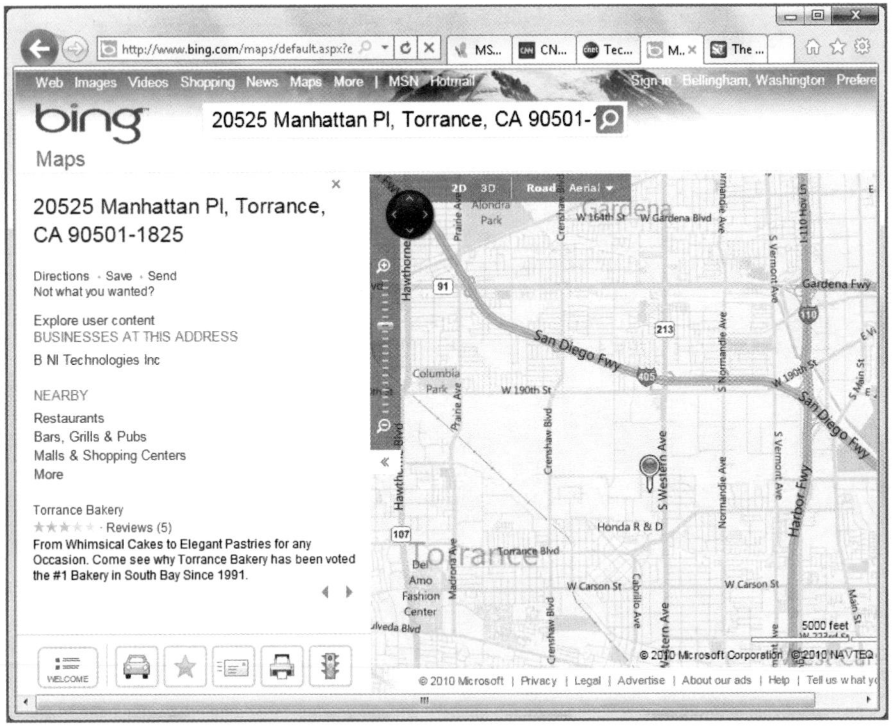

![Bing Maps screenshot showing a map of Torrance, CA with address 20525 Manhattan Pl, Torrance, CA 90501-1825 and nearby business listings]

Figure 2-13: Excellent maps are available online with many features not available any other way.

GOOGLE DIRECTIONS

Both Google and Microsoft provide detailed driving directions between two or more locations.

1. In the Internet Explorer address bar, type google.com to open the Google search site. At the top of the page you should see a row of options; if not immediately, they should appear after a few seconds.

2. Click **Maps**. In the page that opens, note you can put in an address or a location just as you did with Bing. Here, though, we'll get driving directions.

3. Click **Get Directions**. In the first text box, labeled "A," type the starting location. This can be a street address, a city or airport, or some other location identifier.

4. Press **TAB** and type the ending location or the location's first intermediate point. If you want to enter more locations, click **Add Destination**, and type that location.

5. Click **Get Directions**. A map will appear along with a detailed set of directions, as you can see in Figure 2-14. Click **Print** above the map to print the directions. If you want the map printed, click **Include Large Map**, and then click **Print** again.

6. Close the print window. Back on the map, if you want to change your route, simply drag the blue line that represents it. You'll see the line move and the directions change accordingly.

7. As with the Bing map, you zoom by simply double-clicking the map, drag the map to show other areas, and look at it either as a road map or as a satellite photograph.

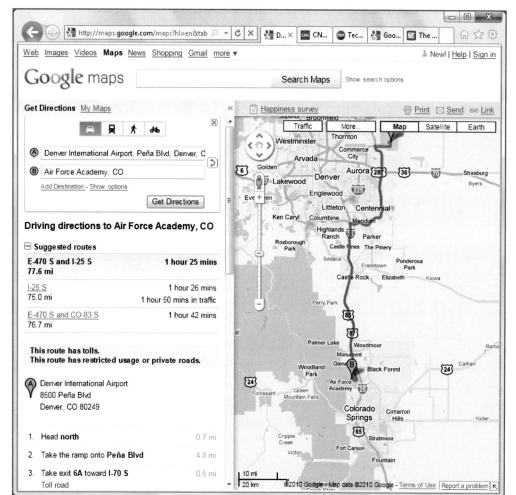

Figure 2-14: **With the advent of online maps and directions, you can more easily find your way.**

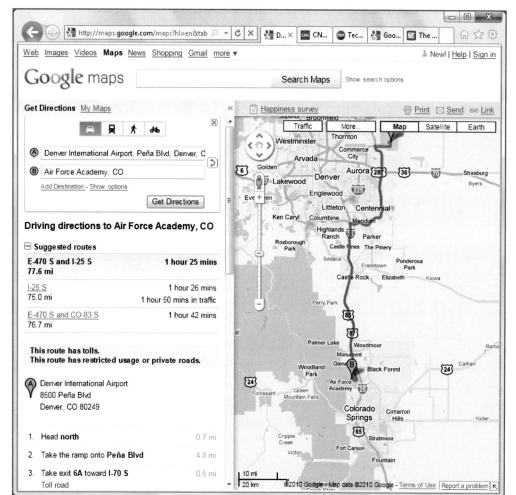

Digital cameras: compare digital camera reviews - CNET Reviews
Digital camera reviews and ratings, video reviews, user opinions, most popular digital cameras, camera buying guides, prices, and comparisons.
reviews.cnet.com/digital-cameras · Cached page

Shop on the Internet

Internet shopping is one of the great benefits of having access to the Internet. You don't have to leave your home, you have access to far more outlets than are available in most places, prices are generally modest, and you have the ability to do comparison shopping to find the best products at the best prices. Look at three examples of online shopping for a digital camera, narrow shoes, and airline tickets.

DIGITAL CAMERA

You may be aware that digital cameras are improving quickly and getting cheaper at the same time. If you are interested in getting a new one, you may be in a quandary as to which to buy. Start by searching for camera reviews and then do some comparison shopping before finally buying a camera (you can't do this with all products, but electronics in particular can be handled in this way).

1. In either the Google or Internet Explorer Bing search box, type <u>digital camera reviews</u> and press **ENTER**. A page of sites that review digital cameras will appear.

2. Open several of the sites and look at what they offer. Some may be more comparison shopping than reviews of cameras. One site that I have found to be good is CNET Reviews. Click that to open it.

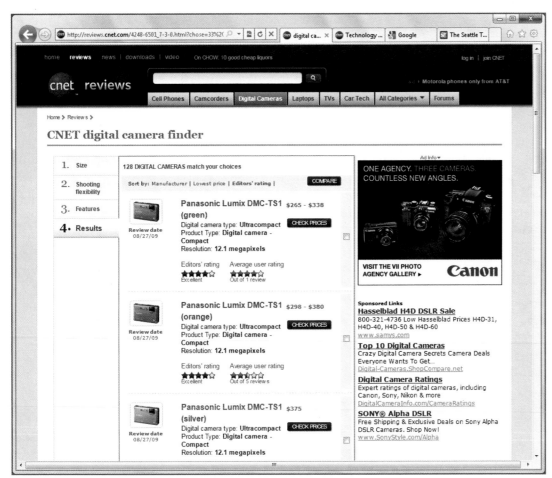

Figure 2-15: *For electronics, there is a wealth of information that allows you to find what you want, compare alternatives, and shop for the best price and terms.*

3. On the CNET site, in the middle of the page, click **Digital Camera Product Finder** to pick the camera that is right for you. Click the size you want, and click **Next**. Click the level of sophistication desired, and click **Next**. Click the features you want, and click **See Results**. A page of possibilities is displayed, an example of which you can see in Figure 2-15.

4. Pick the camera you want to investigate further, and click the title of the camera to open a page devoted to it. Read the review and other information on the page.

5. Click **Compare Prices** in the Price Range section. Here you see a list of several stores with their customer rating, price, and whether the camera is in stock and has free shipping (enter your ZIP code to determine this).

6. If you are ready to go ahead, click **Shop Now** and follow the instructions to purchase the camera.

AIRLINE TICKETS

Airlines now prefer and reward buying tickets online. You often save money, sometimes a lot; may also be entitled to fast electronic check-in at the airport; and sometimes get bonus miles. There are many sources of airline tickets on the Internet, including the airlines

TIP

When comparison shopping, make sure that you compare the price with shipping and tax, because, as you can see, not all the stores are the same.

themselves and numerous travel sites. Sometimes the sites can save you money, but often, the cheapest fares are from the airlines, and some airlines, such as Southwest, do not allow sales through the travel sites, so you need to look at both the airlines and the travel sites. Also, some travel sites, such as Fly.com, will compare the fares on several other travel sites. What I recommend is that you start by comparing travel sites with Fly.com, then go to the site that looks best, and finally go to the airline that looks best. Also, if you are going along a Southwest route, you want check them (Southwest does not charge for up to two pieces of checked luggage, which on other airlines can be $25 to $35 a bag).

1. In the Internet Explorer's address bar, type fly.com and press **ENTER**. Type the from and to cities, select the departure and return dates and times, the number of travelers, and click the travel sites you want to compare, as in the illustration.

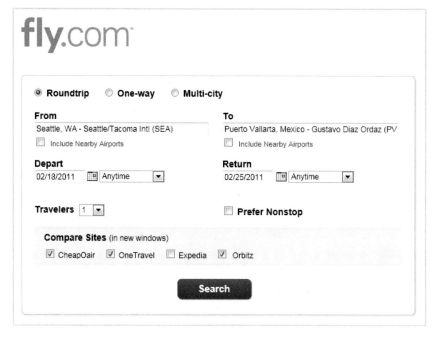

2. Click **Search**. Your screen becomes very busy and you may see a message that a pop-up window has been blocked. Click to allow the pop-up. You see a Fly.com summary, shown next, and then a narrow window for each of the travel sites you selected, as you can see in Figure 2-16.

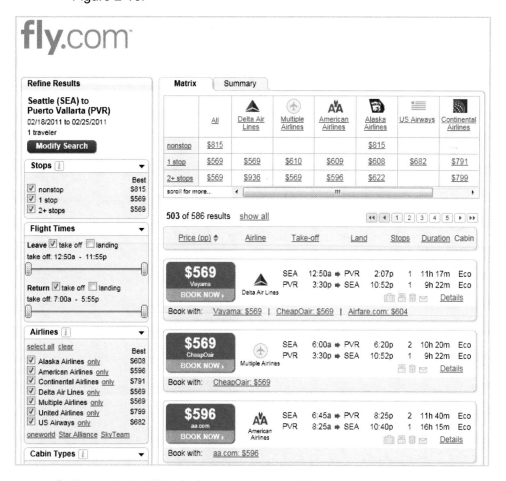

3. Expand (click **Maximize** on the right of the title bar) and review each of the travel sites (be sure to get the *total price* with *both* taxes and fees included, not just the advertised price).

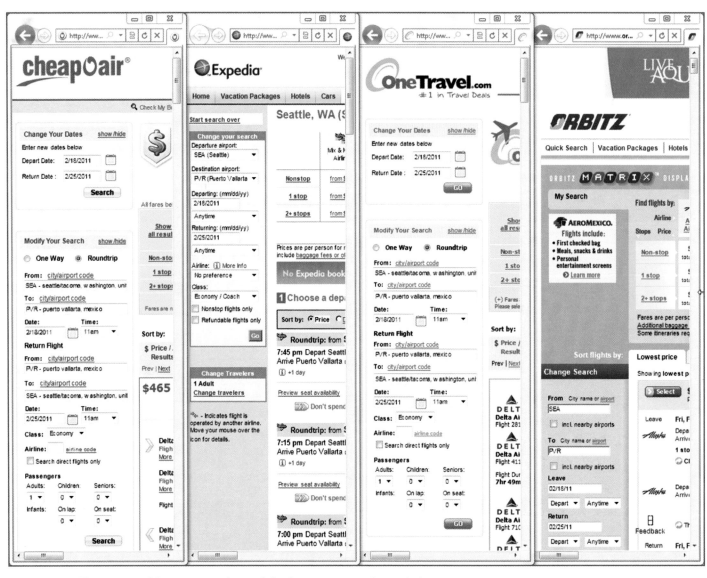

Figure 2-16: Fly.com provides a comparison of the fares on several travel sites.

TIP

Priceline.com has a Name Your Own Price program that allows you to enter from and to locations and the dates you want to fly, and then enter the round-trip fare before taxes and fees that you want to pay. (You can also do this for hotels and rental cars.) Priceline says you can save up to 40 percent on flights. The catch is that you have to pay for the tickets ahead of time; you can't specify the airline or the time of day you will fly; the ticket must be roundtrip and for economy class only; and if your price is accepted, your money is nonrefundable and nontransferrable, the ticket cannot be changed, and you don't get mileage credits. Priceline does promise that domestic flights will leave only between 6 A.M. and 10 P.M., unless the city pairs require off-peak travel, and that there will be no more than one connection each way. If you have some flexibility (and don't mind the William Shatner stare), it can save you some money.

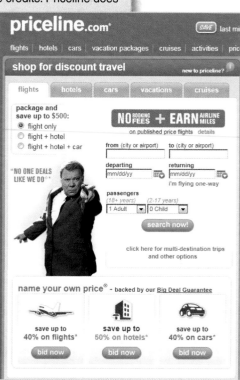

4. Pick an airline and enter their name in the Internet Explorer address bar (don't click their name in Fly.com or another travel site, because you want the best fare the airline itself will offer). Re-enter the from and to cities and dates and times. Click **Search** or the equivalent button (Alaska Airlines uses "Shop"). The results for that airline will be displayed. It may surprise you.

5. If Southwest flies the route you want to fly (type southwest.com in the address bar and try—because Southwest flies to only selected cities— to enter your from and to cities), check their fares. Initially, the fares are displayed one-way without fees and taxes, so you need to select a departing and a returning flight. Click **Continue** to go to the Price page and see the total cost.

It may take some work and perseverance to find the lowest fare.

Chapter 3
Computing Security

Computing, like most things in life, requires prudent caution. You should not let yourself be petrified by it; on the other hand, you want to do what's needed to protect yourself, your information, and your computer. Controlling computer security is a multifaceted subject because of the different aspects of computing that need protection. In this chapter you'll see how to control who uses a computer, control what users do, protect data stored in the computer, and review the security you need with the Internet.

Control Who Is a User

Controlling who uses a computer means identifying the users to the computer, giving them a secure way of signing on to the computer, and preventing everyone else from using it. This is achieved through the process of adding and managing users and passwords.

With Windows 7, like previous versions of Windows, the first user of a computer is, by default, an administrator; however, the Windows 7 administrator operates like a standard user until there is a need to be an administrator. Then a Windows 7 feature called *User Account Control* (UAC) pops up and asks if the administrator started the process. If so, click **Continue** to proceed. A nonadministrative user in the same circumstance would have to enter an administrator's password to continue.

Even though you may initially be an administrator, *it is strongly recommended that your normal everyday account be as a standard user*. The reason for this is that if you are signed on as an administrator and a hacker or malevolent software (called "malware") enters your system at the same time, the hacker or software might gain administrator privileges through you. The best solution is to use a separate administrator account with a strong password just for installing software, working with users, and performing other tasks that require extensive administrator work.

Set Up Users

If you have several people using your computer, each person should be set up as a separate user. To add users to your computer, or even to change your user characteristics (as well as to perform most other tasks in this chapter), you must be logged on as an administrator, so you first need to accomplish that. Then you may want to change the characteristics of your account and add a Standard User account for yourself. Finally, if you have multiple people using your computer, you may want to set up separate user accounts and have each user sign in to his or her account.

NOTE

There are three views of the Control Panel: the Category view, which is the default, the Large Icon view, and the Small Icon view. The Category view is a hierarchical one in which you first select a category and then the item you want to control. In the two icon views, you directly select the item you want to control. To change the view, click the **View By** down arrow and then click the view you want. This book assumes you are looking at the Category view.

If your personal account on your computer is currently set up as an Administrator account, it is strongly recommended that you create a new Standard User account and use that for your everyday computer use. Only use the Administrator account for installing software, changing and adding user information, and performing other tasks requiring an administrator.

LOG ON AS AN ADMINISTRATOR

The procedure for logging on as an administrator depends on what was done when Windows 7 was installed on your computer:

- If you installed Windows 7 on your computer, or if you bought a computer with it already installed and did nothing special to the default installation regarding administrator privileges, you should be the administrator and know the administrator's password (if you established one).

- If you did not do the installation or you got the computer with Windows 7 already installed and you are unsure about your administrator status or password, the instructions here will help you log on as an administrator. The first step is to determine the administrator status on your computer.

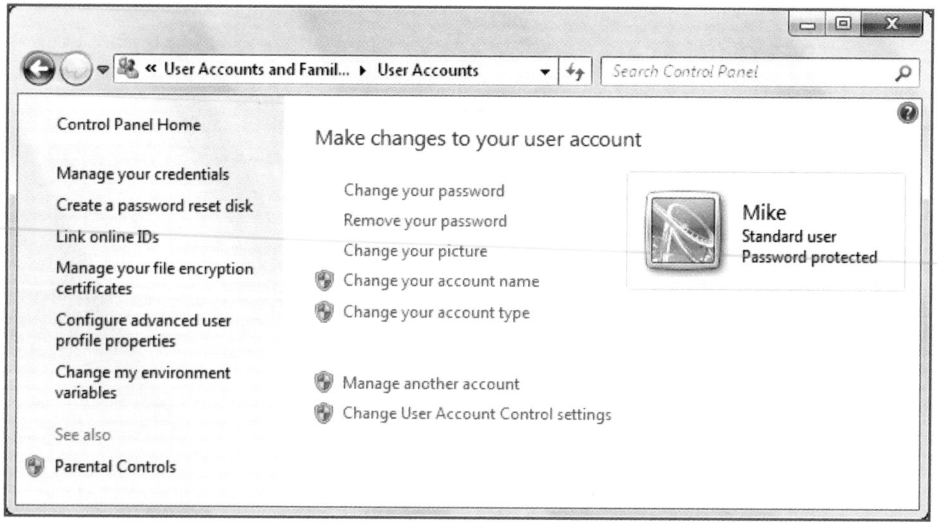

Click **Start** and in the Start menu click **Control Panel**. In Category view, click **User Accounts And Family Safety**, and then click **User Accounts**. The User Accounts window opens, as shown in Figure 3-1.

If the window shows you are an administrator, you can skip these steps. To make changes to an account, see "Change Your Account" later in this chapter.

–Or–

If you are not an administrator someone else on your computer must be. Ask that administrator to change your account type or facilitate your signing on as an administrator. Once that is done skip to "Change Your Account" later in the chapter.

Figure 3-1: Setting up users provides a way of protecting each user from the others and the computer from unauthorized use.

QUICKFACTS

UNDERSTANDING USER ACCOUNT CONTROL

Windows 7 has a feature called User Account Control, or UAC. UAC monitors what is happening on the computer, and if it sees something that could cause a problem, like installing a program, adding a new user, or changing a password, it interrupts that process and asks for physical user verification. When it does this, it also freezes all activity on the computer so that nothing can happen until verification is provided—either using the mouse or the keyboard. If the user has administrator privileges, this person is asked if he or she wants to allow changes to be made and, if so, to click **Yes**. If the user doesn't have administrator privileges, he or she is asked for the administrator's password. By requiring a physical action, UAC ensures that an actual person is sitting at the computer and that malware is not attempting to modify it.

All operations that require administrative privileges have a little shield icon beside them, as you can see in Figure 3-1.

For a while, especially if you are installing several programs, the UAC dialog boxes can be irritating. You can turn it off in the User Accounts Control Panel, but this is strongly discouraged. If you do turn it off while you are installing several programs, it is strongly recommended that you turn it back on when you are finished.

CHANGE YOUR ACCOUNT

You can change an account name, the display picture, add or change a password, and possibly change the account type.

1. Click **Start** and click **Control Panel**. In Category view, click **User Accounts And Family Safety**, and then click **User Accounts**.

2. Click **Change Your Account Name**. If you are not already logged on as an administrator, the User Account Control dialog box will appear and ask you to type an administrator's password.

3. Type a new name, and click **Change Name**.

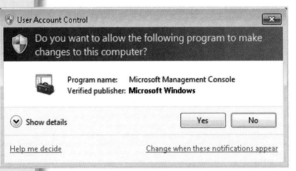

In a similar manner, you can change your display picture. If you are the only administrator, you will not be allowed to change your account type or delete your account. Changing and setting passwords are discussed in the "Setting Passwords" QuickSteps in this chapter.

SET UP ANOTHER USER

To set up another user account, possibly a Standard User account for your use:

1. Click **Start** and click **Control Panel**. In Category view, click **User Accounts And Family Safety**, and then click **User Accounts**. The User Accounts window opens.

2. Click **Manage Another Account**, and, if needed, type a password and click **Yes** to open the Manage Accounts window, as shown in Figure 3-2.

3. Click **Create A New Account**. Type a name of up to 20 characters. Note that it cannot contain just periods, spaces, or the @ symbol; it cannot contain " / \ [ ] : ; | = ,+ * ? < >; and leading spaces or periods are dropped.

QUICKSTEPS

SETTING PASSWORDS

Passwords are the primary keys used to allow some people to use a computer and to keep others away. While there are recent alternatives to passwords, most computer protection depends on them.

CREATE A PASSWORD

After setting up a new user account, you can add a password to it that will then be required to use that account.

1. Click **Start** and click **Control Panel**. In Category view, click **User Accounts And Family Safety**, and then click **User Accounts**. The User Accounts window opens.

2. If it is not your account that you want to add a password to, click **Manage Another Account**. If needed, type a password, click **Yes**, and click the account you want. In your account or in the other account that opens (this cannot be the Guest account because that cannot have a password), click **Create A Password**.

The Create Password window will open, as shown in Figure 3-3. Note the warning message. This is true only if the user already has a password that has been used to encrypt files, create certificates, and access websites and network resources. If you create a new password for this person, it will replace the old one, and all the places where the old one has been used will no longer be available even with the new password. This is the case every time you create, change, or delete a password.

Continued . . .

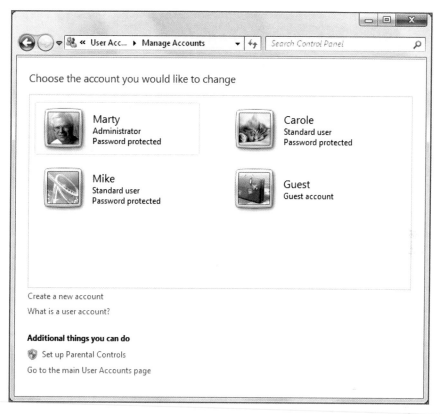

Figure 3-2: The Manage Accounts window provides password and user account management.

4. Accept the default account type, **Standard User**, or click **Administrator** as the account type. You can see a summary of the privileges available to each user type.

SETTING PASSWORDS *(Continued)*

3. Type the new password, click in the second text box, type the new password again to confirm it, click in the third text box, type a nonobvious hint to help you remember the password, and click **Create Password**.

4. Close the Change An Account window.

CHANGE A PASSWORD

It is a good idea to change your password periodically in case it has been compromised.

1. Click **Start** and click **Control Panel**. In Category view, click **User Accounts And Family Safety**, and then click **User Accounts**. The User Accounts window opens.

2. If it is not your account that you want to change, click **Manage Another Account**. If needed, type a password, click **Yes**, and click the account you want to change. In your account or in the other account that opens, click **Change Your/The Password**.

3. In your account, type the current password, and click in the second text box. In either your or another's account, type a new password, click in the next text box, and type the new password again to confirm it. Click in the final text box, type a nonobvious hint to help you remember the password, and click **Change Password**.

4. Close the Change An Account window.

Continued . . .

Figure 3-3: Creating, changing, or deleting a password will lose all items that are based on passwords, such as encrypted files, certificates, and other passwords.

5. Click **Create Account**. You are returned to the Manage Accounts window. Changing other aspects of the account is described in later sections of this chapter.

Reset a Password

Windows 7 allows you to reset a password you have forgotten if you have previously created a password reset disk, which can be a USB flash drive, CD, or floppy disk. A reset disk can hold the password reset for only one user at a time, but it can hold other information if you want.

SETTING PASSWORDS *(Continued)*

REMOVE A PASSWORD

If you move a computer to a location that doesn't need a password—for example, if it is not accessible to anyone else, or if you want to remove a password for some other reason—you can do so.

1. Click **Start** and click **Control Panel**. In Category view, click **User Accounts And Family Safety**, and then click **User Accounts**. The User Accounts window opens.

2. If it is not your account in which you want to remove the password, click **Manage Another Account**. If needed, type a password, click **Yes**, and click the account you want. In your account or in the other account that opens, click **Remove Your/ The Password**.

3. If it is your account, type the current password, and, in any case, click **Remove Password**.

4. Close the Change An Account window.

TIP

For a password to be *strong,* it must be eight or more characters long; use both upper- and lowercase letters; and use a mixture of letters, numbers, and symbols, which include ! # $ % ^ & * and spaces. It also should *not* be a recognizable word, name, or date. Instead of a password such as "mymoney," consider using something like this: "my$Money23."

CREATE A RESET DISK

1. Insert a USB flash drive in its socket, or insert a writable CD or a formatted and unused floppy disk into its respective drive. Close the AutoPlay window if it opens.

2. Click **Start** and click **Control Panel**. In Category view, click **User Accounts And Family Safety**, and then click **User Accounts**. The User Accounts window opens.

3. Click **Create A Password Reset Disk** in the list of tasks on the left. If needed, type a password and click **Yes**.

4. The Forgotten Password Wizard starts. Click **Next**. Click the drive down arrow, and select the drive on which you want to create the password key. Click **Next**.

5. Type the current user account password, and again click **Next**. The disk will be created. When this process is done, click **Next**. Then click **Finish**. Remove and label the disk, and store it in a safe place.

6. Close the User Accounts window.

USE A RESET DISK

If you have forgotten your password and there isn't another person with administrator permissions on your computer who can reset it, you can use a reset disk you have previously created.

1. Start your computer. When you see the Welcome screen, click your user name. If you have forgotten your password, click the right arrow. You will be told that the user name or password is incorrect.

2. Click **OK** to return to the password entry, and look at your hint.

3. If the hint isn't of any help, click **Reset Password**. The Password Reset Wizard starts.

4. Click **Next**. Insert your reset disk in its socket or drive. Click the drive down arrow, select the drive the reset disk is in, and again click **Next**. Type a new password, confirm it, type a password hint, click **Next**, and click **Finish**. (You do not have to create a new reset disk with your new password; Windows updates the reset disk for you.) Remove the reset disk.

5. Enter your new password, and press **ENTER**.

Switch Among Users

When you have multiple users on a computer, one user can obviously log off and another log on; however, with the Welcome screen, you can use Fast User Switching (which is not available in the Starter Edition of Windows 7). This allows you to keep programs running and files open when you temporarily switch to another user. To use Fast User Switching:

1. Click **Start**, click the **Shut Down** right arrow, and click **Switch User**. The Welcome screen will appear and let the other person click his or her account and log on.

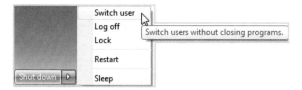

2. When the other person has finished using the computer and has logged off (by clicking **Start**, clicking the **Shut Down** right arrow, and clicking **Log Off**), you can log on normally. When you do, you will see all your programs exactly as you left them.

Control What a User Does

User accounts identify people and allow them to log on to your computer. What they can do after that depends on the permissions they have. Windows 7 has two features that help you control what other users do on your computer: Parental Controls and the ability to turn Windows features on and off for a given user.

Set Parental Controls

If you have a child or grandchild as one of the users on your computer and you are an administrator with a password, you can control what your child can do on your computer, including hours of usage, programs he or she can run, and access to the Internet. When your child encounters a blocked program, game, or website, a notice is displayed, including a link the child can click to request access. You, as an administrator, can allow one-time access by entering your user ID and password.

1. Click **Start** and click **Control Panel**. In Category view, click **User Accounts And Family Safety**, and then click **Parental Controls**. If needed, type an administrator password and click **Yes**. The Parental Controls window opens.

2. Click the user for whom you want to set Parental Controls to open the individual User Controls window.

3. Click **On** under Parental Controls, as shown in Figure 3-4.

4. Click **Time Limits**, drag the hours to block or allow (you only need to select one or the other, and you can drag across multiple hours and days), and then click **OK**.

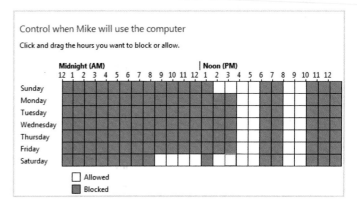

Figure 3-4: Parental Controls allows you to determine what a child can do and see on your computer.

NOTE

A child for whom you want to set up Parental Controls must have a Standard User account. To set up the Parental Controls, you must have an Administrator account with a password.

NOTE

In addition to the parental controls that are described here, additional controls such as Web filtering and activity reporting are available for download and use at the bottom of the window that opens when you first open Parental Controls in step 1 of the "Set Parental Controls" section of this chapter.

5. Click **Games** and choose if any games can be played. Click **Set Game Ratings**, choose if games with no rating can be played, click a rating level, choose the type of content you want blocked, and click **OK**. Click **Block Or Allow Specific Games**, click whether to block or allow specific games installed on the computer, and click **OK**. Click **OK** again to leave Game Controls.

6. Click **Allow And Block Specific Programs**, and choose whether to allow the use of all programs or only the ones you choose. If you choose to pick specific programs to allow, a list of all the programs on the computer is presented. Click those for which you want to allow access, and click **OK**.

7. Click **OK** to close the User Controls window.

Control What Parts of Windows Can Be Used

As an administrator, you can control what parts of Windows 7 each user can access.

1. Log on as the user for whom you want to set Windows feature usage.

2. Click **Start** and click **Control Panel**. In Category view, click **Programs** and then click **Programs And Features**.

3. Click **Turn Windows Features On Or Off** in the left column. If needed, type a password and click **Yes**. The Windows Features dialog box appears.

4. Click an unselected check box to turn a feature on, or click a selected check box to turn a feature off. Click the plus sign (+) where applicable to open the subfeatures and turn them on or off.

5. When you have selected the features the user will be allowed to use, click **OK**.

6. Close the Programs And Features window.

LISBETH HAS BECOME COMFORTABLE WITH HER COMPUTER

I had always depended on my husband to help me use the computer or do it for me. After he passed away, I decided to get a new computer and learn how to use it in earnest. A friend helped me get started with a long lesson and then answer several questions as I had them, although I didn't want to abuse that privilege. For a while, I was very frustrated and at times wanted to throw the computer out the window. I stuck at it, though, because I really wanted to exchange email with my family in Europe. Now, after a couple of years, I'm reasonably comfortable and doing a number of things with the computer, in addition to a fair amount of email.

Lisbeth H., 67, Washington

Set File and Folder Sharing

Files are shared by being in a shared folder or drive. Folders and drives are shared by their creator or owner or by an administrator. To share folders and drives, as well as printers and other devices, both locally and over a network, you must address three components of Windows 7 that allow you to control access to your computer and its components (see Figure 3-5):

- **The Windows Firewall**, which protects your computer and its contents from network access
- **The Network And Sharing Center**, which is the primary means of controlling sharing in Windows 7
- **Sharing individual drives and folders**, which lets you determine if a drive, folder, or other device is shared; who has permission to access it; and what they can do with the contents

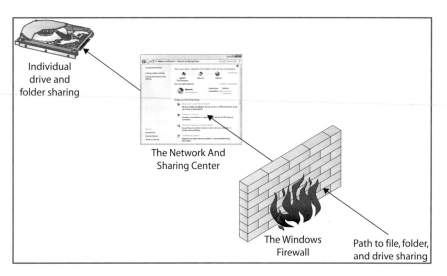

Individual drive and folder sharing

The Network And Sharing Center

The Windows Firewall

Path to file, folder, and drive sharing

Figure 3-5: The sharing of your computer requires that you set up your firewall, the Network And Sharing Center, and the individual drives and folders to accomplish that.

SET UP THE WINDOWS FIREWALL

Windows 7 includes the Windows Firewall, whose objective is to slow down and hopefully prevent anybody from accessing your computer without your permission, while at the same time allowing those who you want to use your computer to do so. The Windows Firewall is turned on by default. Check to see if it is; if it isn't, turn it on.

1. Click **Start** and click **Control Panel**. In Category view, click **System And Security**, and then click **Windows Firewall**. The Windows Firewall window opens and shows your firewall status.

2. If your firewall is not turned on, or if you want to turn it off, click **Turn Windows Firewall On Or Off** in the pane on the left. If needed, type a password and click **Yes**. The Windows Firewall Settings window opens. Click the respective option button to turn on your firewall (highly recommended) or to turn it off (not recommended). You can do this for both your local network and for a public network to which you may be connected. Click **OK**.

3. To change the settings for what the firewall will and won't let through, click **Allow A Program Or Feature Through Windows Firewall** at the top of the left column. The Allowed Programs window opens, as shown in Figure 3-6. In the Windows Firewall Allowed Programs window, you can determine what each option does by highlighting it and clicking Details at the bottom of the dialog box.

4. In the Programs And Features list, select the services running on your computer that you want to allow people from the Internet to use. To share information across a LAN, click the following items:

   ● Core Networking

   ● File And Printer Sharing

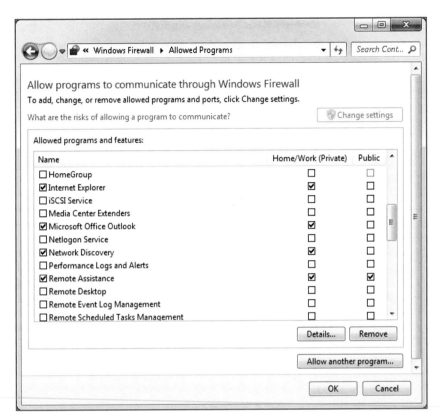

Figure 3-6: The Windows 7 Firewall can be configured to allow certain programs and features to come through.

TIP

If you have a specific program not on the Windows Firewall Allowed Programs And Features list, you can include that program by clicking **Allow Another Program** at the bottom of the Windows Firewall Allowed Programs window. Select the program from the list or browse to its location, and click **Add**.

- HomeGroup
- Network Discovery
- Windows Collaboration Computer Name Registration Service (optional)
- Windows Peer To Peer Collaboration Foundation (optional)

You will probably have other programs selected, such as Internet Explorer and Windows Live Messenger, that can be used on the Internet.

5. Click to select each program or feature you want to allow through the firewall. Click **OK** to close the Windows Firewall Allowed Programs window, and then click **Close** to close the Windows Firewall Control Panel.

USE THE NETWORK AND SHARING CENTER

The second layer of file-sharing protection in Windows 7 is controlled with the Network And Sharing Center, shown in Figure 3-7, which allows you to turn on or off the primary components of sharing information among users on a computer and across a network.

The first time Windows 7 was run, a choice was made between a public and private network. The Network And Sharing Center allows you to change that. If you are primarily sharing your computer with other computers within an organization or a residence, you should select either Home or Work Network, where network sharing is relatively simple. If you are primarily using public wireless or cable Internet connections and allow very little sharing of your computer,

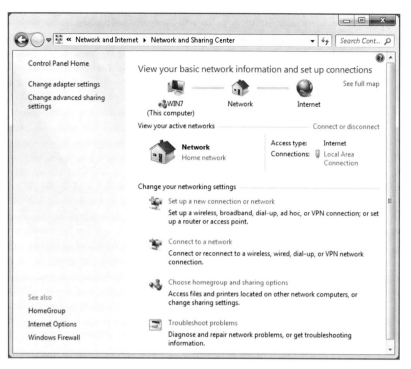

Figure 3-7: The Network And Sharing Center is the primary means of sharing your computer.

select Public, which makes it more difficult for someone to get into your computer.

1. Click **Start** and click **Control Panel**. In Category view, click **Network And Internet**, and then click **Network And Sharing Center**. The Network And Sharing Center window opens, as shown in Figure 3-7.

2. If you want to change the type of network (home, work, or public) you are connected to, click the current type of network to the right of the icon (in Figure 3-7, it is Home Network). The Set Network Location dialog box will appear.

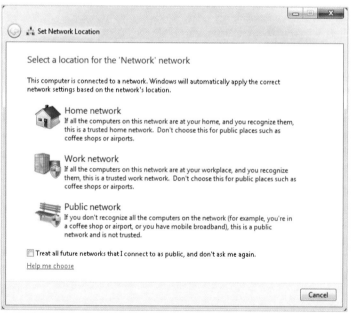

3. Read the conditions that are expected in each network type, and then click the type that is correct for you. If needed, type a password and click **Yes**. Your choice will be confirmed. Click **Close**.

A *homegroup* is a group of networking computer users who want to easily share information and resources on their computers. Such a group can be in a residence or in a smaller organization. Only Windows 7 computers can join a homegroup.

Figure 3-8: The HomeGroup default is to share three of your libraries plus your printer within your homegroup.

4. Each type of network has sharing settings that are automatically set. Home Network is the most open, with just about everything shared; Public Network is the other extreme.

5. When you have finished with the Network And Sharing Center, click **Close**.

USE HOMEGROUP FOLDER SHARING

The final layer of sharing settings is the determination of the disks and folders you want to share. Windows 7's HomeGroup makes sharing files and folders within the homegroup much easier. When Windows 7 is first installed or started, you are asked if you want a home, work, or public network. If you choose Home, which may also be a good idea for small businesses, a homegroup is either set up or joined, depending on whether a homegroup already exists. You are then shown a list of your libraries and asked if you want to share them. By default, your pictures, music, printers, and videos are shared for anyone to read, view, or use but not to change. Documents are not shared, but you can change this at the time of installation or at a later time. You can make these changes at the library level or at the disk and folder level. To do this at the library level:

1. Click **Start** and click **Control Panel**. In Category view, click **Network And Internet**, and then click **HomeGroup**. The HomeGroup window opens. If this is the first time you are looking into HomeGroup, you'll be asked if you want to share any libraries. Click **Choose What You Want To Share**. The Share Libraries And Printers window will open, as shown in Figure 3-8.

   If you have previously reviewed HomeGroup, the Share Libraries And Printers window will open (see Figure 3-8).

2. Make any changes that you feel you need, and then, if you made changes, click **Save Changes**. If needed, enter the password and click **Yes**. Otherwise, click **Cancel**.

To go beyond the sharing of libraries within the homegroup, and even then only for someone to read, view, or use your libraries, you need to go to the individual drives and folders. You can change the sharing of libraries so that other users can change contents in addition to reading or viewing them. To do that:

1. Click **Start** and click **Computer**. In the folders (left) pane, click **Libraries** so the detail libraries (documents, music, pictures, or videos) are shown in the right pane.

2. Right-click the library whose sharing you want to change, and click **Share With**. The context menu and file-sharing submenu will appear.

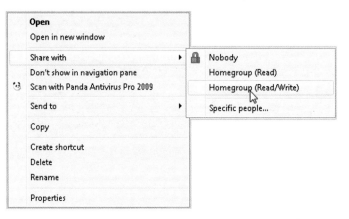

3. By default, the libraries are shared among the homegroup to be read only. You can allow homegroup members both read and write access to your libraries, or you can select specific people and give them specific permissions. Click the option you want, and, when you are finished, close the Windows Explorer window.

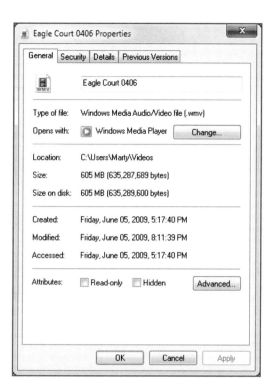

Figure 3-9: Protecting files and folders is
accomplished from the files' and folders'
Properties dialog boxes.

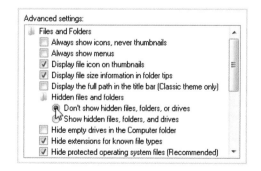

Protect Files and Folders

Protecting files and folders is another layer of protection. It makes it
harder for someone who manages to break through the other layers
of protection to use whatever is found on the computer. The easiest
way to protect files and folders is to hide them. Start by opening the
Properties dialog box for the file or folder.

1. Click **Start** and click **Computer**. In the navigation pane, open the disk
   and folders necessary to locate in the right pane the file or folder you
   want to protect.

2. Right-click the file or folder you want to protect, and click **Properties**. The
   Properties dialog box will appear, as shown for a file in Figure 3-9 (there
   are slight differences among file and folder Properties dialog boxes).

Hiding files and folders lets you prevent them from being displayed by
Windows Explorer. This assumes the person from whom you want to
hide them does not know how to display hidden files or how to turn
off the hidden attribute. To hide a file or folder, you must both turn on
its hidden attribute and turn off the Display Hidden Files feature.

1. In the file or folder Properties dialog box, on the General tab, click
   Hidden, click **OK**, and click **OK** again to confirm the attribute change.
   If needed, type a password and click **Yes** (the object's icon becomes
   dimmed or disappears).

2. In the Windows Explorer window, click the **Organize** menu, click
   Folder And Search Options, click the **View** tab, and make sure
   Don't Show Hidden Files, Folders, Or Drives is selected. Click **OK**
   to close the Folder Options dialog box. Close and reopen the parent
   folder, and the file or folder you hid will disappear.

3. To restore the file or folder to view, click the **Organize** menu, click
   Folder And Search Options, click the **View** tab, click **Show Hidden
   Files, Folders, And Drives**, and click **OK**. Then, when you can see
   the file or folder, open its Properties dialog box, and deselect the
   Hidden attribute.

TOM BELIEVES COMPUTER SECURITY IS CRITICAL

During a long career, I have worked as a real estate broker and advisor, nonprofit board member/ officer, and, for several terms, as a county assessor. Throughout my career, I have felt that the security of my client's or taxpayer's information to be of upmost importance. I feel the same about information on a personal computer. A person must feel as secure about information stored on a computer as information stored in a safety deposit box. In this day and age, peace of mind is directly related to the security of information on one's computer.

Tom B., 79, Washington

Back Up Your Information

Computers are a great asset, but like any machine, they are prone to failures of many kinds. Once you have started using your computer regularly, it becomes important to make a copy of your information and store it in another location should your hard drive fail or something else happen to your computer.

There are several solutions to copying and saving your information. The term normally used for this is *backup* (or to back up—the verb form). This means storing a copy of your information in a location other than on your computer. You can back up both on your computer and on the Internet.

BACK UP ON YOUR COMPUTER

Within your computer, you can back up your information to a CD or DVD, to another drive that is connected to your computer (including an external hard drive and a USB flash or thumb drive), or to a hard drive on another computer. You may want to perform backups to a couple of these items on a periodic basic, and a couple of times a year back up your data to a CD and put it in your bank safety deposit box.

Windows 7 has a backup program, but without a lot of setup, it backs up things you don't really care about, like your programs you already have on CDs or DVDs. A simpler way to do a backup is to simply copy your files from the hard disk in your computer to an external device, like a CD, DVD, USB flash drive, or external hard drive. Here's how to copy some files to a writable (or "burnable") CD:

1. Click **Start**, click **Computer**, and open (click the triangle on the left) the drive and folders in the left column needed to display the files you want to back up in the right column, as you see in Figure 3-10.

⊿ 🖭 Data (F:)
    📁 Files 100701
    📁 Marty2 1002

2. Open your CD/DVD drive, insert a blank writable disc, and close the drive. An AutoPlay dialog box will open offering you several options.

Your AutoPlay dialog box may look different from the one shown here, depending on the options that have been selected in the past.

3. Click **Burn Files To Disc** to open the Burn To Disc dialog box. Type a title, click **Like A USB Flash Drive**, and click **Next**. You will see a message that the disc is being formatted and then another AutoPlay dialog box will appear.

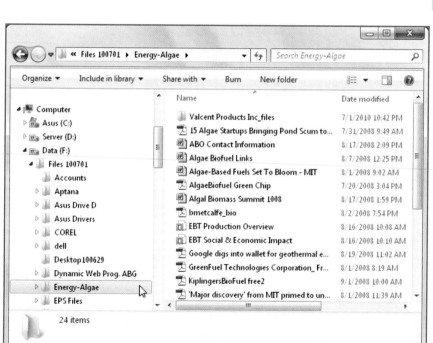

Figure 3-10: You must first locate the files on your computer that you want to back up.

4. Click **Open Folder To View Files** to open another window with a blank right pane with the message "Drag Files To This Folder To Add Them To The Disc."

5. In your original folder, similar to the one shown in Figure 3-10, select the files you want to back up by clicking the first file, and pressing and holding **SHIFT** while clicking the last file, if the files are contiguous. If not, press and hold **CTRL** while individually clicking the other files.

6. When all the necessary files in a folder are selected, drag them (point on the selected files, press and hold the left mouse button, and move the mouse) to the right pane of the new folder for the CD or DVD, as you can see in Figure 3-11, and release the mouse button.

7. You can open other folders and drives and drag other files to the CD/DVD folder. Periodically look at how much space on the CD/DVD has been used by right-clicking the drive in the left pane of its window and clicking **Properties** in the context menu. In the Properties dialog box (shown below on the right), look at how much free space you have left, and then click **OK**.

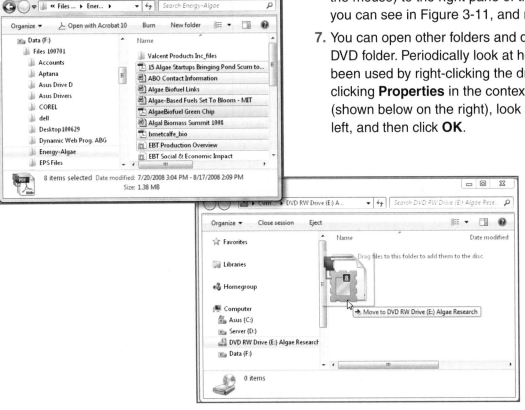

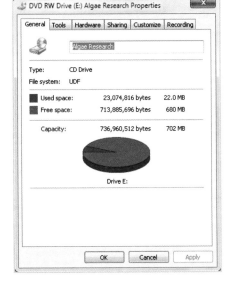

Figure 3-11: An easy way to back up files is to drag them to an external disc or drive.

Disc Ready ✕
Your disc is now ready to be used on other computers.

NOTE

A disc created with the Like A USB Flash Drive option can be put into the CD/DVD disc drive again and have files deleted and added to it, as well as edited and restored to the disc.

8. When you have all the files you want to back up in the CD/DVD, click **Close Session**. You'll see a message that the disc is being closed. When that is done, you'll get a message that the disc is ready. Click **Eject**, remove the disc, label it with a soft felt-tip pen, and store it with a paper or plastic sleeve in a safe place, preferably away from your computer and in a fireproof container.

BACK UP OVER THE INTERNET

Recently, many people are choosing to save their information to the *cloud*, meaning that they back up the data on their computer to a location (a server) accessed through the Internet. This method makes it easy to access your data from any location, as well as your new computer, should your old computer fail. These services are reasonable in cost or even free and easy to set up.

Some programs, once you have subscribed to them, install a small software program on your computer. These programs work behind the scenes, copying new photos, data files, deposits, or letters to a secure, encrypted location. Should your old computer break down, you can restore your files and data to your new computer.

Some personal financial management programs also offer this service for their data. For example, Quicken's Online Backup service charges a nominal fee per month to protect your financial information.

An example of a currently free cloud service is Microsoft's SkyDrive. Microsoft gives you 25GB of storage. You'll need to set up an account with a user ID and a password.

1. Click the **Internet Explorer** icon on the taskbar to open it. In the address bar, type skydrive.com and press **ENTER**. Windows Live will open, and if you are not already signed up as a Windows Live or Hotmail client, you will be asked to do that. Click **Sign Up**, fill out the form that opens, and click **I Accept**. Your SkyDrive page will open, where you can use existing folders or set up your own, as you can see in Figure 3-12.

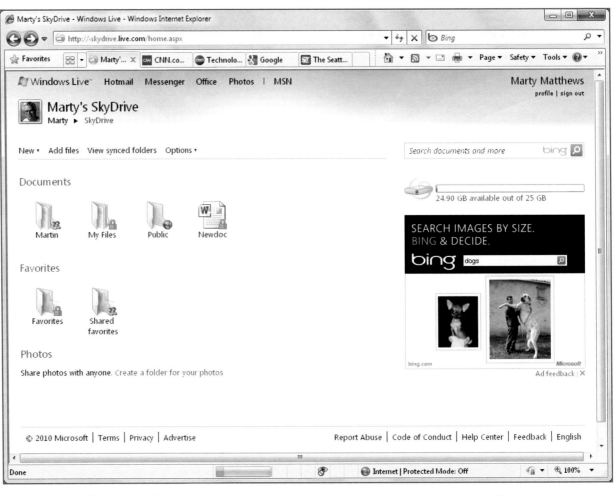

Figure 3-12: Online, "cloud" Internet storage is a good and safe way to back up important files.

2. Click a folder you want to use to open it, and then click **Add Files**; or click **New**, click **Folder**, enter a name for the folder, and click **Next**. In either case, a window will open inviting you to drop documents there or select documents from your computer.

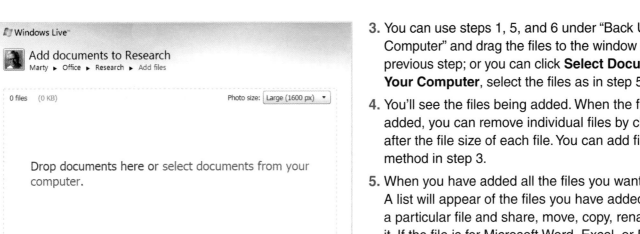

3. You can use steps 1, 5, and 6 under "Back Up on Your Computer" and drag the files to the window shown in the previous step; or you can click **Select Documents From Your Computer**, select the files as in step 5, and click **Open**.

4. You'll see the files being added. When the files have been added, you can remove individual files by clicking the X after the file size of each file. You can add files using either method in step 3.

5. When you have added all the files you want, click **Continue**. A list will appear of the files you have added. You can select a particular file and share, move, copy, rename, and delete it. If the file is for Microsoft Word, Excel, or PowerPoint, you can edit it directly in your browser (Internet Explorer) using the Microsoft Office Web Apps.

6. When you are done close the skydrive.live website and, if desired, the Internet Explorer.

Other cloud sites work similarly.

QUICKSTEPS

LOCKING A COMPUTER

By default, when your screen saver comes on and you return to use your system, you must go through the logon screen. If you have added a password to your account, you have to enter it to get back into the system, which is a means of preventing unauthorized access when you are away from your running computer. If you don't want to wait for your screen saver to come on, you can click **Start**, click the **Shut Down** right arrow, and click **Lock**; or you can press ▦ (the Windows logo key)**+L** to immediately bring up the logon screen, from which your screen saver will open at the appropriate time.

Depending on your environment, having to go through the logon screen every time you come out of the screen saver may or may not be beneficial. To turn off or turn back on the screen saver protection:

1. Right-click the desktop and click **Personalize**. Click **Screen Saver**.

2. Select or deselect **On Resume, Display Logon Screen**, depending on whether you want to display the logon screen upon returning to your system (see Figure 3-13).

3. Click **OK** to close the Screen Saver Settings dialog box, and close the Personalization window.

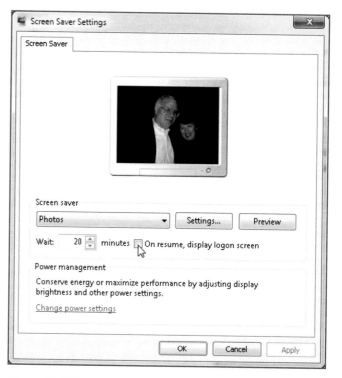

Figure 3-13: *You can password-protect your system when you leave it unattended by having the logon screen appear when you return after using the screen saver.*

Protect Yourself on the Internet

Your connection through your computer to the Internet is your doorway to the cyberworld. It allows you to communicate with others through email and social networking; it allows you to shop for virtually anything without leaving your home; and it provides an enormous resource for gathering information and news. It also is a doorway that can let in things that can harm you, your computer, and your data. It is like the front door to your house—you need it to see and interact with other people, but it also has locks on it to keep out the people you don't want to let in. Similarly, there are a number of barriers you can place in the way of people who want to do damage via the Internet.

Understand Internet Threats

As the Internet has gained popularity, so have the threats it harbors. Viruses, worms, spyware, and adware have become part of our vocabulary. Look at each of these threats to understand what each can do and how to guard your computer and data, as described in Table 3-1.

PROBLEM	DEFINITION	SOLUTION
Virus	A program that attaches itself to other files on your computer. There are many forms of viruses, each performing different, usually malevolent, functions on your computer.	Install an antivirus program with a subscription for automatic updates, and make sure it is continually running.
Worm	A type of virus that replicates itself repeatedly through a computer network or security breach in your computer. Because it keeps copying itself, a worm can fill up a hard drive and cause your network to malfunction.	
Trojan horse	A computer program that claims to do one thing, such as play a game, but has hidden parts that can erase files or even your entire hard drive.	
Adware	The banners and pop-up ads that come with programs you download from the Internet. Often, these programs are free, and to support them, the program owner sells space for ads to display on your computer every time you use the program.	Install an anti-adware program.
Spyware	A computer program that downloads with another program from the Internet. Spyware can monitor what you do, keep track of your keystrokes, discern credit card and other personally identifying numbers, and pass that information back to its author.	Install an antispyware program.

Table 3-1: Security Issues Associated with the Internet and How to Control Them

CHERYL HAS LEARNED TO APPRECIATE COMPUTERS

My first experience was with a computer that filled a large room at college and for which I had to punch a set of cards to enter data—no keyboards then. On more than one occasion I dropped the cards and had quite a puzzle to solve in rearranging them. A few years later, after birthing two children, I went back to teaching and found things had changed—Apple 2Es were in the school computer lab. One of my colleagues taught me to use the word processor, and with much struggle I truly began my long appreciation of computers. Now in 2010, almost 30 years later, using my computer seems effortless and is part of everyday living. There are so many things that I can do to prepare documents for my consulting business that would have taken hours back in the day. I find that if I think like one of my students and just explore, and not be intimidated by the computer, I learn and accomplish wonders.

Cheryl G., 65, Colorado

Use an Antivirus or Security Program

To counter the various Internet threats, you need to install an antivirus or security program. A number of such programs are available, both free and at a cost. You can buy these in computer stores and on the Internet. There is a lot of variability in the pricing, and the opinion of which is the best also varies widely. Table 3-2 shows a few of these programs with which we have had direct experience. The best thing for you to do is go on the Internet and do a search of "antivirus program reviews." Look for the toptenreviews.com site—it gives you a quick comparison, but look at several sites and read the reviews, because there is considerable difference of opinion. When you have decided on the program you want, determine the version to get. Most companies have a basic antivirus program, an Internet security program, and an overall security program (see Figure 3-14). Our opinion is that the Internet security programs are a good middle ground. Finally, do some price hunting, making sure you are looking at the version you want. At the time this was written, Amazon.com was offering Kaspersky Internet Security at $19.99 for three PCs for one year. There have been mail-in rebate deals that allow you to get the program for the price of shipping after the rebate.

NAME	WEBSITE	LIST PRICE (AS OF 2/2011)
AVG Antivirus Free Edition	free.avg.com	Free
AVG Internet Security	avg.com	$68.99 for three PCs, one year
BitDefender Internet Security	bitdefender.com	$49.95 for three PCs, one year
Kaspersky Internet Security	Kaspersky.com	$79.95 for three PCs, one year
Microsoft Security Essentials	microsoft.com/security_essentials	Free
Norton Internet Security	Symantec.com	$69.99 for three PCs, one year

Table 3-2: Antivirus and Security Programs

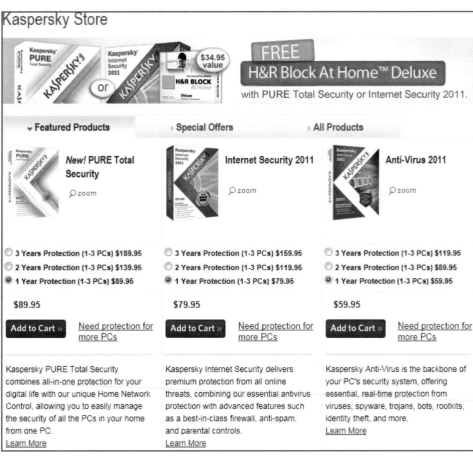

Figure 3-14: *There are often three levels of security protection you can buy.*

Control Internet Security

Internet Explorer allows you to control three aspects of Internet security. You can categorize sites by the degree to which you trust them, determine how you want to handle *cookies* placed on your computer by websites, and set and use ratings to control the content of websites that can be viewed. These controls are found in the Internet Options dialog box.

In Internet Explorer, click **Tools** or the **Tools** icon on the tab row, and click **Internet Options**.

CATEGORIZE WEBSITES

Internet Explorer allows you to categorize websites into zones: Internet (sites that are not classified in one of the other ways), Local Intranet, Trusted Sites, and Restricted Sites (as shown in Figure 3-15).

From the Internet Options dialog box:

1. Click the **Security** tab. Click the **Internet** zone. Note its definition.

2. Click **Custom Level**. Select the elements in this zone that you want to disable, enable, or prompt you before using. Alternatively, select a level of security you want for this zone, and click **Reset**. Click **OK** when you are finished.

3. Click each of the other zones, where you can identify either groups or individual sites you want in that zone.

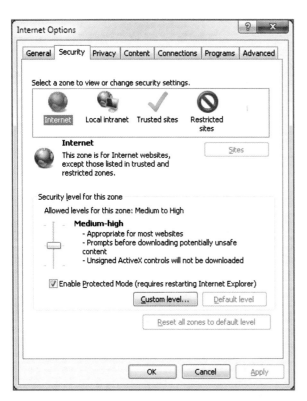

Figure 3-15: Internet Explorer allows you to categorize websites into zones and determine what can be done within those zones.

4. Turn Protected Mode on or off at the bottom of the Security tab (the notice for which you'll see at the bottom of Internet Explorer). Protected Mode produces the messages that tells you a program is trying to run in Internet Explorer or that software is trying install itself on your computer. In most cases, you can click in a bar at the top of the Internet Explorer window if you want to run the program or install the software. You can also double-click the notice at the bottom of Internet Explorer to open the Security tab and turn off Protected Mode (clear the Enable Protected Mode check box).

HANDLE COOKIES

Cookies are small pieces of data that websites store on your computer so that they can remind themselves of who you are. These can save you from having to constantly enter your name and ID. Cookies can also be dangerous, however, letting people into your computer where they can potentially do damage.

Internet Explorer lets you determine the types and sources of cookies you will allow and what those cookies can do on your computer (see Figure 3-16).

From the Internet Options dialog box:

1. Click the **Privacy** tab. Select a privacy setting by dragging the slider up or down.

2. Click **Advanced** to open the Advanced Privacy Settings dialog box. If you wish, click **Override Automatic Cookie Handling**, and select the settings you want to use.

3. Click **OK** to return to the Internet Options dialog box.

4. In the middle of the Privacy tab, you can turn off the pop-up blocker, which is on by default (it is recommended that you leave it on). If you have a site that you frequently use that needs pop-ups, click **Settings**, enter the site address (URL), click **Add**, and click **Close**.

5. At the bottom of the Privacy tab, you can determine how to handle InPrivate Filtering and Browsing. See the following Note on InPrivate.

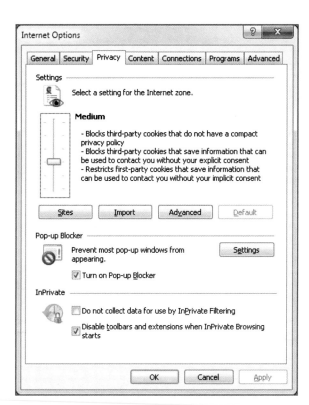

Figure 3-16: *Determine how you will handle cookies that websites want to leave on your computer.*

CONTROL CONTENT

You can control the content that Internet Explorer displays.

From the Internet Options dialog box:

1. Click the **Content** tab. Click **Parental Controls**. Click the user you want to control to open the User Controls window, shown in Figure 3-17. Click **On** to turn on parental controls, and configure any other settings you want to use. Click **OK** when you are done, and then close the Parental Controls window.

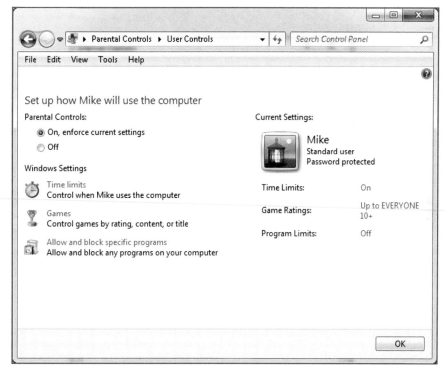

Figure 3-17: *You can place a number of controls on what a particular user can do on a computer using the Parental Controls feature.*

3

4

5

6

7

8

9

10

NOTE

Internet Explorer 8 and 9 have added a new way to browse and view sites, called *InPrivate*, that is opened by clicking **Safety** on the tab row and clicking **InPrivate Browsing**. This opens a separate browser window with this address bar: ⊙⊙ InPrivate 🔗 about:InPrivate . While you are in this window, your browsing history, temporary Internet files, and cookies are not stored on your computer, preventing anyone looking at your computer from seeing where you have browsed. In addition, with InPrivate Filtering, also opened from Safety in the tab row, you can control how information about you is passed on to Internet content providers.

2. Click **Enable** to open the Content Advisor dialog box. Individually select each of the categories, and drag the slider to the level you want to allow. Detailed descriptions of each area are shown in the lower half of the dialog box.

3. Click **OK** to close the Content Advisor dialog box.

When you are done, click **OK** to close the Internet Options dialog box. (Other parts of this dialog box are discussed elsewhere in this book.)

Chapter 4

4

Sending and Receiving Email

For many seniors, having access to the *Internet* and *email* (See "Speaking Internet" QuickFacts) are the primary reasons for having a computer. The Internet, using computer networks connected via telephone wires and satellite links, provides worldwide communications between both individuals and organizations, allowing you to send and receive email, as well as communicate using blogs, forums, and newsgroups. In this chapter we'll talk about how to get, set up, and use Windows Live Mail, including creating, sending, and receiving messages; handling spam; adding attachments and signatures; and applying formatting. We'll also briefly look at a web-based alternative for email, as well as how to use the Calendar, and use Windows Live Messenger.

SPEAKING INTERNET

Here are some common terms you'll encounter when using the Internet:

- **Internet** The means by which you can use your computer to connect to other computers all over the world using networks of telephone, cable, and satellite links.

- **WWW** World Wide Web is a subset of the Internet, but today it represents the majority of Internet usage.

- **ISP** Internet Service Provider, perhaps your telephone or cable TV company, connects your computer with the Internet. You set up an account with the ISP and pay a monthly fee to connect your computer.

- **Email** An electronic message sent over the Internet or a local network to someone or to an organization.

- **Blog** A website where you create and maintain a journal which other people can read and may be permitted to enter their comments or thoughts. Blogs are used to discuss everything from national politics to family vacations.

- **Forum** A website created by an organization or group to discuss a topic or group of topics. Participants can enter opinions, questions, and ideas as part of the discussion.

Continued . . .

Use Internet Email

Windows 7 does not include a mail program, but you can download Microsoft Windows Live Mail for free from as part of Windows Live Essentials. Windows Live Mail allows you to send and receive email and to participate in newsgroups. You can also send and receive email through a Web-mail account using Internet Explorer or an other browser. This section will primarily describe using Windows Live Mail. See the "Using Web Mail" QuickSteps for a discussion of that subject.

Get Windows Live Mail

For email with Windows 7, this book describes the use of Windows Live Mail because it works well, is freely available from Microsoft, and is designed for Windows 7. There are a number of other alternatives that you can buy or get for free, including Outlook from Microsoft, Eudora, Mozilla Thunderbird, and Opera. Conduct an Internet search on "Windows Mail Clients."

To get Windows Live Mail, you must download Windows Live Essentials from Microsoft. To do that:

1. If you have a new computer or new installation of Windows 7, click **Start**, click **Getting Started**, and click **Go Online To Get Windows Live Essentials**.
   If you are using Windows 7 (assumed in this book) and don't see Getting Started, click **Start**, click **All Programs**, click **Accessories**, click **Getting Started**, and double-click **Go Online To Get Windows Live Essentials**, as shown in Figure 4-1.

2. Click **Download Now** and in the File Download–Security Warning box, click **Run**. If a User Account Control dialog box opens, click **Yes** to allow the installation. The Windows Live site will open.

SPEAKING INTERNET *(Continued)*

- **Newsgroups** A collection of discussions or news updates on a particular topic. You may be allowed to participate in the discussions and automatically download updates to your own computer.

- **A Mail Program** A computer program, such as Windows Live Mail, that allows you to use Internet email.

Figure 4-1: By downloading Windows Live Essentials, Microsoft assures that you have the very latest software and allows other manufacturers the opportunity to have you use their software.

3. Click **Choose The Programs You Want To Install**, choose what you would like (I recommend all, but think it is a good idea to look at what you are installing; see Figure 4-2), and click **Install**. If you are asked to close Internet Explorer and possibly other programs, click **Continue**, and the programs will be closed for you.

4. The downloading and installation of Windows Live Essentials will begin and take from one to ten minutes with a broadband Internet connection. When this is completed, you may be asked to restart your computer. If so, make sure all other programs are closed and click **Restart Now**.

FREYA USES MULTIPLE EMAIL ACCOUNTS

Having two email accounts is invaluable for me to keep my multi-task life straight. I have a work email address that receives mail from several work-related sources and keeps all records and information in one place. Then I have a second email address for private conversations, family business, and another enterprise. I am considering setting up a third email box for this new enterprise as well.

Within each email account, I use several folders to further sort my email. For instance, I have a To-Do folder that I use to hold emails containing tasks I need to do. I just drag the email messages into an appropriate folder as they come in.

Having multiple email accounts helps my clarity of focus immensely to be able to physically shift back and forth between them. That way I can always be sure which hat I am wearing!

Freya S., 57, Washington

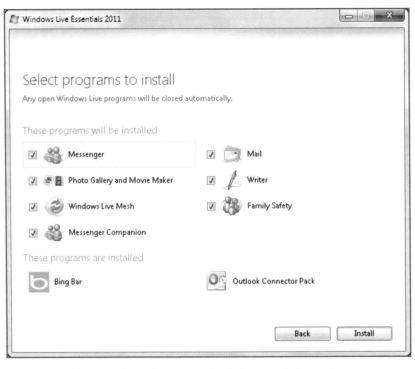

Figure 4-2: Windows Live Essentials includes email, instant messaging, blogging, movie making, and more.

5. When your computer restarts, you are asked to select various settings that, if selected, tend to lock you into Microsoft's Bing search engine and Microsoft's MSN website. This may be subtle, like telling you that several add-ons are ready to use. Click **Enable** if you want the add-ons or **Don't Enable** otherwise (my recommendation).

6. If you do not have a Windows Live, Hotmail, Messenger, or Xbox Live account, you will need to create one. Click **Sign Up** and follow the instructions on the screen to establish an account. If you already have one of those accounts, sign in as indicated.

7. If the Windows Live Messenger window has opened, click **Close**. It will be opened again and discussed at the end of this chapter.

Establish an Email Account

To send and receive email with Windows Live Mail, you must have an Internet connection, an email account established with an *ISP* (Internet service provider, or the service that connects your email address with the Internet), and that account must be set up in Windows Live Mail.

For an email account, you need:

- Your email address, for example: mike@anisp.com
- The type of mail server the ISP uses (POP3, IMAP, or HTTP—POP3 is the most common)
- The names of the incoming and outgoing mail servers, for example: mail.anisp.com
- The name and password for your mail account

With this information, you can set up an account in Windows Live Mail.

1. Click **Start**, click **All Programs** and click **Windows Live Mail** if you see it on the Start menu; if not, click the **Windows Live** folder, and then click **Windows Live Mail**.

2. If Windows Live Mail has not been previously set up, the Add Your Email Accounts dialog box will appear (see Figure 4-3); if it doesn't, click the **Accounts** tab and click **Email** on the left to open it.

3. Enter your email address, press **TAB**, enter your email password, press **TAB**, enter the name you want people to see when they get your email, click the **Manually Configure Server Settings** check box, and click **Next**.

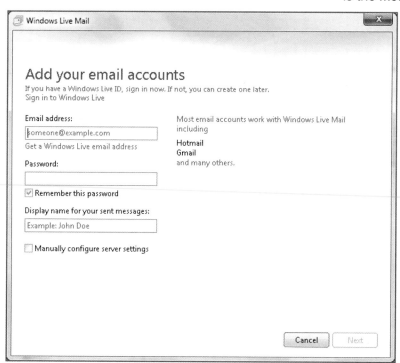

Figure 4-3: You need to get your email address and password from your ISP before you set up an email account.

The *ribbon* is the container at the top of Microsoft Office applications, such as the Windows Live Mail and New Message windows, for the tools and features you are most likely to use to accomplish the task at hand (see Figure 4-4). Microsoft's Web Apps also use the ribbon, as you'll see in Chapter 6.

The ribbon collects tools in *groups*; for example, the New group provides the tools to start an email message or add a new event to the calendar. Groups are organized into tabs, which bring together the tools to work on broader tasks. For example, the Folders tab contains groups that allow you to add and work with folders.

The ribbon provides space so each of the tools (or commands) in the groups has a labeled button you can click. Depending on the tool, you are then presented with additional options in the form of a list of commands, a dialog box or task pane, or galleries of visibly accurate choices that reflect what you'll see in your work.

Other features that are co-located with the ribbon include the Windows Live Mail button on the left of the tab row, and the Quick Access toolbar on the left of the title bar. The Windows Live Mail button lets you work *with* your mail, as opposed to the ribbon, which centers on working *in* your mail. The Quick Access toolbar provides an always available location for your favorite tools. It starts out with a default set of tools, but you can add to it.

4. Select the type of mail server used by your ISP (commonly POP), and then enter the name of your ISP's incoming mail server (such as mail .anisp.com), and whether this server requires a secure connection (most don't, but your ISP will tell you if it does and how to handle it). Unless your ISP tells you otherwise, leave the default port number and logon authentication.

5. Enter your logon ID or user name, the name of your ISP's outgoing server (often the same as the incoming server), leave the default port number, and select the relevant check box if your ISP tells you that the server requires a secure connection or authentication.

6. When you have completed these steps, click **Next** (if you have other email accounts you want to add, click **Add Another Email Account** and repeat the necessary steps), and then click **Finish**. Before Windows Live Mail can read messages from certain accounts, it might need to download the existing folders in those accounts. Click **Download** to do that. Windows Live Mail will open. Figure 4-4 shows it after receiving several email messages.

Use the next two sections, "Create and Send Email" and "Receive Email," to test your setup.

Create and Send Email

To create and send an email message:

1. Open Windows Live Mail, as described above, and in the Home tab, click **Email Message** in the New group. The New Message window will open, similar to the one in Figure 4-5.

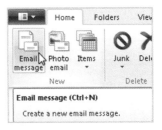

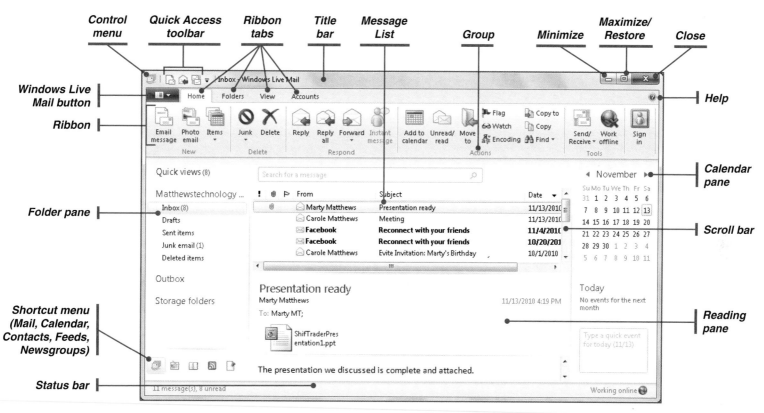

Control menu | Quick Access toolbar | Ribbon tabs | Title bar | Message List | Group | Minimize | Maximize/ Restore | Close

Windows Live Mail button

Ribbon

Help

Calendar pane

Folder pane

Scroll bar

Shortcut menu (Mail, Calendar, Contacts, Feeds, Newsgroups)

Reading pane

Status bar

Figure 4-4: Windows Live Mail provides access to email, a calendar, contacts, feeds, and newsgroups.

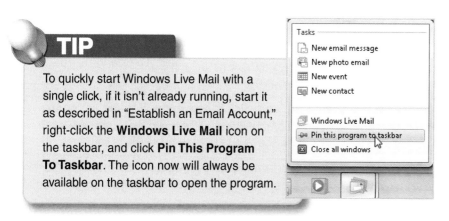

TIP

To quickly start Windows Live Mail with a single click, if it isn't already running, start it as described in "Establish an Email Account," right-click the **Windows Live Mail** icon on the taskbar, and click **Pin This Program To Taskbar**. The icon now will always be available on the taskbar to open the program.

2. Start to enter a name in the To text box. If the name is in your Contacts list (see the "Using the Contacts List" QuickSteps in this chapter), it will be automatically completed and you can press **ENTER** to accept that name. If the name is not automatically completed, finish typing a full email address (such as billg@microsoft.com).

3. If you want more than one addressee, type a semicolon (;) and a space after the first address, and then type a second one as in step 2.

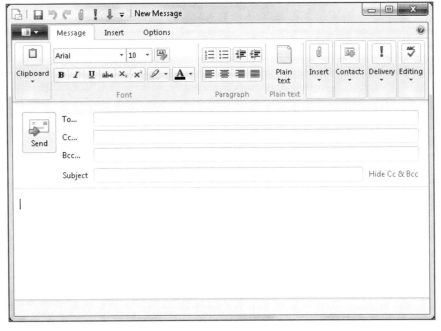

Figure 4-5: Sending email messages is an easy and fast way to communicate.

4. If you want to differentiate the addressees to whom the message is principally being sent from those for whom it is just information, click **Show Cc & Bcc**, if they are not already displayed, press **TAB**, and put the second or subsequent addressees in the Cc text box as you did in the To text box.

5. If you want to send the message to a recipient and not have other recipients see to whom it is sent, click **Show Cc & Bcc**, if they are not already displayed, click in the Bcc text box, and type the address to be hidden. (Bcc stands for "blind carbon copy.")

6. Press **TAB**, type a subject for the message, press **TAB** again, and type your message.

7. When you have completed your message, click **Send** opposite the addresses. For a brief moment, you may see a message in your outbox and then, if you open it, you will see the message in your Sent Items folder. If you are done, close Windows Live Mail.

Receive Email

Depending on how Windows Live Mail is set up, it may automatically receive any email you have when you are connected to your ISP or you may have to direct it to download your mail. To open and read your mail:

1. Open **Windows Live Mail**, and click **Inbox** in the Folders list on the left to open your inbox, which contains all of the messages you have received and haven't deleted or organized in folders.

2. If new messages weren't automatically received, in the Home tab click the top of the **Send/Receive** area in the Tools group. You should see messages being downloaded.

TIP

Have a friend send you an email message, so you know whether you are receiving messages. Then send the friend a message back and ask them to let you know when they get it, so you know you are sending messages.

MADELYN KEEPS HER PRIVACY

At first email felt like an invasion of my privacy, with too many people, organizations, and businesses, beyond my circle of family and friends, vying for my attention.

Learning to disregard and delete unwanted emails has helped, but sorting takes time and I prefer to spend as little time as possible at the computer.

That said, email has become a valuable tool of communication for social and business purposes. The Sent folder has become a record keeping device that I find very useful. I have to admit though, when I am at home I still prefer the telephone over the computer for many personal communications. But when I travel, email makes keeping in touch wonderfully easy.

Madelyn P., 67, Washington

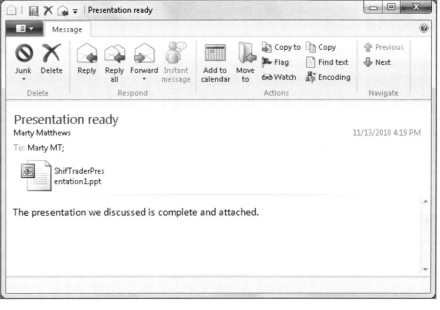

Figure 4-6: Work with a message you have received in the Message List (see Figure 4-4) or in its own window (shown here).

3. Click a message in the inbox Message List to read it in the Reading pane on the bottom or right of the window, as shown in Figure 4-4 (which shows the message on the bottom), or double-click a message to open the message in its own window, as shown in Figure 4-6.

4. Delete a message in either the inbox or its own window by clicking the relevant button on the toolbar. Close Windows Live Mail if you are finished with it.

Respond to Email

You can respond to messages you receive in three ways. First, click the message in your Message List or open the message

TIP

Normally, the contents of your Message List are sorted by the date and time in the Date column, with the most recent message at the top. You can sort on any of the elements in the message by clicking in the column heading for that element. Click in the column heading a second time to sort in the opposite direction. You can also click **Sort By** in the View tab Arrangement group and click the element you want to sort on.

USING THE CONTACTS LIST

The Contacts list contains your list of email addresses and other information about the people with whom you correspond or otherwise interact. An example of a contact list is shown in Figure 4-7.

OPEN THE CONTACTS LIST

To open the Contacts list:

Click **Contacts** 🕮 in the lower-left area of the Windows Live Mail window.

ADD A NEW CONTACT

To add a new contact to the Contacts list:

1. With Contacts Windows Live Mail open, click **Contact** in the Home tab New group. The Add A Contact dialog box opens.

2. Enter as much of the information as you have or want. For email, you need a name and an email address, as shown in the Quick Add category. If you have additional information, such as a nickname, several email addresses, several phone numbers, or a home address for the contact, click the other categories on the left and fill in the desired information.

3. When you are done, click **Add Contact** to close the Add A Contact window.

ADD CONTACT CATEGORIES

You can group contacts by category and then send messages to everyone in the category. To categorize a group of contacts:

Continued . . .

Figure 4-7: The Contacts list provides a place to store information about the people with whom you correspond.

in its own window, and then in the Home tab of the inbox or the Message tab of the message click:

- **Reply** to return a message to just the person who sent the original message.

    –Or–

- **Reply All** to return a message to all the people who were addressees (both To and Cc) in the original message.

    –Or–

- **Forward** (upper half) to relay a message to people not shown as addressees on the original message.

QUICKSTEPS

USING THE CONTACTS LIST *(Continued)*

1. In Contacts Windows Live Mail, click **Category** in the Home tab New group. The Create A New Category dialog box appears.

2. Enter the category name, and click the names in your Contacts list that you want in the category. When you have selected all the names, click **Save**.

3. When you are done, click the **Mail** icon in the lower left to close the Contacts list and reopen Windows Live Mail.

When you want to address a message to a category of people, start typing the category and its name will be displayed. Click the category name to send the message to everyone in the category.

Click the plus sign to the left of the category to expand it and list the contacts that are included in it.

If the sender of an email is not in your Contacts list, you can easily add her or him by clicking **Add Contact** next to the From email address.

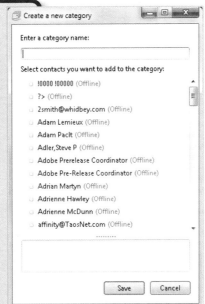

In all three cases, a window similar to the New Message window opens and allows you to add or change addressees and the subject, and add a new message.

TIP

If you see an email address in an email message that you want to add to your Contacts list, right-click the email address, and click **Add To Contacts**. This opens the Add A Contact window so that you can enter the necessary information.

Deal with Spam

Spam, or unsolicited email, often trying to sell something, from Viagra to designer watches, can be harmful as well as irritating. Spam can contain viruses or malware buried inside a harmless looking link or sales offer. If you do not handle spam, it can overwhelm your inbox. There are essentially three ways to deal with it:

- **Your ISP (Internet Service Provider) often can filter email for their clients if the clients choose**. If you are suffering from too much spam, your first attack is to ask your ISP to increase the filtering level for your account. They capture email that is suspicious and present it

ANNE FINDS EMAIL A MIXED BLESSING

Email for me is a way to stay current on what's going on in others' lives. I see it as a surface connection, and often follow up with a phone call. It reminds me of connections in my life and the value of networking. I can't imagine not having email, although I find it a mixed blessing.

I try to save email communication for family, friends, and professional peers, but I confess I haven't managed to keep the intruders out. My current junk mail volume is outrageous! Email address information is a standard question on most applications now, be it for employment or opening a bank account. Who knows who has access to my address so it seems virtually impossible to keep it all private. At one time, I considered changing my email address, but I believe that would only be a short-term diversion. So I put up with the nonsense that shows up in my mailbox and delete tons of incoming mail regularly. Really, people are quite creative in how they can annoy you, anonymously, of course!

Perhaps an anti-spam product is the my way out of my dilemma. There must be something that will solve this problem—too many people have had to march down this same road. Somewhere there is an answer....bring it on!

Anne T, 61, New Mexico

to you in a list for you to check. If you see valid email, you can rescue it. If your ISP cannot do this, or if it doesn't guide you through finding a way to do it, you might look for a different ISP. This can be a serious problem.

- **Your email program, such as Windows Live Mail, will usually have a filtering mechanism available.** You may have several options. Windows Live Mail, for example, can set a level for email protection, filter for phishing attacks (phishing is described in the following section), block specific senders, allow specific senders, restrict international email, use digital IDs, or block images in email and put the offending messages in a Junk email folder (see Figure 4-8). To access these features in Windows Live Mail, see "Set Safety Options in Windows Live Mail."

- **You can find third-party software that specializes in filtering email and providing a way for you to safely sift through your email without a lot of hassle.** We have used MailWasher for this

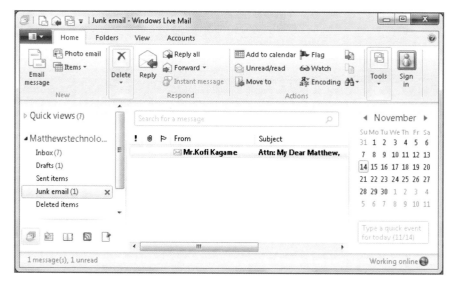

Figure 4-8: To keep from being inundated with spam, it is important to use all the filtering mechanisms at your disposal.

Figure 4-9: You can set Safety Options for dealing with spam and other threats to your email in Windows Live Mail.

NOTE

Many malware protection packages labeled "Internet Security" include anti-spam capability. Examples of two highly rated programs include Norton Internet Security and Kaspersky Internet Security.

with good results (see mailwasher.net for a free download). You can get a list of products that are rated from cnet.com. Type http://cnet.com into your browser's address bar, type anti spam software into the search text box and click **Search** (the magnifying glass). You'll find a list of reviewed anti-spam software (look at the date and make sure it is a current review).

SET SAFETY OPTIONS IN WINDOWS LIVE MAIL

To set the options for handling spam and other email threats in Windows Live Mail:

1. Click the **Windows Live Mail** tab on the left of the tab bar (left of the Home tab), click **Options**, and then click **Safety Options**. You'll see a dialog box, shown in Figure 4-9, with several approaches to safely dealing with email.

   - **Options**, the default tab, allows you to set a level of protection you want. High, the default, is a good choice, although you may prefer Low if you already have a good ISP or third-party spam handler. If you don't want to deal with suspected spam at all, you might click **Permanently Delete Suspected Junk Email Instead Of Moving It To The Junk Email Folder**. Although this can be a viable solution, we don't recommend it because occasional valid emails get trapped this way—you'll lose the ability to rescue them.

   - **Safe Senders** allows you to enter specific email addresses or domain names that you trust. Click **Add** and enter the email address/domain name. Also click **Also Trust Email From My Contacts** to allow people from your Contacts list to be automatic trusted senders.

   - **Blocked Senders** blocks specific email addresses or domain names. If you have a specific offender, you can simply block them. Click **Add** and enter the address/domain name. You can also choose to send an offending email back to the sender or unsubscribe from the mailing list. I don't recommend either of these in order to retain your privacy.

   - **International** allows you to block email from specific countries or languages. Click **Blocked Top-Level Domain List**, and click in the check box to block messages from countries on the list based on their top-level domain, such as BE for Belgium or RU for Russia. Click **Blocked Encoding List** and click in the check box to block the selected languages based on the way they are encoded.

- **Phishing** is when an email message pretends to be from a reputable organization and tries to get you to give them sensitive information like a credit card number or your password. This tab allows you to remove suspicious emails that potentially contain invalid links to the source of the message (it says it is from one source, but is really from another). Select both check boxes to protect against phishing and to place the email in your Junk email folder. You'll want to check your Junk folder occasionally and delete the contents after you verify that no valid email was selected.

- **Security** gives you several opportunities for protection. You can select a "security zone" to use. We recommend the Internet Zone; otherwise, it is too restrictive. We also select the **Warn Me When Other Applications Try To Send Mail As Me**. We do not recommend blocking the downloading of images. Again, this is too restrictive. It is better to just open images from trusted sources. Do not open forwarded images without knowing who it is from and trusting that they forward only nonthreatening links. Finally, you can purchase a Digital ID and use it to send and receive email that contains a digital signature. You can encrypt the contents and attachments for all your email or digitally sign your outgoing email. These are fairly strict security measures that we do not use. However, if you have a special need for them, they are available.

2. Click **OK** to save your changes and close the dialog box.

Apply Formatting

The simplest messages are sent in plain text without any formatting. These messages take the least bandwidth and are the easiest to receive. If you wish, you can send messages with formatting using Hypertext Markup Language (HTML), the language with which many websites are created. You can do this for an individual message or for all messages.

CAUTION

Not all email programs can properly receive HTML messages, which results in messages that are not very readable. However, most programs released in the last ten years can handle HTML.

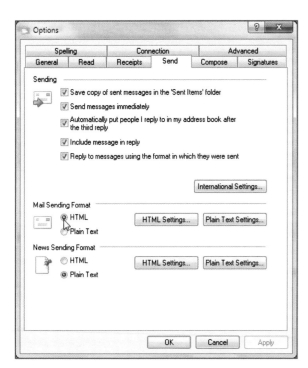

Figure 4-10: *If you send your mail using HTML instead of plain text, you can apply fonts and color and do many other things not available with plain text.*

APPLY FORMATTING TO ALL MESSAGES

To turn HTML formatting on or off:

1. Click the **Windows Live Mail** tab on the left of the tab bar (left of the Home tab) and click **Options**, and then click **Mail**.

2. Click the **Send** tab. Under Mail Sending Format, click **HTML** if you want it and it is not selected, or click **Plain Text** if that is what you want (see Figure 4-10).

3. Click **OK**, and, if desired, close Windows Live Mail.

SELECT A FONT AND A COLOR FOR ALL MESSAGES

To use a particular font and font color on all of your email messages (you must send your mail using HTML in place of plain text—see "Apply Formatting to All Messages"):

1. Click the **Windows Live Mail** tab, click **Options**, and then click **Mail**.

2. Click the **Compose** tab. Under Compose Font, click **Font Settings** opposite Mail.

3. Select the font, style, size, effects, and color that you want to use with all your email; click **OK** twice; and then, if desired, close Windows Live Mail.

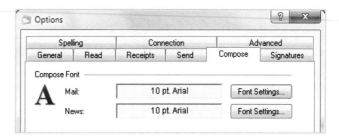

ATTACH A SIGNATURE

To attach a signature (a closing) on all of your email messages:

1. Click the **Windows Live Mail** tab, and click **Options**, and then click **Mail**.

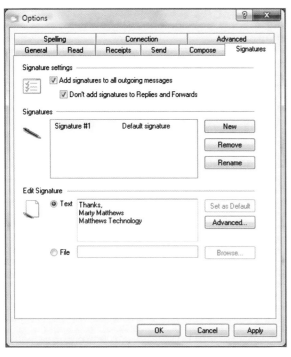

Figure 4-11: A "signature" in Windows Live Mail is really a closing.

2. Click the **Signatures** tab, and click **New**. Under Edit Signature, enter the closing text you want to use, or click **File** and enter or browse to the path and filename you want for the closing. The file could be a graphic image, such as a scan of your written signature, if you wished.

3. Click **Add Signatures To All Outgoing Messages**, as shown in Figure 4-11, and click **OK**. Then, if desired, close Windows Live Mail.

Attach Files to Email

You can attach and send files, such as documents or images, with email messages.

1. Open Windows Live Mail, and click **Email Message** in the Home tab New group.

2. Click **Attach File** in the Message tab Insert group. Select the folder and file you want to send, and click **Open**. The attachment will be shown below the subject.

3. Address, enter, and send the message as you normally would, and then close Windows Live Mail.

Use Calendar

The Windows Live Mail Calendar, which you can use to keep track of scheduled events, is open by default in the right pane, as you have seen in several figures in this chapter, beginning with Figure 4-4.

To close the Calendar or open it if it is closed:

Click the **View** tab and click **Calendar Pane** in the Layout group. The calendar pane will close, or open if it was closed.

UICKSTEPS

USING WEB MAIL

Web mail is the sending and receiving of email over the Internet using a browser, such as Internet Explorer, instead of an email program, such as Windows Live Mail. There are a number of web mail programs, such as Windows Live Hotmail (hotmail.com), Yahoo! Mail (mail.yahoo .com), and Google's Gmail (gmail.com). So long as you have access to the Internet, you can sign up for one or more of these services. The basic features (simple sending and receiving of email) are often free. For example, to sign up for Windows Live Hotmail:

1. Open Internet Explorer. In the address bar, type <u>hotmail.com</u>, and press **ENTER**.

2. If you already have a Windows Live account, enter your ID and password, and click **Sign In**. Otherwise, under Windows Live Hotmail, click **Sign Up**, fill in the requested information, and click **I Accept**.

3. When you are done, the Windows Live Hotmail page will open and display your mail, as shown in Figure 4-12.

4. Click the envelope icon to open and read a message.

5. Click **New** on the toolbar to write an email message. Enter the address, a subject, and the message. When you are done, click **Send**.

6. When you are finished with Hotmail, close Internet Explorer.

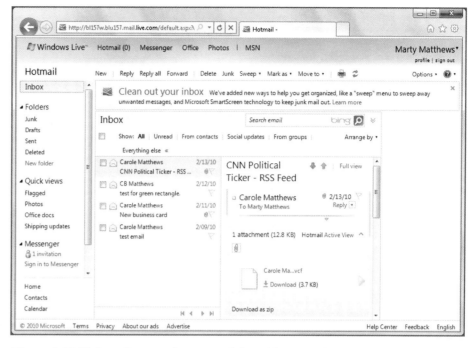

Figure 4-12: Web mail accounts are a quick and free way to get one or more email accounts.

You can also expand the Calendar to fill the Windows Live Mail window:

Click the **Calendar** icon in the lower-left corner of the Windows Live Mail window. The Calendar opens, as you can see in Figure 4-13.

To return from the Calendar to Windows Live Mail:

Click the **Mail** icon in the lower-left corner of the Windows Live Mail window.

TIP

A way to quickly open Windows Live Hotmail is to add it to your Favorites list or Favorites bar. With Hotmail open in Internet Explorer, click the **Favorites** icon ☆ in the upper-right corner of the Internet Explorer window, click the **Add To Favorites** icon, and then click **Add to Favorites** or click the **Add To Favorites** down arrow and click the **Add To Favorites Bar**. Windows Live Hotmail will appear either in the Favorites list or on the Favorites bar. In either place, click the name or icon once to open Windows Live Hotmail.

TIP

With a New Message window open, you can drag a file from Windows Explorer or the desktop to the message, and it will automatically be attached and sent with the message.

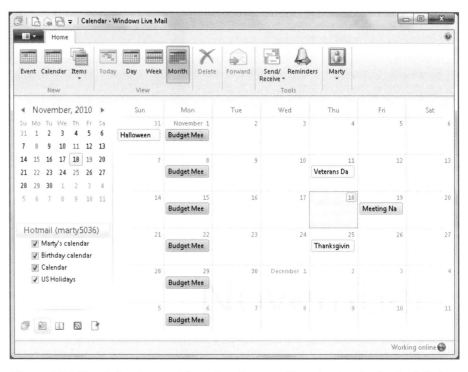

Figure 4-13: The Calendar provides a handy way of keeping track of scheduled events, especially those scheduled through email.

DIRECTLY ADD EVENTS TO A CALENDAR

To add an event to a calendar date:

1. With the calendar pane open, right-click a date on the Calendar, and click **Create New Event**. The New Event window will open.

2. Enter the subject, location, dates and times, and a message, as shown in Figure 4-14.

3. If you have multiple calendars, click the **Calendar** down arrow, and select the calendar you want to use. Also, select how you want the calendar to reflect your time during the event.

SUSAN TRACKS, SIGNS, AND FORMATS EMAIL

In my work in a law office, I use the Calendar, Signatures, and formatting. The Calendar tracks my office priorities. For instance, for upcoming trials, I track deadlines or activities needing my assistance. My personal calendar is private, but a common office calendar allows me to track the activities of the firm, so that I can schedule my own activities around them.

My signature reduces decisions about how to end emails. I keep several signatures: office, personal, and for a side business I have. Then I simply select the proper signature for the recipient who gets the correct "flavor" of me from the signature. I also maintain signatures for attorneys signing legal correspondence. This way I don't have to remember all the varying details, such as phone numbers or email addresses. I simply choose the right signature and the information is automatically included.

Formatting makes my correspondence more professional. In the office we adhere to a standard style—such as font or font size, so that emails look similar, regardless of the sender. I don't have to think about making email look professional; I just format according to the standard.

Susan S., 57, Michigan

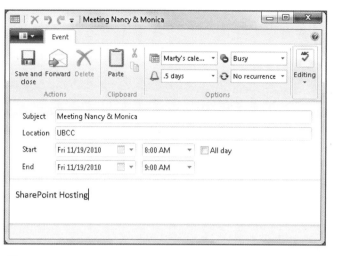

Figure 4-14: *The Windows Live Mail Calendar allows you to send scheduled events to others to put on their calendars.*

4. If the event will happen on a repeated basis, click the **Recurrence** down arrow, and click the period for this event.

5. When you have completed the event, click either **Save & Close** to store the event on your Calendar or **Forward** to send this to others for their schedules.

6. If you selected Forward, an email message will open. Address it, make any desired changes to the message, and click **Send**.

ADD AN EMAIL MESSAGE TO A CALENDAR

When you receive an email message with scheduling ramifications, you can directly add its information to your Calendar.

1. In Windows Live Mail, click the message that has calendar information and click **Add To Calendar** in the Home tab Actions group.

   –Or–

   Right-click the message and click **Add To Calendar**.

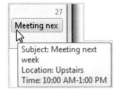

In both cases, an event window will open. Unfortunately, the subject and the body are the only fields that are filled in for you from the email (the current date is in the Start and End Date fields, but you probably need to change that). You must fill in the location, dates and times, and whether it is recurring.

2. After filling in the pertinent information, click **Save & Close**. The event will appear on your Calendar.

Use Windows Live Messenger

Windows Live Messenger allows you to instantly send and receive instant messages (or *chat*) with others who are online at the same time as you. This is frequently called "instant messaging" or IM.

Set Up Windows Live Messenger

When you downloaded and installed Windows Live Essentials to get Windows Live Mail, you probably also installed Windows Live Messenger; it is selected by default. If so, its icon 🐾 may be on your taskbar, or at least it is in the Start menu. If you didn't install it and want to now, return to the "Get Windows Live Mail" section and follow the instructions there.

The use of Windows Live Messenger requires that you first have a Microsoft Live account or an MSN or Hotmail account, which you may have signed up for earlier in this chapter in the "Using Web Mail" QuickSteps. Once you have an account, you are able to set up your contacts and personalize Messenger to your tastes.

ESTABLISH A WINDOWS LIVE ACCOUNT

With Windows Live Messenger installed, open it and establish a Windows Live account.

1. Click **Start**, click **All Programs,** and click **Windows Live Messenger**; or click the **Windows Live** folder, and click **Windows Live Messenger**. The Windows Live Messenger window will open, as you can see here.

2. If you already have a Windows Live account, enter your email address and password, and click **Sign In**. Go to the next section, "Add Contacts to Messenger."

3. If you don't have a Windows Live account, click **Sign Up**. Internet Explorer will open and the Windows Live registration will appear. Enter the information requested, click **I Accept**, and when you are told you have successfully registered your email address, close your browser. You will be returned to Windows Live Messenger.

4. Enter your email address and your password, and then click **Sign In**.

ADD CONTACTS TO MESSENGER

To use Windows Live Messenger, you must enter contacts for people you want to "talk" to.

1. If Windows Live Messenger is not already open, click its icon in the taskbar. If the icon isn't there, click **Start**, click **All Programs**, and click **Windows Live Messenger**.

2. The first time you start Windows Live Messenger you will see some introductory screens asking if you want to connect with Facebook and other social media sites. Following that you are asked if you would like either Social Networks or MSN news in a side panel of Messenger. Click your choice. If you choose Social Networks, you are given a choice of Facebook, MySpace, or LinkedIn. Again, click your choice.

3. Click **Add** in the upper-right corner of the Windows Live Messenger window to open a context menu of choices for IM contacts. Click:

- **Add A Favorite** to open your list of contacts so that you can select one or more that you want to contact with IM. Click in the **Search Contacts** text box and type the person's name as best you can.

People that fit what you have typed will appear (you can see if that person is online). Double-click the name you want.

- **Create A Group**. Click **OK** to start a group so you can have group conversations. Type a name for the group and click **Next**. Click **Select From Your Contact List**, click the contacts you want, and click **OK**. Click **Next** and then click **Done**. After the contacts accept your invitation, they will become members of the group.

- **Create A Category**. Click **OK** to create a new a new category, such as "church" or "club," within which you can organize your contacts. Type a name for the category, click to select the contacts you want in the category, and click **Save**.

- **Add A Friend**. Type your friend's email address; optionally, if you want to send text messages, select a country and type the friend's cell phone number, and click **Next**. If you want to make the person a favorite, click that option and click **Next**. An invitation will be sent to the friend. Depending on the person's status—whether they are online and whether they accept your invitation—you will get a response accordingly. Click **Add More Friends**, if desired, or click **Close**.

- **Search For Someone**. In the Windows Live search page, type the name you want to search for. As you type the name a drop-down list appears with options to search your contacts, your documents, or the Web, or select a few choices. Click your choice. Depending on your choice a Bing search will open and display either a list matching your search or a list of people in your contacts or documents. Click the one you want to find.

- **Add People From Other Services**. Type a name or email address and click **Next** to add people in that way, or click one of the services and follow the instructions to connect that service with Windows Live. If you see a dialog box labeled "Set Up Your Privacy Settings," choose among Public, Limited, or Private settings and click Save.

4. When you are done adding contacts, close Internet Explorer. Back in Windows Live Messenger, you should now have a list of contacts, as you can see in Figure 4-15. If you want to exit Windows Live Messenger, click **Close**.

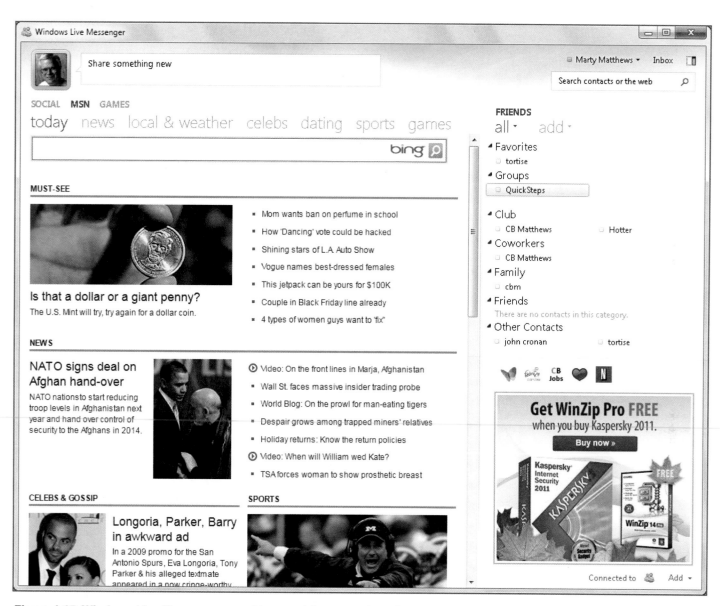

Figure 4-15: *Windows Live Messenger provides a quick way to chat, share photos, and exchange files with family, friends, and associates online.*

CUSTOMIZE MESSENGER

There are several ways to customize Windows Live Messenger.

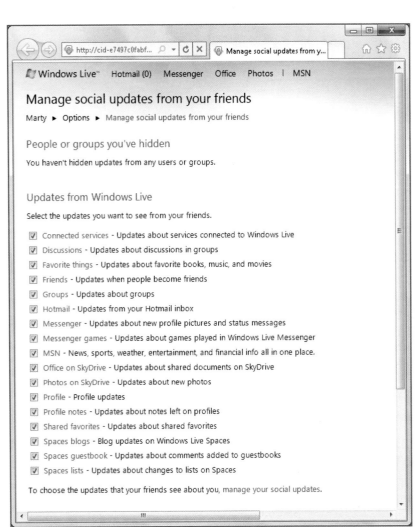

Figure 4-16: Setting Windows Live Messenger options allows you to customize how your services work with mail.

1. Open **Windows Live Messenger**. Change from full view, as was shown in Figure 4-12, to compact view, shown below, by clicking the **Switch To Compact View** icon in the upper-right corner of the window.

2. Assuming you have connected with social networking sites, click the **Edit Messenger Social Settings** icon. You are presented with a number of options for working with the various services you have selected, as shown in Figure 4-16.

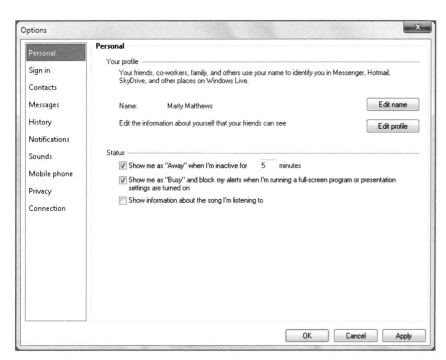

Figure 4-17: You can customize Windows Live Messenger in a number of areas using the Options dialog box.

3. When you have chosen the options you want, click **Save** and close Internet Explorer.

4. In Windows Live Messenger, click the down arrow to the right of your name. Here you can choose how you appear to IM users and a number of other options.

5. Click **More Options** to open the Options dialog box. Here you have a number of options you can use to customize Messenger, as you can see in Figure 4-17.

6. Click each of the areas on the left and review the options and selections on the right. Make the changes that are correct for you, and then click **OK**.

Use Windows Live Messenger

Using Windows Live Messenger is simple: double-click a contact. If they are online, the Conversation window will open, as shown in Figure 4-18. If they are not online, you will be told the contact will be given the message the next time they are online.

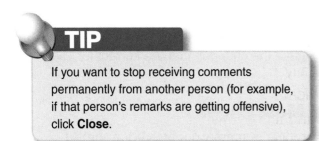

Figure 4-18: *When a conversation is in process, you can see who said what in the Conversation window.*

SEND A MESSAGE

With the Conversation window open (done by double-clicking a contact), send a message by typing it in the bottom pane and pressing **ENTER**. You can add emoticons (smiley faces), change the font, and/or change the message background with the icons below the text box.

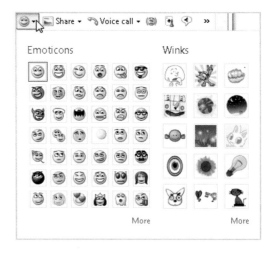

RECEIVE A MESSAGE

With a conversation in process, a received message appears in the Conversation window, as you can see in Figure 4-18. If someone sends you an instant message without a Conversation window open, you will see a little pop-up message in your notification area. Double-click this message to open a Conversation window with the sender.

TIP

If you want to stop receiving comments permanently from another person (for example, if that person's remarks are getting offensive), click **Close**.

Chapter 5

Socializing and Communicating Online

According to Wikipedia, Georg Simmel (1858–1918) was the first person to document the concept of social networking in considering interactions between people around the beginning of the 20th century. So as a concept, social networking is not new, but on the Internet, it is a relatively recent science. It is still very much in its infancy, and like a growing child, today's social networking, available to anyone with a computer, is flourishing both scientifically and socially. It is a global phenomenon. How people communicate and interact with each other is studied to understand the spread of disease, how it affects people's states of mind and happiness, how rumors spread and cliques form, how people meet and establish ties to each other, how and when advertising works

> **NOTE**
>
> Some studies have shown that the separation between any two people on the planet can be as small as five to seven other people—one early experiment for this was conducted by Stanley Milgram in 1967 and called "A Small Experiment." His findings are known as "six degrees of separation."

(or doesn't), how cultures differ, how social networking may diminish tolerance for people with different views, and yet paradoxically how global social networking broadens the availability of diverse views, the effects of social networking on politics, and on and on.

The impact of social networking on our lives is significant. Of course, our youth seemingly are born for social networking, they adapt to it so easily. Seniors are beginning to take it up in increasing numbers. An article written by Joshua Brockman (Aug 27, 2010) for npr.org, quoting a recent poll by the Pew Research Center's Internet & American Life Project, stated that social networking by seniors has doubled from 22 percent to 42 percent over the last year. That same article quoted comScore, a digital measurement company, as saying that the number of seniors who are now social networking is up to 27.4 million people from 16 million only a year ago. This chapter describes some of the ways that we seniors are engaging in social networking.

Understand Social Networking with Computers

One of the ways we can understand social networking using computers is to see how it is played out in our lives. Where are the "mainstream" places that we engage with others socially on a computer? Why would

QUICKQUOTES

DEBORAH USES SOCIAL NETWORKING EFFECTIVELY

I use social networking to stay aware and connected. I use email, Facebook, Twitter, blogging, and Ning—each program is a microcosm; together forming a complex, interwoven ecology.

Facebook is the most intriguing and engaging. I'm a visual artist, and the image orientation and relational aspects of Facebook appeal to me. It presents a live and dynamic landscape of family and friends around the world and from different phases of my life, as well as collegial connections. In viewing friends' Facebook postings, I find varied ideas, and entertaining ones, too. I like that Facebook is not invasive: I choose who to accept as friends and when to look at it.

Twitter is less engaging to me. However, I do use it professionally to post upcoming events or announce a new blog entry. Twitter is more oriented to using on an iPhone or Blackberry—and currently I don't use those. However, for many people, Twitter provides a great sense of immediacy and connectedness.

Ning allows me to set up my own specialized online art community. With it, I provide an interactive area for my art students, seamlessly integrated into my own website. I don't need programming skills to change anything.

Deborah C., 58, Washington

we want to spend our time that way? How do we get started? These are some of the questions we hope to address in this chapter. Facebook is where we will start.

Use Facebook

Facebook, a private online website, is perhaps today's most visible social networking presence. More than 500 million active users (http://en.wikipedia.org/wiki/Facebook) spend time on Facebook, some for hours a day. Facebook allows you to connect with other Facebook users—you choose which ones. You first set up your own webpage, which can be private for your designated family or friends, or public where anyone can find you and initiate a connection. You can include a photo and personal information, or not, and then you can send invitations to others to be "your friend," or respond to other's invitations. You can correspond with all your "friends" at one time or individually, depending on your choice. You have to be over age 13 to use Facebook; most likely, that is not a problem if you're reading this book!

SET UP A FACEBOOK ACCOUNT

Setting up an account is easy. You simply fill in the form on the home page, shown in Figure 5-1, and then fill in your own webpage with your personal data.

1. Open your browser, such as Internet Explorer, type <u>facebook.com</u> in its address bar, and click **ENTER**. The home page will be displayed.

2. Fill in the form with your name, email address, and a password. Enter your gender and birth date (needed to verify that you are old enough to register). Click **Sign Up**.

3. Type in the security check words designed to keep drone computers from accessing the system. Click **Sign Up**. If the words are hard to distinguish, you may have to reenter them more than once. The three-step page for completing your webpage will be displayed.

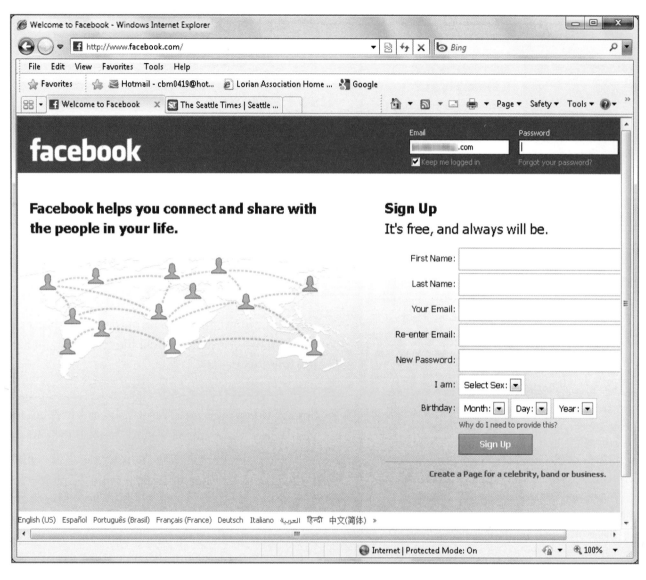

Figure 5-1: *Facebook, one of the most recognizable of the social networking sites, makes signing up easy and quick.*

4. The first step in finalizing your webpage is to find your friends. If you want Facebook to look in your email files and find your friends, enter your email address and email password, and click **Find Friends**. Otherwise, click **Skip This Step**—there will be other opportunities to find your friends.

5. If you want to enter your profile information now, type your high school, college, or university; the years you graduated from each; and then your employer. As you type, a list of possibilities will be presented to you; click the correct one if it is listed. Then click **Save & Continue**. If you want to skip this step, click **Skip**—you'll have another opportunity later. You may see pictures of people you don't know and be asked if you want to add any as friends. Just click **Skip** or **Save & Continue** again.

6. The third step allows you to insert a picture of yourself onto your webpage. You can insert a photo or graphic using one of two techniques. Click **Upload A Photo** to find and retrieve a picture from your hard disk. Click **Take A Photo** to take the photo with your webcam. Click **Skip** to do this later. At this point you'll see the edit profile page of your new Facebook webpage.

7. However, there is one more step. You'll need to go to your inbox and retrieve the **Just One More Step To Get Started On Facebook** email, shown in Figure 5-2. Click the designated link, and you will finalize your setup.

If you have chosen to skip entering your friends or profile, you can see how to do it next.

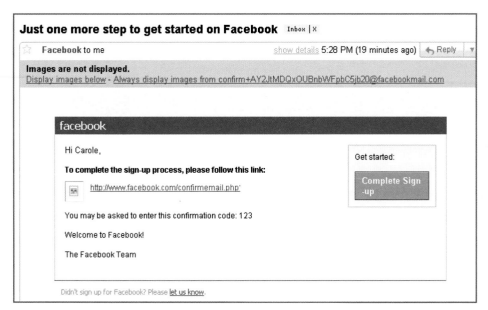

Figure 5-2: *You must reply to an email to finalize and activate your Facebook account.*

5

UICKSTEPS

OPENING FACEBOOK THE EASY WAY

To place a Facebook tab on your Internet Explorer browser so that you can quickly find your webpage whenever you open the browser:

1. Using Internet Explorer, find and open your Facebook page.

2. On the toolbar, click the down arrow on the **Home** icon and click **Add or Change Home Page**.

3. Click one of these options and then click **Yes**. (Click **No** if you don't want Facebook to open automatically when you open the browser.)

   • **Use The Webpage As Your Only Home** When you open your browser, this tab will be the only one that opens.

   • **Add This Webpage To Your Homepage Tabs** This adds Facebook to the other webpages that currently display as tabs when you open your browser.

   • **Use The Current Tab Set As Your Home Page** This makes the tabs that are currently displayed in your browser, the set of pages that will be available when you next open a browser.

4. If you selected one of the options and clicked Yes, the next time you open your browser, a tab with the Facebook webpage will appear. If Facebook is not displayed, click the tab name (click **Login** and click **Facebook**) to open it.

UPDATE YOUR PERSONAL INFORMATION FOR THE FIRST TIME

When you first sign up, your Facebook page welcomes you with a page, as shown in Figure 5-3, that leads you through finding friends, filling in your profile, activating a mobile phone, and specifying which information may be displayed to the public. On each step, just click the appropriate button, such as Find Friends or Edit Profile.

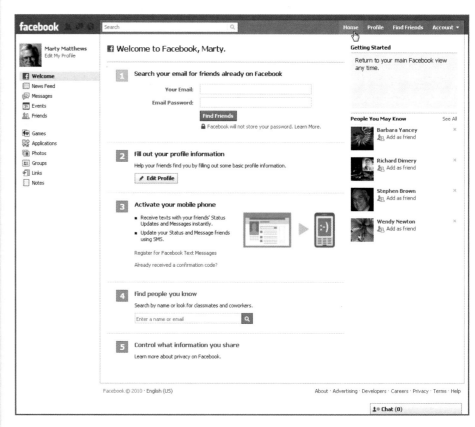

Figure 5-3: Facebook facilitates how you control and update your personal information by making it clear and easy to change.

Current City:	
Hometown:	
Sex:	Female ▾ ☑ Show my sex in my profile
Birthday:	Apr ▾ 20 ▾ 1945 ▾ Show my full birthday in my profile. ▾
Interested In:	☐ Women ☐ Men
Looking For:	☐ Friendship ☐ Dating ☐ A Relationship ☐ Networking
Political Views:	
Religious Views:	
Bio:	
Favorite Quotations:	

Save Changes **Cancel**

Figure 5-4: Facebook provides a form for you to enter the information you want to share.

NOTE

There are three ways you can find friends in Facebook: you can have Facebook search your email contact list, search for people by name or email address, or find people with whom you communicate by Instant Messenger. Click **Find People You Know** on the Home page.

1. If you are just beginning to add friends and update your personal profile, sign in to Facebook and click **Home** in the upper-right area of the Facebook toolbar. The page seen in Figure 5-3 is displayed.

2. Type your email address and your email password, and click **Find Friends** to have Facebook find friends in your email Contact list. You'll need to enter your email address and then approve friends as they are suggested.

3. Click **Edit Profile** to update your personal information. The form displayed in Figure 5-4 is displayed. Fill in the information you want to share, and click **Save Changes**. You can specify who gets to see it next. (See "Protecting Your Online Identity" QuickSteps.)

4. Click **Home** to return there, and then to specify who sees your information, click **Control What Information You Share**. You'll see an explanation of the privacy controls offered by Facebook. Please spend some time reading the text. At the top of the Privacy Controls text, on the right, click **Edit Your Privacy Settings**. The settings, by default, are set to Recommended, where your information is shared by a combination of Everybody, Friends Of Friends (people who see you from a friend's site), and Friends Only (only your own friends), as seen in Figure 5-5.

- You can reset the combination by clicking **Everyone**, **Friends Of Friends**, or **Friends Only**.

PAT FIGHTS BEING A DINOSAUR WITH FACEBOOK!

I never thought about Facebook until my daughters flagged me as a technological dinosaur. They rummaged through my email contacts shouting, "Don't you want to be friends with your buddies?" I thought I was friends with them, but I quickly learned, Facebook carries friendships to a dynamic new level.

Imagine yourself at a party chatting with varied acquaintances, friends, and family. Some you know well; others you have not seen in years or know only tangentially. With some you will have thought-provoking, personal exchanges. Some discussions will be in groups, about books or a football game. Others you will want to track day-to-day events. Facebook enables you to keep up with all, gaining an expanded sense of family and friendship.

I use Facebook for social networking and follow that old advice "Don't talk about sex, religion, or politics" when I write posts available to everyone. For private or select group conversations, I use Facebook messages. I encourage you to learn to use Facebook, set your privacy comfort level, and start reconnecting. Post pictures—they speak thousands of words. Oh, and don't spy on your kids. It's counter-productive.

Pat T., 66, Colorado

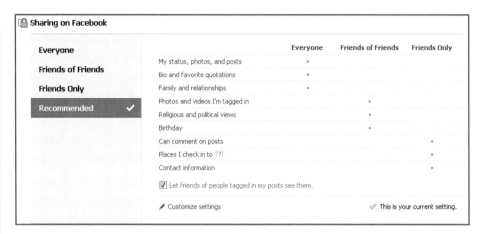

*Figure 5-5: **Facebook provides a recommended way of controlling who will see your page, but you can customize it according to your own comfort zone.***

- Click **Edit Your Settings** under Applications And Websites to control how applications, games, and websites can see information about you when your friends are using them, and how you can be found in a public search. Click **Edit Settings** to set the options, and click **Save Changes** to return to the Applications, Games, And Websites page. Click **Back To Privacy** to return to the Privacy Settings page.

- Click **Edit Your Lists** under Block Lists to set up a list of people to be blocked from your site, and to block application and event invitations from certain people. Click **Back To Privacy** to return to the Privacy Settings page.

- Click **Customize Settings** to set your own preferences for how your personal information will be shared. When you are finished, click **Preview My Profile** on the top of the page to see what others will see when they look at your profile.

UPDATING YOUR PERSONAL INFORMATION LATER

After you have been active on your Facebook page and found a few friends and entered some information, you'll use different ways to update your information.

1. On your Home page or Profile page, click **Edit My Profile** under your name.

Carole Matthews
Edit My Profile

2. Click the category on the left side, and change the information as you want it to be.

3. Click **View My Profile** to see the results.

Play Games in Facebook

Gaming in Facebook is popular with seniors according to a PopCap study of game demographics. It found that 38 percent of people that play social games are ages 50 and up. We seniors seem to like games.

Facebook, and to a lesser degree MySpace, allow you to play games. For example, FarmVille, the most popular game on Facebook, is a real-time simulation on running a farm. You plant virtual crops, raise virtual livestock, and manage your virtual farm. You can use the same technique to find other social networking games.

To sign up to play FarmVille and learn how to access other games in Facebook:

1. On your Facebook Home page, type <u>Farmville</u> in the Search text box at the top of the page. Click **Search** (the magnifying glass icon). As you type the name, you'll see a list of other games that are available. In the list of search results, click FarmVille. You'll go to the Home page for the game. FarmVille's Home page is displayed in Figure 5-6.

facebook   Farmville

2. Click **Play Now**. You will be asked to allow FarmVille to access your Facebook account. This means they can display your name and contact information, and will use your age to verify that you are old enough to play the game. To find out exactly how they will use your information, click **Privacy Policy**.

PROTECTING YOUR ONLINE IDENTITY

It is a wonderful thing to be able to find and exchange information with people with similar interests. Social networking facilitates these communications so that we connect with broader webs of people and with people we simply do not know. In today's world, it is wise to be "street smart" when it comes to the streets of the Internet. Here are a few hard and fast rules for keeping your identity to yourself and your information private.

- Make your password reasonably difficult to figure out by using combinations of numbers, letters, and special characters. Protect your passwords for the various applications you use, such as Facebook; don't share them with others.

- Be wise about the information you put on the Internet. For example, share only that information you are comfortable with unknown persons knowing. Don't put highly personal information or photos in Facebook for instance. Even if you think you are only sharing with friends, you may be surprised with whom they share.

- If you are in a forum or blog that is publicly available, don't put information that could cause your identify or your home to be compromised—don't put your address or even your town or city name. Put a city close by, for instance. Don't use your last name, or use a fake ID. Be aware of the information you are sharing and make it

Continued . . .

Figure 5-6: *FarmVille is a game that is available in several social networking arenas, such as Facebook.*

3. Click **Allow**.

4. Follow the remaining prompts to register, enter your credit card information, and get started learning how to play the game.

Use Twitter

Twitter is another phenomenon in the social networking world—its home page is displayed in Figure 5-7. Twitter provides a way for you to *tweet* about what is going on in your life. A tweet is a message no longer than 140 characters that you can broadcast to your followers. Twitter tracks all the tweets and displays a "billboard" of what the world is thinking about at any one time. Using this, you can find out what people are thinking about in general at the moment, or on a specific subject.

PROTECTING YOUR
ONLINE IDENTITY *(Continued)*

minimal. (However, there are some sites that require you to enter your correct information. In this case, you'll have to enter your real data *if you really want to use the site*, but be stingy when you can.)

- Don't click links from unknown persons. These can be programmed to gather information from you or your computer.

- Keep your computer browser software up to date so that the latest advances in security are on your computer. Equally important is making sure your antivirus or Internet security software is current.

- Be wary about meeting people in person or sharing personal information with strangers in unprotected sites.

Social networking can be fun and a great way to meet people. Just keep in mind that you want to be "street smart" while you are having that great time.

NOTE

MySpace, next in line with regard to number of users after Facebook, is another social networking site. MySpace, with its emphasis in music and video presentations, caters mostly to younger people. Look at myspace.com to compare its suitability for your needs.

Figure 5-7: *Twitter provides a way for you to communicate in short bursts, or tweets, a message to the world of Twitter followers, or to your own smaller, unique community.*

SIGN UP FOR TWITTER

1. Enter twitter.com into your browser address text box, and click **ENTER**. The Twitter home page is displayed. Click **Sign Up**. The sign-up form is displayed.

2. Fill in the form with your first and last name, a user name (which is how you are known to others on the website), a password, and your email address. You may have to experiment with your user name and password to find unique ones.

3. Scroll through the terms of service to understand how your information will be used. You can print a copy by clicking **Printable Version**.

4. Click **Create My Account**.

5. Enter the security code by typing the letters displayed and clicking **Finish**. This ensures that you are not a computer drone. The first of two set-up screens is displayed.

6. For Step 1, beneath "Select The Topics…" on the left, click the link of the topics that interest you. When you click a link, a list of people tweeting on that topic will display below. Scroll through the list and click the person you want to follow. You can just select one or two to get started and then refine your interests later on. When you click a person, the list of their tweets will appear on the right so you can get a sense of what they are tweeting about. You will see a summary of their tweets above the list, such as number of tweets and number of followers. To select someone to follow, click **Follow** (the plus sign) to get an ongoing stream from that source. When you have completed your interest list, click **Next Step: Friends**.

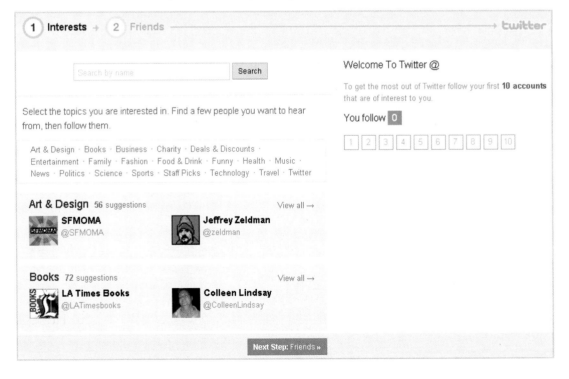

7. For Step 2, you are given the opportunity to get your contacts from an existing contact list. Your email address is displayed and you can click on a service you want to search for contacts, such as Hotmail or Messenger. Below are More Services, such as Gmail or LinkedIn. When you click one of the services, you'll be asked to enter an ID and password and click **Sign In**. This gives your service permission for Twitter to download its contacts. Twitter may take awhile to gather your contacts. When they are imported, you'll see a list of those contacts who have an account on Twitter. When you are finished with this step, click **Finish**. If you want to skip this step, click **Skip Import** to gather your contacts later.

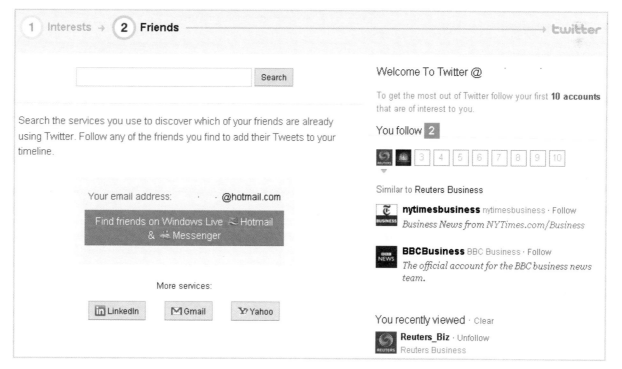

At this point you see your Home page on Twitter.

UNDERSTAND YOUR TWITTER PAGE

On your Twitter Home page, shown in Figure 5-8, you can send tweets, follow your selected tweets, set up or change your profile, send messages, and more.

● Click in the **What's Happening** text box to type a tweet. See "Create a Twitter Message."

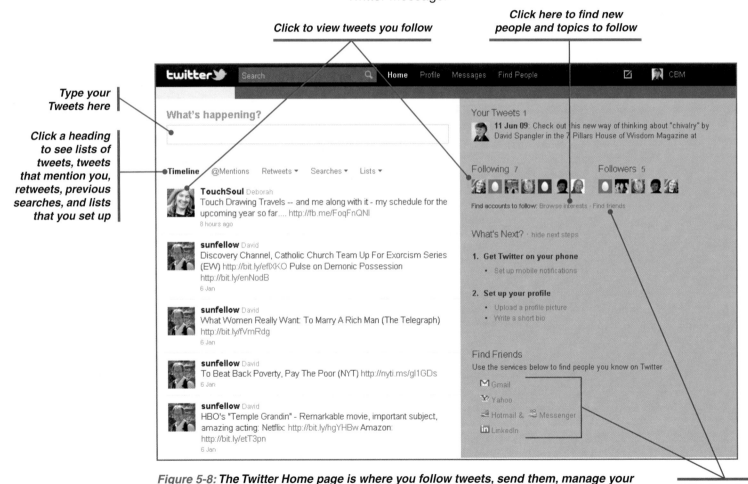

Click to view tweets you follow

Click here to find new people and topics to follow

Type your Tweets here

Click a heading to see lists of tweets, tweets that mention you, retweets, previous searches, and lists that you set up

Click here to find more contacts

Figure 5-8: The Twitter Home page is where you follow tweets, send them, manage your account, and communicate with others.

QUICK**FACTS**

USING TWITTER VOCABULARY

Here are some common Twitter words:

- **Tweet**   A message created, or "to tweet" is to send a message.

- **Tweeter**   One who tweets.

- **Retweet**   Forwarding a tweet to someone else, or a message that has been forwarded to you by someone you follow. Also called "RT."

- **@*username***   A way to indicate that a message is for a specific user. You type @*username* as the first thing in your tweet, and Twitter will place it in the user's timeline.

- **A mention**   Any reference to another user by including @*username* in a tweet. Mentions are placed in a mentioned user's Replies tab.

- **Timeline**   The tweets that are displayed on your home page. As tweets come into your Twitter page, they are listed in sequence by time, the newest on top and the older below.

- **An update**   A tweet you created and sent.

- **Follower**   Someone who wants to know what you are tweeting and signs up to be notified when you tweet. A follower will have your tweets available to them on their Twitter page.

- Click **Timeline** (by default already selected) to see the list of tweets. Click one of the tweets to see a summary of the person tweeting on the right and to find other similar tweeters. (To remove the summary, click the arrow icon on the right of the selected tweet.)

- Click **@Mention** to view tweets that mention you.

- Click **Retweets** to see retweets by you and others.

- Click **Searches** to see a list of your previous searches. When you type a search in the Search text box (next to the Twitter logo), you can click **Save This Search** to review updated results at another time without reentering the search.

- Click **Lists** to see a list you have created or to create a new one. A list allows you to view tweets from several people in one list. Also you can see tweets from others without having them displayed in your Timeline.

- Click a tweet icon on the upper right to see that stream of tweets in your Timeline.

- Click **Browse Interests** to find additional topics to follow.

- Click **Find Friends** to find other contacts.

- Click a link under **Trends** to find what is currently being discussed on Twitter.

CREATE A TWITTER MESSAGE

You can create a message in three ways: create a fresh tweet, reply to someone else's tweet, or forward someone else's tweet.

- To create a new tweet, click in the **What's Happening** text box and write your message. Then click **Tweet**. Your tweet will be broadcast to everyone on your people list and those following you.

What's happening?
This is my first Tweet. Look out world!
⊕ Add your location   101   Tweet

—Or—

- To reply or forward, point to the tweet you want to reply to or forward, and on the bottom of the tweet, you'll have the option to reply or retweet. To forward an existing tweet, click **Retweet**. To create a new reply, click **Reply**.

MANAGE A TWEETER

1. Click the tweeter's icon on the upper right of the Home page. The right column will contain the summary for the tweeter, and several commands to manage the tweets.

- Click **Following** to change it to Unfollow.
- Click the mobile icon to restrict tweets to your mobile device.
- Click the retweet icon to display retweets to this tweeter in your Timeline.
- Click the list icon to create a new list or include the tweeter in one.
- Click the rotary gear icon to mention, block or report the tweeter.

Find and Use Blogs and Forums

The word *blog* is a combination of "web" and "log." The word was first used in 1999 by Peter Merholz, according to Wikipedia (http://en.wikipedia.org/wiki/Widi/Blogs). Although not very old, blogs now are popular with Internet users. (Twitter is a form of a blog, for instance.) Blogs take many forms, but essentially they allow you to keep a public diary/forum where others can read and

NOTE

To add a tweet to your Favorites list, point to the tweet and click **Favorite** on the bottom line.

Reply ↻ Retweet

Retweet

SUZANNE BLOGS FOR WORK AND PLAY

I was inspired to blog when I moved from one state to another and realized that I couldn't possibly write to so many people on a regular basis. Blogging was a way that I could tell people in my old home what I was doing and thinking, all at one time. I used Google's free Blogspot.com. It was fairly easy to set up—they have several templates available. It took me a few times to get the hang of placing photos.

The blog worked! People wrote back to me, and I have kept in touch with many of my friends by using it. Writing the blog turned out to be a lot of fun: writing stories about my family, describing the places I visit, and including photographs. Because I was writing about my family and new home, I declined the setting to allow my blog to pop up in the general search engine. There's no password, but in order to find the blog, a person must know the web address. Even so, I haven't used addresses or full names, just to be on the safe side.

I also began sending it to friends in my new home, and "my readership" has grown for three years now. Many people tell me how much they enjoy reading it, which has made the blog more fun, more challenging, and more rewarding.

Suzanne S., 59, New York

respond to what you say. Blogs are usually, but not always, aimed toward specific topics, such as videos, music, photos, politics, a personal diary (remember Julie/Julia?), etc. One or more people, known as *bloggers*, are responsible for maintaining a blog, keeping it current and active. Some blogs are community-oriented, wherein groups of associated people come together on a blog and socialize, discuss, cuss, and show off. Others are more news-like, and are often commentaries on what official news sources have published. Some blogs are for one individual only, who is both its creator and responder—such as a personal diary or organizing tool. Blogs usually contain links to other blogs, articles, or websites, creating a great network of links within the blog site as well as hyperlinks to sites external to the blog site. *Followers* enhance the network by following, or keeping in touch with, what is being posted on a blog.

You can both find interesting blogs or create your own (see the "Creating Your Own Blog with Blogger" QuickSteps). To find interesting blogs to follow, you can either use specialized blog searches or create your own search.

DO YOUR OWN SEARCH TO FIND BLOGS

1. To find a blog using a search engine such as Google, bring your search engine up in a browser. For instance, for Google, type Google .com in the browser address text box.

2. In the search text box, type what you want to find; for instance, type blog on Obama to find the blogs currently active on President Barack Obama. As you type, as seen in Figure 5-9, you'll see a list of possibilities, including a suggestion that you may be wanting the blog "of" Obama. Find the blog you want and click it.

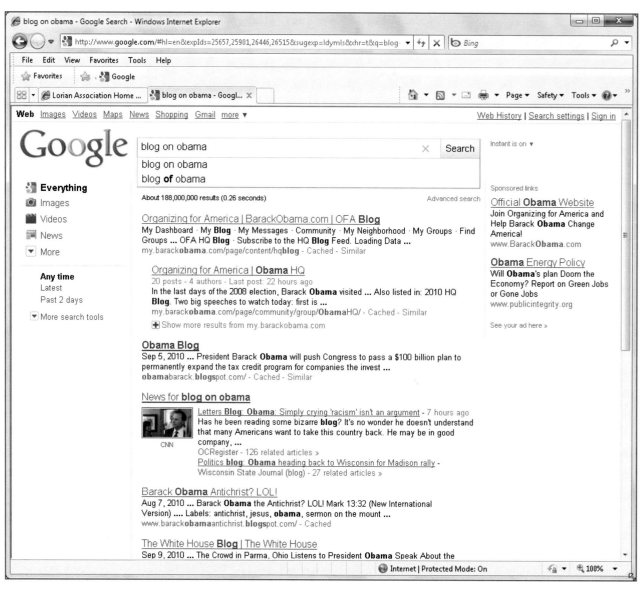

Figure 5-9: *Searching for a blog can be easy—in your search software, type what you are interested in seeing.*

CREATING YOUR OWN BLOG WITH BLOGGER

One of the most common providers of software for creating blogs is Google's Blogger, shown in Figure 5-10. This is free, and available to all who have a Gmail account. Blogger provides templates, or layouts, for a blog with colors and graphics. These can be personalized and customized.

Start your blog as follows:

1. Given you have a Gmail account, type blogger.com in your browser's address bar. The Blogger.com home page will appear as shown in Figure 5-10.

2. Type your Gmail user name and password in the upper-right corner of the page, and click **Sign In**.

3. The Sign Up For Blogger page will display with the first of three steps. Type the name or ID that others will see on the blog. Click whether you want to be notified about Blogger features, and then read the terms of service by clicking that link. Then click the **I Accept The Terms Of Service** check box. You must accept the terms before you can proceed. Finally, click **Continue**.

4. For the second step, type the blog title. Then enter the blog address (URL). This can be anything you want, and it becomes part of the address that people type to find your blog: http://*yourblogaddress*. blogspot.com. Click **Continue**.

☆ Favorite

Continued . . .

*Figure 5-10: **Blogger is one place where you can create your own blog, easily and quickly.***

MAINTAIN YOUR BLOG

Once you have created your blog, you need to maintain it, which involves editing posts, refining your design, adding a profile and photo, and perhaps profiting from some ads. Your posts are

QUICKSTEPS

CREATING YOUR OWN BLOG WITH BLOGGER *(Continued)*

5. On the third step, choose a "look" for your blog based on the templates that are presented. You can change them later. Click **Continue**.

6. Your blog is now ready for you to start blogging. Click **Start Blogging**.

7. Give your blog a name and start typing. When you want to take a look at what it looks like, click **Preview**, as seen in Figure 5-11.

NOTE

To find interesting blogs to follow, check these links:

www.technorati.com/blogs/top100
Tracks the most-used blogs; one of the best search engines for finding the most popular blogs.

www.bloggerschoiceawards.com
Displays a list of blogs that have been vetted (some blogs are not worth your time to even look at, so this is a worthy site).

www.blogsearch.google.com   Click the topics on the left to find blogs in that category.

www.blogsofnote.blogspot.com   Not a large selection, but fascinating and interesting.

Figure 5-11: *Use Preview to take a look at your blog-in-progress.*

considered to be "drafts" until you "publish" them. When they are published, they are placed on the Internet and can be viewed by others. Until they are published, they are unavailable to others.

1. Sign in to your Blogger account, and you will see the *Dashboard*, the blogger home page where you can manage the blog. Figure 5-12 shows an example of a Dashboard page.

Figure 5-12: The Blogger Dashboard is where you maintain your blog's look and content.

2. You have these options:

- Click **View Profile** or **Edit Profile** to see how your profile looks on the blog and to change it if needed.

- Click **Edit Photo** to add a photograph of yourself.

- Click **Edit Notifications** to change how you receive announcements and other information on how to use your blog most effectively.

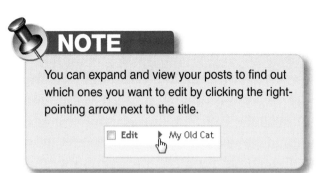
- Click **New Post** to initiate a new entry in a blog. Enter a name in the Title text box, and press **TAB** to move to the blog text box and begin typing your text. The toolbar above the text box contains formatting tools, such as Bold, Italic, and Font Color. When you're finished, click **Preview** to see what it will look like on the blog, and then click **Save Now**.

- Click **Edit Posts**, and then click **Edit** next to the post you want to work with. The text you have entered will be displayed with the editing toolbar. Make your changes. When you are finished, click **Save Now** and click **Edit Posts** to return to your list of posts. When you are ready, click the check box next to the blog title, and then click **Publish Selected** to put the blog on the Internet. If you want to get rid of the selected blog, click the check box and click **Delete Selected**.

- Click **Comments** to look at the comments from others. Blogger will place comments into the Spam area when it detects a questionable one. You can monitor this by clicking **Spam** and retrieving comments that are not spam or deleting those that are. In the Comments list, select the comments you want to delete, and click **Delete**. Click **Remove Content** if you want to remove selected text.

- Click **Settings** to set defaults for how your site will be monitored and made available to others. When you click Settings, you will see a bar of menus of the types of settings. You should scan them all and verify that they are set according to your needs. Some important ones are **Basic** for overall access, **Comments** if you want all comments to be monitored before they are published to the Internet, **Email & Mobile** to notify others when you publish a post or to add a mobile device, and **Permissions** to restrict access to the blog.

- Click **Design** to change the look and placement of your blog. Click **Edit** to change the text or other aspects of a blog. Click **Add A Gadget** to add functionality to the page, such as a search engine, or a Really Simple Syndication (RSS) feed, such as seen in Figure 5-13. To rearrange items on a page, click an outlined section and drag it to another location.

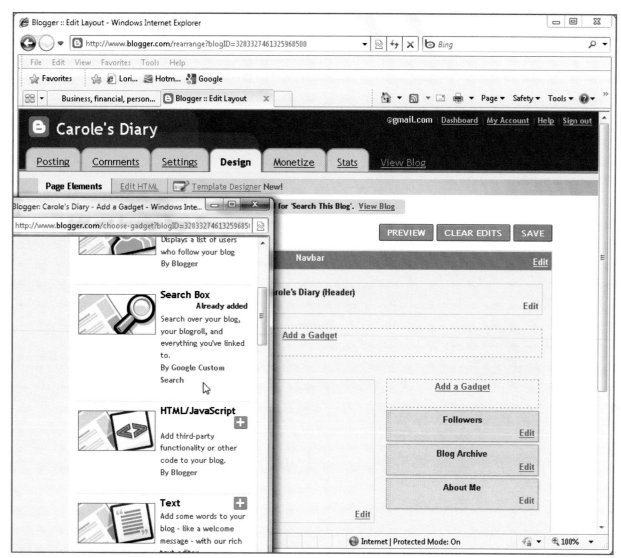

Figure 5-13: You can change the look of your blog and add "gadgets" that give you greater presence in the web environment, such as RSS feeds.

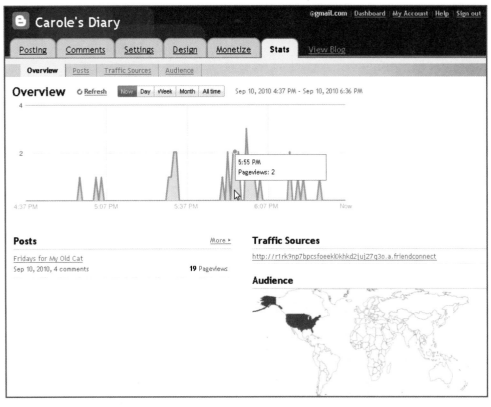

- Click **Monetize** to earn money on ads placed on your blog. Google will place selected ads based on your content. If anyone clicks the ad on your blog, you will earn money. You can determine where to place the ads by clicking the **Display Ads** option you want. Click **Learn More** (middle-right area) to find out how much you might earn and when.

- Click **Stats** to track how you're doing with your viewers. Stats enables you to see how many people are viewing your blog by time, day, week and month, and geography, as seen in Figure 5-14. Click **Audience** in the Stats toolbar to see Pageviews by Browsers and Pageviews by Operating System.

3. Click **Save** to save the changes (some options do not have a save function).

4. Click **View Blog** to see the results.

*Figure 5-14: **Stats show you how you are doing with regard to viewers.***

Find Dating Services

Some websites are more specialized. For instance, there are dating sites that work well for seniors. Seniors are one of the fastest-growing population using online dating. Let's face it: these are the years when increasingly we find ourselves widowed or divorced—and previously the possibilities for dating have been limited for seniors. In today's world, the potential for finding compatible matches is much greater with online dating. In addition, actively seeking dates is simply more comfortable in front of a computer, in the privacy of our homes.

 **NOTE**

LinkedIn, shown in Figure 5-15, is another social networking site for business people and professionals. It allows you to connect with others in your line of work, to keep current and find colleagues for networking. When you access linkedin.com, you will be asked to fill in some forms with your name and email address, and confirm your email address by clicking a link in an email sent to your email address. Once you have confirmed your email, you will be asked to select people who you might know and trust. Then, you choose the plan level you want: the Basic, which is free, or the Premium, which has a monthly fee ($24.95 at this writing). Your LinkedIn page is designed to facilitate setting up your connections to email contacts, business colleagues, classmates, and others. You can even find or post jobs.

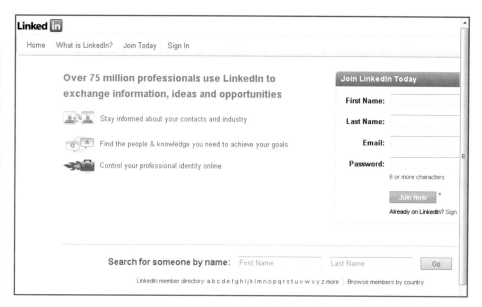

Figure 5-15: LinkedIn is used to maintain and initiate professional and business networking.

Date Online

Dating online for seniors is available from several sites. Consumer-ranking.com shows Match.com (followed by eHarmony) as the highest ranked, and claims that it is the fastest-growing dating site in the world, with around 29 million registrants, 17 percent of them being seniors.

The procedures to become active with dating services are similar, but have differences. One of the differences is cost; some are free and some have fees. The advice on the Web is to go for the fee-based, as these sites offer more features and are safer, filtering out the curious

"ANONYMOUS" FINDS DATING ONLINE TRICKY

I resisted online dating at first, partly old school upbringing, distaste for impersonal, electronic dating, and reluctance to buy into this mode of communication. Also, I had ethical concerns about putting my profile out there in the city where I had practiced medicine for years, fearing that some patients would glimpse my personal life.

When I finally tried online dating I used eHarmony and Match.com for three and six months, respectively. eHarmony has a detailed profile to fill in, and I wondered about my matches which were poor fits as far as I was concerned. With Match .com, I had a much larger selection, but I had to plow through a lot of "no ways."

I used my intuition for whom to contact, assessing what and how they wrote. Checking photos was helpful, not so much for looks as for assessing kindness, integrity, and "squirreliness." My first contacts were always in a public coffee shop. I let a friend know where I was going on my first date and I called them immediately afterwards. I was uneasy, as there were no common acquaintances and therefore no references or endorsements. I finally stopped the online process and am now back to my tried and true more personal approaches.

Anonymous, 60, Washington

or deviant with the cost (see "Date Online Safely"). The costs are very similar between services. In general, the longer the plan, the less you pay per month. Special features may be available at an additional cost, such as mobile phone chats with dating candidates, consultants that help you refine your profile, and access to online advice and "tricks of the trade." Notice any specials that are being offered. You can get reduced fees and even free access at times.

Another difference is the questions you are asked to establish a profile for yourself that is used to find potential matches. These profiles are what others look at to evaluate whether they are interested in taking a next step. The better the questions and the more truthful and complete you are in answering them, the more valid the matches will be. This, of course, is what the online dating services sell—their own way to find suitable matches. One difference is how your profile information is made available to potential suitors; how your privacy is respected.

There is also a difference between dating services as to what their goal really is. Some are just trying to get you casual dates; others are trying for long-term relationships. You'll have to do research (such as with consumer-ranking.com) and do some experimentation to find the one that exactly meets your needs. Two that are known to be effective and safer are Match.com and eHarmony.

Here is an example of the procedure to get started with Match.com and eHarmony.

- After registering, enter your email, birthday, country, zip code, what you are seeking, and password. Click **Continue**.

- You then enter a series of questions, such as shown in Figure 5-16 which are intended to capture information about you, including basic information such as your age, what age partner you are looking for, where you live, what your interests are, what your values are, what your lifestyle choices are (smoking, drinking, for example), and other

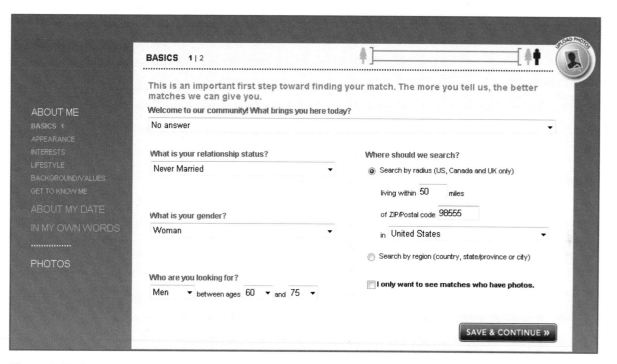

ABOUT ME
BASICS ‹
APPEARANCE
INTERESTS
LIFESTYLE
BACKGROUND/VALUES
GET TO KNOW ME

ABOUT MY DATE

IN MY OWN WORDS

PHOTOS

Figure 5-16: **Start your Match.com online dating experience by answering questions.**

questions about your likes and dislikes, and what choices you might make in a particular situation. The more complete and considered your answers are, the better the match will be. eHarmony's questions are a bit longer and more detailed, and they claim to be excellent at long-term relationships. Match.com guarantees you'll find a serious contender within six months, or, with certain restrictions, you'll get a second six months for free.

- You will be asked to enter a photo. Match.com claims that people with a photo are 15 times more likely to get a match than those without a photo. The photo should be one that clearly shows your face as it is. Many people enter pictures showing themselves years younger, but this really doesn't serve your interests in the long run.

- You might be able to immediately see matches (eHarmony, see Figure 5-17), or you might have to wait for 24 hours while someone verifies that your information is acceptable (Match.com).

Match Details	Communication Stage	Next Steps
John, 59 Lakewood, CO matched on: September 12, 2010	(1) Get to know each other	Send him a Message last communication: September 12, 2010
Glen, 66 phoenix, AZ matched on: September 12, 2010	(1) Get to know each other	Send him a Message last communication: September 12, 2010
Fred, 69 Mesa, Arizona, AZ matched on: September 12, 2010	(1) Get to know each other	Send him a Message last communication: September 12, 2010
jeff, 67 New Phoenix, AZ matched on: September 12, 2010	Introduction	View Match Details
jim, 68 New Centennial, CO matched on: September 12, 2010	Introduction	View Match Details

*Figure 5-17: **eHarmony immediately shows you possible matches for free; if you subscribe, you can see photos too.***

Once you see some potential matches you'd like to explore, you can begin the process of getting to know each other. The other person has to agree to meet you, and then, depending on the service, you are started through a series of emails, telephone conversations, and then actual meetings.

Date Online Safely

Because you are asked to share personal information, dating online contains risks. Millions of people have had good experiences, so the risk should not put you off if you are really interested in

MARY AND RAY MEET ONLINE

My children were my instigators, pushing me to try online dating until I finally gave in. I did want to meet someone, as I had been single for about seven years. Ray, too, was ready to get on with life. We each filled in the eHarmony profiles as honestly as possible and waited.

I remember returning from a trip to Mexico and finding a message in my email from eHarmony: **Ray, from C… wants to meet you**. The process began.

Looking back on it now, we are both amazed at how perfectly the process worked. After the contact procedure, we began an email exchange through eHarmony and found each other to be funny and interesting. One night, Ray gave me his cell phone number. We had a great time talking, and soon decided we should meet in person. Needless to say, we hit it off and enjoyed our date. Unfortunately, Ray lived about 81 miles away so our follow-up meetings were by phone, only seeing each other on some weekends. Our relationship grew and we met each other's friends and families.

We were married one and a half years later. We now have been married for almost four years— bringing together seven grown children and 20 grandchildren between us. We are grateful to eHarmony, knowing that we might not have met otherwise.

Mary D., 61, Washington

finding a serious relationship. But, you need to be "street smart." While the dating service can help you be safe, they ultimately are not responsible—you are. Take control of your own security. Use your common sense and your intuition to keep yourself safe. Trust yourself and your gut instincts. Follow, without exception, rules for keeping your personal information and your physical body safe. Here are some ideas about that:

- Use a for-pay dating service that is well known and is about matching people for serious relationships rather than sexual encounters.

- Although you will need to give the dating service your credit card information to subscribe to the service, do not give any of your dating contacts any personal financial information, credit card numbers, or Social Security numbers. Do not give information, including how you select your user ID, that would enable them to guess about your financial circumstances. In your initial emails, do not give out any contact information that will reveal how to reach you or your location, including your real name.

- Do not use sexually suggestive names or write them in text you write about yourself or what you want. You may feel flirty and adventurous, but you can convey your playfulness without being suggestive— thereby attracting the wrong type of match. Do not choose to meet with a date who presents themselves in an inappropriate way.

- Use an email account different from your own service (set up a separate email account with Hotmail or Gmail), and use a name that cannot be used to identify you or your location. Keep a barrier between yourself and your dates until you know they are safe.

- When you meet someone for the first time, let others know where you will be—have a time to end the meeting and call your friends to let them know you are safe. You might even have someone accompany you. Do not accept a ride either to the location or back home from your date—get yourself there and back.

TIP

One of the biggest drawbacks to getting involved in dating online is a reluctance to put personal information and photos out for the world to see. But this is becoming more accepted now as people get used to banking online and such sites as Facebook. The truth is that the more complete your information is, the more likely you'll find a serious contender. And people do find marriage partners every day using online dating services. The secret is to use common sense and be selective in the information you reveal.

- Meet during the day in a place with lots of other people around.
- Carry your cell phone.
- Be restrained in drinking alcohol.
- If someone asks you for money, or seems to be setting you up to do that, run, don't walk away. Beware of stories about job losses, unfair divorce settlements, etc.
- Ask your date for his or her driver's license so that you can verify that he or she is who they say they are. Keep in mind that before meeting, you can check a name to see if he is a sexual predator if you feel something is not quite right.
- Keep in mind that if you are sexually molested, stalked, or threatened, you should notify both the police and the online dating service so that they will remove the person from the database.

Chapter 6
Using Applications

In our lifetimes, the computer has replaced the faithful typewriter, spiral notebooks of spreadsheets, manila folders filled with sheets of paper, and a pencil sharpener next to cups filled with freshly sharpened pencils. Even the smell of an office is different. The office, and therefore the home office, was clearly transformed with computers. Our productivity is also transformed with computers. We type and edit, with automatic spellcheckers and grammar checkers, and when our manuscript or letter is perfect, we print it or send it via email. Our computer calculates spreadsheet equations, graphing them for presentations and visual interpretations. Our backup files are stored on CDs in a small case or nearby shelf. Or maybe not. Today, our backups may be stored on an online server. When we need to find something, we search through files on our computer or on our online server, not in a

QUICKFACTS

UNDERSTANDING WEB APPS

Microsoft Office Web Applications, called "Web Apps" for short, are a browser-based set of applications for viewing and lightweight editing in a familiar layout of your existing Word, Excel, and PowerPoint files over the Internet or an intranet wherever there is a PC or Mac attached. Although these are the same programs you could purchase for a desktop computer, they do not have the sophistication and complexity that you have with the desktop programs. The Web Apps are "Office light." However, they are also free, and allow you to try out the software before paying money for more comprehensive desktop versions.

This book introduces you to Web Apps on the Internet using Microsoft SkyDrive, which can also store your data files. When you want to view or edit a Word file, for instance, you bring up a browser, sign on to skydrive.live.com, and scroll through your folders, just as you would with your own computer folders. When you find the document you want to open, you click it, click **View** or **Edit**, and Microsoft Word Web App opens to do that.

file cabinet. The computer search programs do the work that our fingers used to do, in a fraction of the time.

In this chapter we will explore some of the most common applications seniors use, including Microsoft Office applications Word and Excel. We will see how we access these programs and store our files on an online server. Then we'll take a look at Windows built-in applications, such as Calculator and Sticky Notes. We will also take a look at another common application, Adobe Acrobat Reader.

Use Web Apps for Office Programs

With the appearance of *cloud computing*, or working with computer files and applications hosted on a remote server and viewable in a browser rather than your own computer and Office applications, Microsoft is moving Office to the Internet. This means that your files and programs are stored on an Internet server rather than on your standalone desktop computer, and that Office programs are accessed through a browser working on the Internet rather than from programs stored on your computer. This is a new world! Why this is even remotely a good idea really revolves around expanded ways of working with data files and other people and making them available any place, any time. The approach is much more about accessing and sharing data and collaboration than it is about an isolated person working alone. When you store data and have programs available from an Internet server (or "on the cloud"):

- You don't have to worry about whether you have the latest program updates.

To set up your SkyDrive credentials and upload a file, you must first establish a Windows Live ID and account. Chapter 4 describes how to sign up for a Windows Live ID. When you have one, you can simply log in and get access to SkyDrive.

• You don't have to worry about whether you have access to your computer at home, for instance, when you are traveling.

• You don't have to worry about someone else being able to read your documents when they don't own the program, or the same version.

• You don't have to pay for a generous amount of storage, until (or unless) you want to upgrade to higher capacity storage.

Use SkyDrive

SkyDrive (skydrive.live.com), the Microsoft server hosting platform for its Web Apps, is where you can save your Office documents, enabling viewers not having Office applications or the latest version of them to view the document and do lightweight editing with a browser. If you have created a document on your own computer, saving your files to SkyDrive preserves the links, color schemes, and other design elements created with your local Office application. The file and all the supporting objects are saved to a web folder that you create on SkyDrive or to a public folder.

ADD A FOLDER TO SKYDRIVE

SkyDrive contains a number of folders to hold your presentations and other documents. Some of these are standard and are in the account at the beginning. Others, such as the PowerPoint Albums in Figure 6-1, are your personal folders that you create. (See "Understanding SkyDrive Folders" QuickFacts.)

Figure 6-1: **You can save your documents to SkyDrive, where viewers can access them with a browser.**

ANN BENEFITS FROM BOD ONLINE DOCUMENTS

The way I see it, the Internet has enormously benefited organizations with boards of directors. I have served on nonprofit boards for over 30 years, and staff always seems to scramble getting board packets out. They hustle around to copy, deliver or mail the information, while board members hope they will receive it before the meeting. During the last couple of years, some of my boards have taken a different approach to distributing board packets that works well—the board members log on to organizational websites to get the materials they need for the meeting. The staff does have to post the information, but this takes far less time than before. Costs to the organization are reduced in terms of time (copying, collating, packaging) and materials (paper, stamps, envelopes). In addition, I have trouble filing things so I can find them when I want them. The material available to me online solves the problem; I can find the budget or 990 or minutes from a previous meeting without spending hours shuffling through the piles of paper (or confessing my shortcomings by requesting yet another copy). I am convinced this use of the Internet is a great way to help organizations and board members be more effective.

Ann K., 66, California

To log on to SkyDrive and create a new folder to hold your documents:

1. In your browser, type skydrive.com, click **Sign Up** if you don't have a Windows Live or Hotmail ID, and follow the instructions. If you do have an ID, click **Sign In**, click the **Windows Live** logo, and click **SkyDrive** from the menu. The SkyDrive page will display; an example is shown in Figure 6-1. Or, from anywhere in the Windows Live site, click the **Windows Live** logo and click **SkyDrive**.

2. Under your name on the upper-left area, click the **New** down arrow and select **Folder** to add a new folder to the account. The Create A Folder view will appear.

3. Type the Name for the folder.

4. Click **Change** opposite Share With to choose those permitted to see the contents of the folder, as shown in Figure 6-2. Choose between Everyone (Public), My Friends And Their Friends, Friends, Some

Figure 6-2: **You can define how private you want the files in your folder to be.**

Friends, and Me. This sets the level of privacy you want for this folder, ranging from anyone to just you.

● Beneath Add Additional People, enter the email addresses of those allowed to see your folder's contents.

● Click **Select From Your Contact List** to choose the permitted viewers from your email contact list.

5. Click **Next**. The Add Documents To *foldername* window is displayed. Follow steps in "Add Files to SkyDrive" next.

ADD FILES TO SKYDRIVE

You can add files directly to an existing folder or when the folder is created. You can either upload files to SkyDrive by dragging them from your computer to a designated folder, or save them when you create a file using Web Apps.

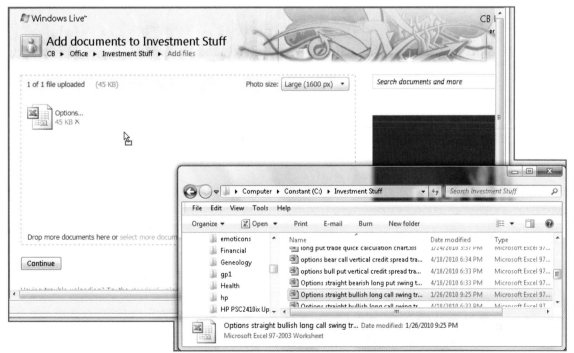

1. If you have added a folder, you will see the Add Documents To *foldername* page when you click **Next**. You can skip to step 4.

2. If you are adding a file to an existing folder, click **Add Files** on the SkyDrive home page. You will see a list of folders.

3. Click the folder you want to use. The Add Documents To *foldername* window appears, as shown in Figure 6-3.

Figure 6-3: Adding files to SkyDrive is as easy as dragging the files from your Windows Explorer, or using the browse function.

4. You can upload files in two ways:

- If you have Windows Explorer open, place that window next to your SkyDrive window, then click your file in Explorer and drag it to the Add Documents To *Foldername* window, as is being done in Figure 6-3.

- Click **Select Documents From Your Computer**, find your file, and click **Open** to place it into the SkyDrive window.

5. When all the files you want to be uploaded are displayed in the SkyDrive Add Files window, click **Continue**. You'll see a message informing you that the upload has been successful, along with icons of your other uploaded files.

You've created the folder Investment Stuff. Let people know

Today

Options straight bearish lo...   CB Matthews   3 minutes ago

Options straight bullish lon...   CB Matthews   5 minutes ago

Shared with: People I selected

Create or Edit Documents Using Web Apps

We just described how, with a Windows Live ID and a SkyDrive account, you can upload files to Microsoft's SkyDrive location in order to keep them in the "cloud" so you, or others with your permission, can access them at any time or place from a browser. Besides simply storing files there, you can also create new documents or view, edit, and download documents saved in the Word 2007 and Word 2010 default .docx file format, without having Word installed on your device. (You can view documents saved in the earlier .doc file format, but you cannot edit them with the Web Apps.)

The editing capabilities in the Word Web App are a subset of those in the desktop version of Word. However, if you are creating a simple document or primarily just editing your information and sharing it with others, SkyDrive and the Word Web App provide you a great opportunity to access your information from anywhere with only a browser and Internet connection.

Create a Document Using Web Apps

When you are signed in to Windows Live, you have some of the Microsoft Office applications available to you through the Office Web Apps. Simplified versions of Word, Excel, PowerPoint, and OneNote can be accessed online so that you don't need the desktop version of Office to work with your Office files. Here is how to use the Web Apps:

1. In the Windows Live toolbar on the top of the window, click the **Office** menu, and click an application; in this case, **Word**.

2. Type the name of the document. Click **Save**. The Word window will open, as shown in Figure 6-4.

3. Type your document, formatting it as needed. See "Understanding the Typical Ribbon" QuickFacts in Chapter 4 and "Edit Documents in the Word Web App," later in this chapter. Figure 6-5 displays an overview of the ribbon functions.

4. When you are finished, click **File** and then click **Save**.

TIP

For information on how to use the desktop versions of Office applications, please look for *Microsoft Word 2010 QuickSteps, Microsoft Excel 2010 QuickSteps, Microsoft PowerPoint 2010 QuickSteps,* or *Microsoft Office 2010 QuickSteps,* all published by McGraw-Hill.

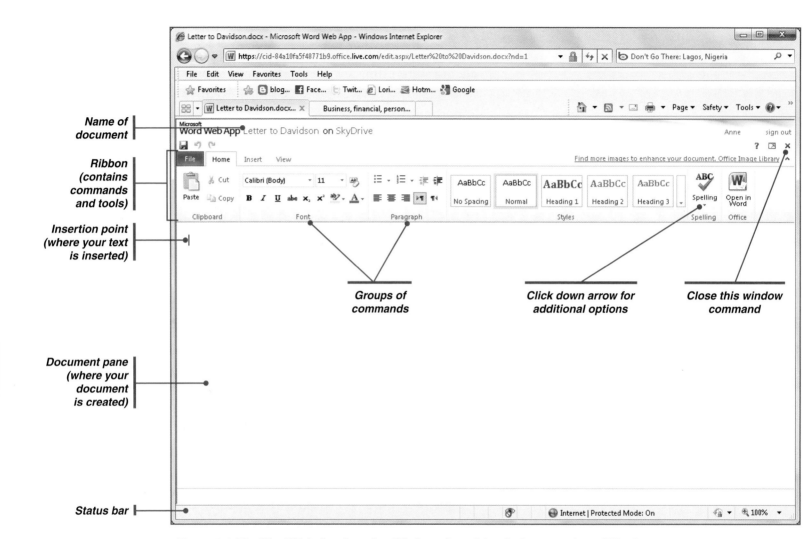

Name of document

Ribbon (contains commands and tools)

Insertion point (where your text is inserted)

Document pane (where your document is created)

Status bar

Groups of commands

Click down arrow for additional options

Close this window command

Figure 6-4: **The Word Web App is a simplified version of the desktop version of Word.**

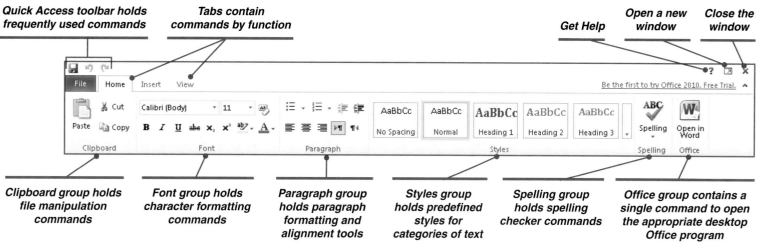

Quick Access toolbar holds frequently used commands

Tabs contain commands by function

Get Help

Open a new window

Close the window

Clipboard group holds file manipulation commands

Font group holds character formatting commands

Paragraph group holds paragraph formatting and alignment tools

Styles group holds predefined styles for categories of text

Spelling group holds spelling checker commands

Office group contains a single command to open the appropriate desktop Office program

Figure 6-5: **The ribbon, here the Word ribbon, is the source of the tools and commands for the Web Apps.**

Edit Documents in the Word Web App

To read and edit a document in the Word Web App:

1. Click the SkyDrive folder that contains the document you want to view or edit.

2. Point your cursor at the file you want to edit. A menu opens up to the right, allowing you to select from several tasks.

- **Edit In Browser** opens the document in the Word Web App.

- **Open In Word** opens the document in your desktop version of Word, assuming it is on your computer.

- **Share** allows you to change your sharing options.

- **More** opens a submenu with additional options.

SUZANNE MAKES GOOD USE OF WORD

I am an adult educator who is always developing curriculum, teaching online, and writing articles and books. Microsoft Word allows me to write, rewrite, rearrange, check spelling and grammar, and do all the creative "thinking" and "fussing" necessary to create something worth reading.

It also gives me a written copy of my lecture notes. When teaching online, I easily "copy" my notes from Word and "paste" them into the online learning site. I also use Word to write comments and feedback to students. This creates written records of comments and feedback for both my students and me.

There are two features of Word that I use a lot. The first feature is the Spelling Checker. One feature of it that I particularly like is the ability to "teach" the Spelling Checker's dictionary a new word. The second feature is the Mark Up menu box. This allows me to work collaboratively with others. I can review and add comments to a document, and can see comments that others have contributed. I can choose to add comments either right in the text or in the right margin next to the sentence I am editing. I can also accept or reject any changes to my document. Whether I am correcting a student paper or editing my own writing, this feature makes it incredibly easy and quick.

Suzanne F., 60, Washington

3. Click **Edit In Browser**. The document opens the Word Web App window, as displayed earlier in Figure 6-4. This window is similar to the desktop Word 2010 user interface, but if you're used to the desktop version, you'll notice the lack of several features, including the tools located on missing ribbon tabs and many of the options found on a standard File tab. See "Work with Your Documents" to find more explanation of what you can do with your document.

4. After editing the document using the tools on the available ribbon tabs, click **File** and select whether you want to open the file in your desktop version of Word, save it to your own computer's hard disk (you don't need to save the document, as Word Web App does that automatically), print it, or share it with others.

5. When finished, return to your SkyDrive folders to work with other Web App documents in the same manner, navigate to other webpages, or simply close your browser.

Work with Your Documents

When you are creating or editing your documents, there are some simple guidelines about using the Web Apps that facilitate your experience and make it smoother.

USE TABS AND MENUS

Tabs are displayed at the top of the ribbon or a dialog box. Menus are displayed when you click a down arrow on a button on the ribbon, a dialog box, or a toolbar. Here are some of the ways to use tabs and menus:

- To open a tab or menu with the mouse, click the tab or menu.
- To select a tab or menu command, click the tab or menu to open it, and then click the option.

ENTER TEXT

To enter text in a document that you have newly created or opened, simply start typing. The characters you type will appear in the document pane at the insertion point and in the order that you type them.

INSERT LINE BREAKS

In Word, as in all word processing programs, simply keep typing and the text will automatically wrap around to the next line. Only when you want to break a line before it would otherwise end must you manually intervene. At the end of a paragraph, to skip to the next line or start a new paragraph, press **ENTER**.

SELECT TEXT

In order to copy, move, or delete text, you first need to select it. *Selecting text* means to identify it as a separate block from the remaining text in a document. You can select any amount of text, from a single character to an entire document. As text is selected, it is highlighted with a colored background, as seen in Figure 6-7. You can select text using either the mouse or the keyboard. See Table 6-1 for details of how to do this.

TYPE OF SELECTION	HOW TO DO IT
Select a single word	Double-click that word.
Select one or more characters in a word, or select two or more words by clicking:	• Click to place the insertion point to the left of the first character. • Press and hold **SHIFT** while clicking to the right of the last character. The selected range of text will be highlighted.
Select one or more characters in a word, or select two or more words by dragging:	• Move the mouse pointer to the left of the first character. • Press and hold the mouse button while dragging the mouse pointer to the right or left. The selected text will be highlighted.
Select text with the keyboard	• To select text to the right or left as you move the arrow keys, press and hold **SHIFT** while using the arrow keys. • To select a line, place the pointer at the beginning of a line by pressing **HOME**. Press and hold **SHIFT**, and press **END**. • To select multiple words at a time, press **CTRL+SHIFT** and press the **RIGHT ARROW** or **LEFT ARROW** key. • To select a whole document, press **CTRL+A**.

Table 6-1: *Ways to Select Text*

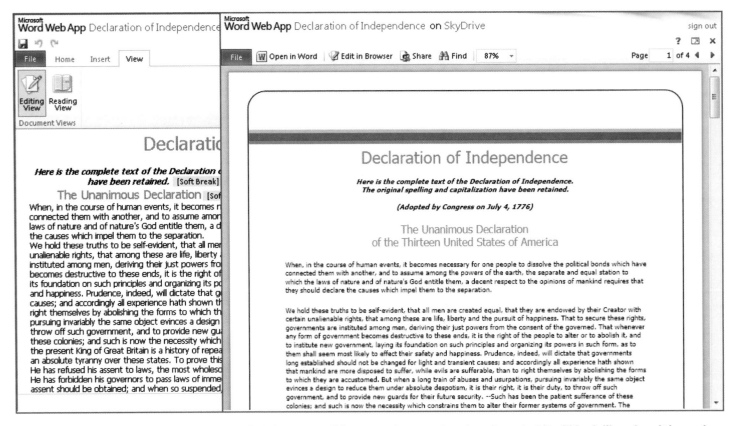

Figure 6-6: *You can use the View tab to switch between editing your document and seeing what it will look like when it is read or printed.*

If you want more sophisticated breaks, such as column breaks, section breaks, or even page breaks, edit the document in the desktop version of Word.

COPY, MOVE, AND PASTE TEXT

Copying and moving text are similar. Think of copying text as moving it and leaving a copy behind. Both copying and moving are done in two steps.

1. Selected text is copied or cut from its current location to the Clipboard. See Table 6-2 for how to do it.

2. The contents of the Clipboard are pasted to a new location identified by the insertion point.

Microsoft Word Web App Declaration of Independence on SkyDrive

CB Matthews sign out

File Home Insert View

Tahoma 9

Paste

B *I* U abc x₂ x² ab₂ A ≡ ≡ ≡ ¶↓ ¶¶

Clipboard | Font | Paragraph | Styles | Spelling | Office

Here is the complete text of the Declaration of Independence. [Soft Break] *The original spelling and capitalization have been retained.* [Soft Break] [Soft Break] *(Adopted by Congress on July 4, 1776)*

The Unanimous Declaration [Soft Break] of the Thirteen United States of America

When, in the course of human events, it becomes necessary for one people to dissolve the political bonds which have connected them with another, and to assume among the powers of the earth, the separate and equal station to which the laws of nature and of nature's God entitle them, a decent respect to the opinions of mankind requires that they should declare the causes which impel them to the separation. We hold these truths to be self-evident, that all men are created equal, that they are endowed by their Creator with certain unalienable rights, that among these are life, liberty and the pursuit of happiness. That to secure these rights, governments are instituted among men, deriving their just powers from the consent of the governed. That whenever any form of government becomes destructive to these ends, it is the right of the people to alter or to abolish it, and to institute new government, laying its foundation on such principles and organizing its powers in such form, as to them shall seem most likely to effect their safety and happiness. Prudence, indeed, will dictate that governments long established should not be changed for light and transient causes; and accordingly all experience hath shown that mankind are more disposed to suffer, while evils are sufferable, than to right themselves by abolishing the forms to which they are accustomed. But when a long train of abuses and usurpations, pursuing invariably the same object evinces a design to reduce them under absolute despotism, it is their right, it is their duty, to throw off such government, and to provide new guards for their future security.—Such has been the patient sufferance of these colonies; and such is now the necessity which constrains them to alter their former systems of government. The history of the present King of Great Britain is a history of repeated injuries and usurpations, all having in direct object the establishment of an absolute tyranny over these states. To prove this, let facts be submitted to a candid world.

He has refused his assent to laws, the most wholesome and necessary for the public good.
He has forbidden his governors to pass laws of immediate and pressing importance, unless suspended in their operation till his assent should be obtained; and when so suspended, he has utterly neglected to attend to them.
He has refused to pass other laws for the accommodation of large districts of people, unless those people would relinquish the right of representation in the legislature, a right inestimable to them and formidable to tyrants only.

Figure 6-7: **You will always know what you are moving, copying, or deleting because it is highlighted on the screen.**

TIP

After selecting one area using the keyboard, the mouse, or the two together, you can select further independent areas by pressing and holding **CTRL** while using any of the mouse selection techniques.

NOTE

You select a picture by clicking it. Once selected, a picture can be copied, moved, and deleted from a document in the same ways as text, using either the Windows or Office Clipboards.

The *Clipboard* is a location in the computer's memory that is used to store information temporarily. The Windows Clipboard can store one object, either text or a picture, and pass that object within or among Windows programs. Once an object is cut or copied to the Windows Clipboard, it stays there until another object is cut or copied to the Clipboard, or until the computer is turned off. The Windows Clipboard is used by default.

DELETE TEXT

● *Deleting text* removes it from its current location *without* putting it in the Clipboard. You can always recover deleted text using Undo in the same way you can reverse a cut or a paste. To delete a selected piece of text: Press **DELETE**, or **DEL**.

● On the Home tab, click **Cut** in the Clipboard group.

TASK	WITH KEYBOARD	WITH RIBBON
Cut	Press **CTRL+X**.	Click **Home** and click **Cut** on the Clipboard group.
Copy	Press **CTRL+C**.	Click **Home** and click **Copy** on the Clipboard group.
Paste	Press **CTRL+P**.	Click **Home** and click **Paste** on the Clipboard group.
Undo	Press **CTRL+Z**.	Click **Undo** in the Quick Access toolbar.
Redo	Press **CTRL+Y**.	Click **Redo** in the Quick Access toolbar.

Table 6-2: **Ways to Move and Copy Text**

CHECK SPELLING AND GRAMMAR

By default, Word checks spelling and grammar as you type the document. You can tell if Word is checking the spelling and grammar by noticing if Word automatically places a wavy red line under words it thinks are misspelled. You can also ask Word to perform a spelling check whenever you want—most importantly, when you are completing a document.

1. Click the **Spelling** down arrow, and click **Spelling**. If a misspelling is found, a menu with a suggested replacement will appear. You have these options:

   ● Click the suggested word if it is correct, or select another word.

   ● Click **Set Proofing Language** to change the language used, for example, French instead of English.

   ● Click **Cut** to delete text, **Copy** to copy it, or **Paste** to replace the current word with a previously copied or cut word.

2. Click the document outside the menu to remove the spelling menu from the screen.

APPLY STYLES TO DOCUMENTS

A *style* applies a specific set of formatting characteristics to individual characters or to entire paragraphs within the theme. For example, you can apply styles to headings, titles, lists, and other text components. Consequently, styles determine how the overall design comes together in its look and feel. Styles are beneficial to document creation, because they provide a consistent look and feel to all text selected for formatting.

Word 2010 provides a gallery of styles that provides you with sets of canned formatting choices, such as font, boldface, and color, that you can apply to headings, titles, text, and lists. You use styles by identifying what kind of formatting a selected segment of text needs,

TIP

It is a great idea to manually save your document frequently (like a couple of times an hour). Doing this can save you from the frustration of working several hours on a document only to lose it. Click **Save** 🖫 in the Quick Access toolbar, or click **File** and then click **Save**. These actions save your document on the online server.

such as for a header or title. Then you select the style of formatting you want to apply to the document.

1. Select the text to be formatted, for example, a title or heading.

2. Click **Home**, and click the **More Styles** down arrow in the Styles group. The Styles gallery is displayed, as shown in Figure 6-8. (If you do not find the style you want in the Quick Styles gallery for a segment of text, click **Apply Styles** from the More Styles menu to display the Apply Styles dialog box. Scroll down the Style Name list to find the style you want.)

3. Click the thumbnail of the style you want to apply.

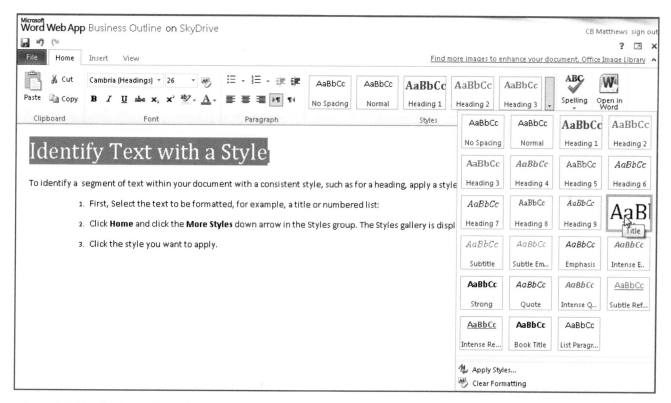

Figure 6-8: **The Styles gallery shows you canned options for formatting headings, text, and paragraphs.**

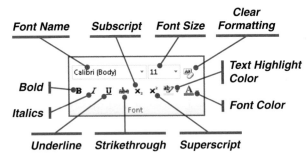

Font Name   Subscript   Font Size   Clear Formatting

Bold

Italics

Text Highlight Color

Font Color

Underline   Strikethrough   Superscript

Figure 6-9: **The Font group on the Home Tab contains character formatting tools.**

CAUTION

When you have a link to a .doc or .docx file (a Word document) on the Internet, and someone opens it by double-clicking the link, it opens in Word Web Apps, with many of the editing tools available. So if you have a document you want to protect, but you want people to be able to read it, consider saving it on the website in a PDF format. PDF documents, when double-clicked, open in the Acrobat Reader with no editing tools available. People can still edit them, but not without opening them in another form of Acrobat.

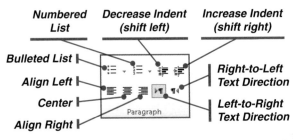

Numbered List   Decrease Indent (shift left)   Increase Indent (shift right)

Bulleted List

Align Left

Center

Align Right

Right-to-Left Text Direction

Left-to-Right Text Direction

Figure 6-10: **The Paragraph group on the Home tab provides fast formatting for paragraphs.**

APPLY CHARACTER FORMATTING

Character formatting can be applied using keyboard shortcuts or the Home tab on the ribbon. The Home tab, in the Font group, provides a visual selection of character formatting and spacing alternatives. See Figure 6-9 to identify which tools are available for character formatting. Keyboard shortcuts (summarized in Table 6-3) allow you to keep your hands on the keyboard while doing the same tasks.

FORMAT A PARAGRAPH

Paragraph formatting, which you can apply to any paragraph, is used to manage alignment, indentation, line spacing, and bullets or numbering. In Word, a paragraph consists of a paragraph mark (created by pressing **ENTER**) and any text or objects that appear between that paragraph mark and the previous paragraph mark. A paragraph can be empty, or it can contain anything from a single character to as many characters as you care to enter.

The Home tab, Paragraph group contains the tools for formatting a paragraph. First you must click in the paragraph you want to align, and then click the command in the Paragraph group, as identified in Figure 6-10. The keyboard can also be used for some formatting. See Table 6-3.

APPLY FORMATTING	SHORTCUT KEYS
Align left	**CTRL+L**
Align right	**CTRL+R**
Center	**CTRL+E**
Justify paragraph	**CTRL+J**
Bold	**CTRL+B**
Italic	**CTRL+I**
Underline continuous	**CTRL+U**

Table 6-3: **Keyboard Character Editing**

EDITING WORKBOOKS IN THE EXCEL WEB APP

As with Word, you can upload Excel files to Microsoft's SkyDrive location in order to keep them in the "cloud" so you, or others, can access them at any time or place from a browser. Besides simply storing files there, using the integrated Microsoft Excel Web App, you can also create, view, edit, and download workbooks saved in the Excel 2007 and Excel 2010 default .xlsx file format without necessarily having a version of Excel installed on your device. (You can view workbooks saved in the earlier .xls file format, but you cannot edit them.) The editing capabilities in the Excel Web App are limited to the more basic features of Excel, such as those described in this chapter, as well as minor formatting actions and working with tables. In fact, if the workbook contains more advanced features such as shapes or a watch window, you cannot edit it (although you can view and download it). However, for those cases where your edits are predominately data-centric, SkyDrive and the Excel Web App provide you a great opportunity to access your information from anywhere with only a browser and Internet connection.

To use a workbook in the Excel Web App:

1. Open the SkyDrive folder that contains the workbook you want to view or edit.

2. Point to the file you want, and in the pop-up menu, click **Edit In Browser**.

Continued . . .

PRINT A DOCUMENT

To print a document using the Web App, you must first save the document.

1. Click **File** and then click **Print**. If you have not saved the document, you will be prompted to do so. Click **Save And Print**. The Print dialog box is displayed, as shown in Figure 6-11.

2. You have these options:

   - If your printer is contained in the Select Printer list and is not selected, click its name. If it is not contained in the list, click **Find Printer** and find the path to the printer you want.

   - In the Page Range area, click **All** to print all pages of the document; click **Selection** if you have selected text you want to print; click **Current Page** to print only the current active page; click **Pages** and then type the page numbers you want (separate individual pages with a comma and page ranges with a hyphen, such as 3,4-9,12.

*Figure 6-11: **The Print dialog box gives you options for printing your document.***

- Click the **Number Of Copies** arrows to find the number of copies, or type it in the text box.

- If you want uncollated copies, clear the **Collate** check box.

- Click **Preferences** to change printer and print preferences, such as page size and arrangement of pages on the printed copy, whether a border is printed, color considerations, and more.

3. Click **Print** to begin the print process.

Use Excel

An Excel worksheet is a matrix, or grid, of lettered *column headings* across the top and numbered *row headings* down the side. The first row of a typical worksheet is used for column *headers*. The column headers represent categories of similar data. The rows beneath a column header contain data that is further categorized either by a row header down the leftmost column or listed below the column header. Figure 6-12 shows an example of a common worksheet arrangement. Worksheets can also be used to set up *tables* of data, where columns are sometimes referred to as *fields* and each row represents a unique *record* of data. To understand Excel in all its capacity, refer to *Microsoft Excel 2010 QuickSteps* by John Cronan, published by McGraw-Hill.

Each intersection of a row and column is called a *cell*, and is referenced first by the column location and then by the row location. The combination of a column letter and row number assigns each cell an *address*. For example, the cell at the intersection of column D and row 8 is called D8. A cell is considered *active* when it is clicked or otherwise selected as the place in which to place new data.

Figure 6-13 shows the ribbon for the Excel Web App.

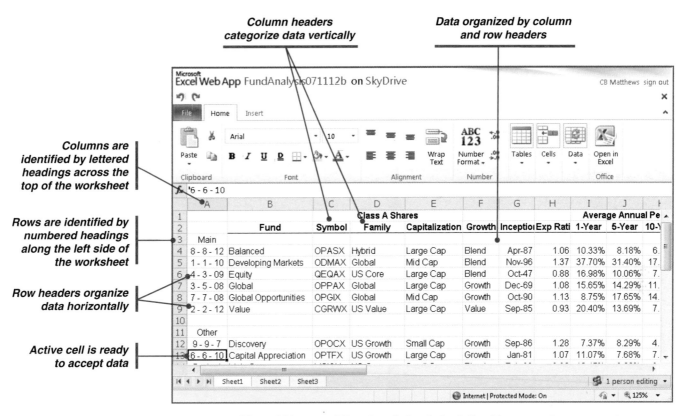

Column headers categorize data vertically

Data organized by column and row headers

Columns are identified by lettered headings across the top of the worksheet

Rows are identified by numbered headings along the left side of the worksheet

Row headers organize data horizontally

Active cell is ready to accept data

Figure 6-12: **The grid layout of Excel worksheets is defined by several components.**

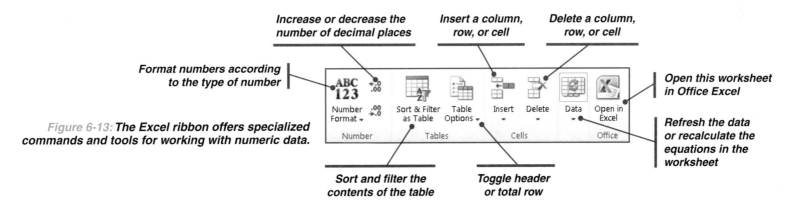

Increase or decrease the number of decimal places

Insert a column, row, or cell

Delete a column, row, or cell

Format numbers according to the type of number

Open this worksheet in Office Excel

Figure 6-13: **The Excel ribbon offers specialized commands and tools for working with numeric data.**

Refresh the data or recalculate the equations in the worksheet

Sort and filter the contents of the table

Toggle header or total row

BOB USES EXCEL FOR FINANCE AND INVESTING

I use Microsoft Excel every day. My wife and I run a small business, and I swing trade in the stock market. Microsoft Excel tracks aspects of our personal financial world.

I use Excel to track tax withholdings for our employees and to create daily time cards. I create flyers to distribute to potential new clients. There are endless possibilities for the type of worksheets and content I can create to better use my valuable time.

For my stock-market trading, I create formulas in spreadsheets that calculate the value for a particular stock. Doing this replaces the need for a hand-held calculator. I spend an evening creating a worksheet for a particular trade strategy to use in the stock market. Then, each time I see an opportunity for that type of trade, I simply input the relevant values and the worksheet tells me when to get in and out of the trade. I even use the "If" function to set up a series of requirements in the stock for the trade to happen. If the criteria in those functions are not met, the worksheet will tell me that it's not ideal to enter into that trade. I enjoy posting my worksheets on a shared investing group website, and I look forward to feedback on my ideas from fellow students.

Bob P., 53, Washington

Enter and Format Text into a Worksheet

In an Excel worksheet, text is used to identify, explain, and emphasize numeric data. Textual data cannot be used in calculations.

- Enter text by typing, just as you would in a word processing program.
- Format text using the commands in the Font group for character formatting as shown earlier for Word in Figure 6-9.
- Align cell data using commands in the Alignment group, which is similar to the paragraph formatting illustrated in Figure 6-10.
- Wrap text within a cell by clicking **Wrap Text** in the Alignment group.

Enter and Format Numeric Data

Numbers are numerical data, from the simplest to the most complex. Excel provides several features to help you work more easily with numbers used to represent values in various categories, such as currency, accounting, and mathematics.

1. Enter numbers by simply selecting a cell and typing the numbers.

2. To format the numbers, select them and click the **Number Format** menu in the Numbers group. You have these options:

   - **General** formats alphanumeric data—data composed of numbers and/or text. Only general formatted data that is purely numeric can be used in calculations.

   - **Number** formats the data as numeric data, which then can be used for calculations. Use **Increase Decimal** or **Decrease Decimal** in the Number group to add or remove decimal places.

TIP

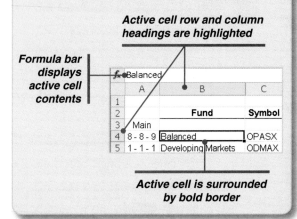

*Active cell row and column
headings are highlighted*

*Formula bar
displays
active cell
contents*

*Active cell is surrounded
by bold border*

TIP

The biggest differences between the Currency
and the Accounting formats are that negative
numbers in the Accounting format are in
parentheses and both the dollar sign and the
number itself are offset to the left to make room
for parentheses.

- **Currency** formats for dollar and cents. Click **Increase Decimal**
  or **Decrease Decimal** in the Number group to set the number of
  decimal places if it is not two places.

- **Accounting** formats data into numeric data that may or may not be
  currency, and that may or may not have decimal places.

- **Short Date** formats the data with numeric dates, such as 1/06/2012.

- **Long Date** formats the data with alphanumeric dates, such as
  Thursday, January 6, 2012. Both types of dates can be used in
  calculations.

- **Time** formats data as time, which can be used in calculations. Enter
  the time format you want; that is, with or without AM/PM or seconds.

- **Percentage** formats the data as a percentage, with the percent sign.

3. Press **ENTER** to accept the formatting and number.

Create Charts

One of the advantages of Excel is its charting capability. You can
take numeric data and give it a visual twist. To create a chart from
a worksheet:

1. Select the range of data you want included in the chart, including the
   headings.

2. Click **Insert**, and click the type of chart you want. The chart will be
   displayed in the worksheet, as shown in Figure 6-14.

3. Using the Chart Tools Design tools, change and edit your charts as
   you need, adding titles, legends, and data labels, for instance.

Choose a Chart Type

The Excel Web App organizes charts into seven types, categorized
by the function they perform. Within each chart type are variations
called *subtypes*. For example, the Line chart type has several ways to
display trends. The main chart types are summarized in Table 6-4.

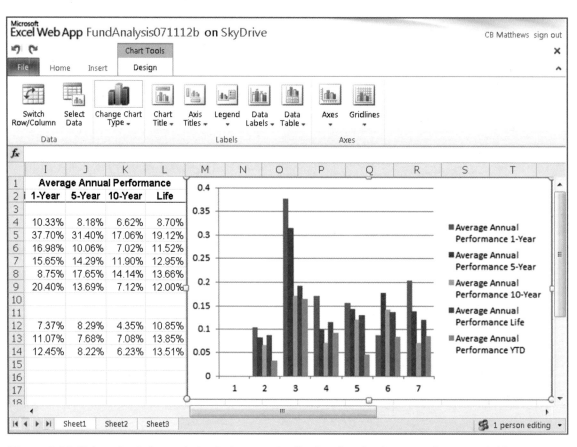

Figure 6-14: *Using charts in worksheets is a way to display data in clearer and more quickly understood terms.*

CHART TYPE	FUNCTION
Column, Bar, Line	Compare trends in multiple data series in various configurations, such as vertical or horizontal; available in several subtypes, such as 3-D line, cylinder, cone, and pyramid
Pie and Doughnut	Display one data series (pie) or compare multiple data series (doughnut) as part of a whole or 100 percent
XY (Scatter)	Displays pairs of data to establish concentrations
Area	Shows the magnitude of change over time; useful when summing multiple values to see the contribution of each

Table 6-4: *Seven Functional Types of Excel Web App Charts*

TOM WORKS ON EXCEL AND PDF DOCUMENTS

Computers are not second-nature to me, but I find them extremely important in communicating in today's world. I am more productive and, in some ways, better able to grasp the implications of data than previously, when I was buried in the details of generating information myself on a manual spreadsheet.

I mainly use the Internet and email, but I use other programs as well. For instance, as a member of a nonprofit organization for seven years, I receive budgets and financial statements created in Excel from our treasurer. The treasurer attaches the information to an email, and I download it and look at it with Excel. Now I know only the basics about using Excel, but I can read an Excel worksheet just fine, and reading the worksheets allows me to concentrate on the financials of the organization rather than on the steps in creating them. I add comments to the email and return it to the treasurer. This has been an effective and worthwhile way to quickly communicate with other board members.

In a similar way, I can read a PDF document with Acrobat Reader—for free. I don't have to purchase Acrobat Pro or another program that might have been used to create that document.

Tom B., 79, Washington

Use Other Common Applications

Windows 7 comes equipped with several useful accessory programs. Among these are WordPad, a simple word processing program; Paint, for drawing and modifying pictures; and Windows Photo Viewer, for viewing photos and graphics. Here is a brief overview of them. In addition, Adobe Acrobat is a program computer users use to read PDF documents.

Run Accessory Programs

You can open the accessory programs by clicking **Start**, clicking **All Programs**, and choosing the folder **Accessories**. Calculator, Character Map, Notepad, and Paint are part of these accessories.

USE CALCULATOR

The *Calculator*, started from Accessories, has four alternative calculators, each with its own view:

- Standard desktop calculator, shown in Figure 6-15
- Scientific calculator
- Programmer calculator
- Statistics calculator

In addition, there are a unit converter, a date calculator, and four worksheets for calculating a mortgage, a vehicle lease, and fuel economy in both mpg and L/100 km, that are extensions to the current view. To switch from one view

Figure 6-15: *The Standard view of the Calculator provides a number of standard mathematical functions, including addition, subtraction, division, and multiplication.*

QUICKSTEPS

USING STICKY NOTES

Sticky Notes are exactly what the name implies: little notes to yourself that you can place anywhere on your screen. You can type messages on these notes; change their color; cut, copy, and paste the text on them with the Clipboard to and from other programs; create additional notes; and delete the note. Here's how:

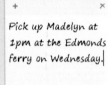

Pick up Madelyn at 1pm at the Edmonds ferry on Wednesday.

1. If you don't already have a note on your desktop, click **Start**, click **All Programs**, click **Accessories**, and click **Sticky Notes**. A note will appear.

   If you already have one or more notes on the desktop, the most recent one will be selected. If you want a new note, click **New Note** (the plus sign in the upper-left corner).

2. On the new note, type the message you want it to contain, or, having copied some text from another source, right-click the note and click **Paste**.

3. Right-click the note, click the color you want the note to be, and then drag the note to where you want it.

4. When you no longer want the note on the desktop, click **Delete Note** (the x in the upper-right), and click **Yes**.

to the other, click **View** and click the other view. To use a calculator, click the numbers on the screen or type them on the keyboard.

USE CHARACTER MAP

The *Character Map*, found in System Tools in Accessories, allows the selection of special characters that are not available on a standard keyboard.

1. Click the **Font** down arrow, and click the font you want for the special character.

2. Scroll until you find it, and then double-click the character; or click the character and click **Select** to copy it to the Clipboard.

3. In the program where you want the character, right-click an open area, and click **Paste** or press **CTRL+V**.

USE NOTEPAD

Notepad is a simple text editor you can use to view and create unformatted text (.txt) files. If you double-click a text file in Windows Explorer, Notepad will likely open and display the file. If a line of text is too long to display without scrolling, click **Format** and click **Word Wrap**. To create a file, simply start typing in the Notepad window, click the **File** menu, and click **Save**. Before printing a file, click **File**, click **Page Setup**, and select the paper orientation, margins, header, and footer.

USE PAINT

Paint is a program that lets you view, create, and edit bitmap image files in .bmp, .dib, .gif, .ico, .jpg, .png, and .tif formats. Several drawing tools and many colors are available to create simple drawings and illustrations (see Figure 6-16).

Use Acrobat Reader

The Adobe Acrobat Reader is a program most computer users find essential. It enables you to read documents created in *PDF* format. This format is often used so that readers don't have to have a particular

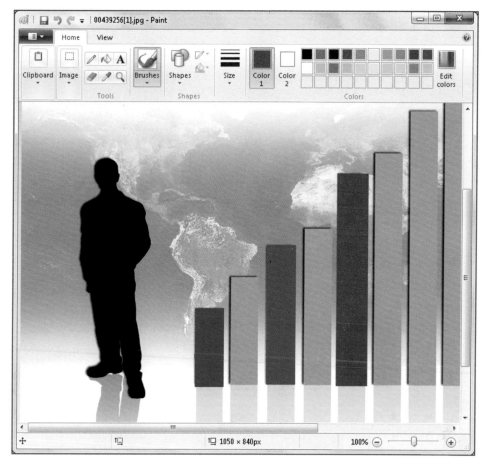

Figure 6-16: *Paint allows you to make simple line drawings or touch up other images.*

program, such as Word, to read it. Acrobat also comes in a more sophisticated package that allows you to create and edit PDF documents as well. However, the simple reader is what we're sure you will someday need, and it is free.

1. In your browser, type <u>adobe.com/reader</u> in the address bar, and press **ENTER**. The Adobe Reader page will display with the system disk requirements.

Adobe Reader

Download the latest version of Adobe Reader

Adobe Reader 9.3.4   53.47 MB
Includes Adobe® AIR®
Windows 7, English

Different language or operating system?

Learn more | System Requirements | License | Distribute Adobe Reader

2. If you do not want Google's free toolbar, clear the check box. (I have Google in my Favorites toolbar, but not its own toolbar.) Click **Download**.

3. Click **Yes** to allow Adobe to continue to download the program onto your computer. You will see a display of the downloading progress.

4. You will need to restart the computer, which you can do either when prompted or later. Click **Yes** to do it now. After the computer has rebooted, you'll find a shortcut to Adobe Reader on your desktop.

5. To open a PDF file, either double-click the **Acrobat Reader** shortcut or double-click a PDF file. When you first bring Acrobat Reader up, you'll have to accept the reader's license agreement. Click **Accept**.

6. Point your cursor at the icons on the toolbar. You'll see how you can navigate through the document, share it with others, change the magnification, change the display of the page, or use the search feature to find specific words or phrases. Figure 6-17 shows how the reader displays a PDF file.

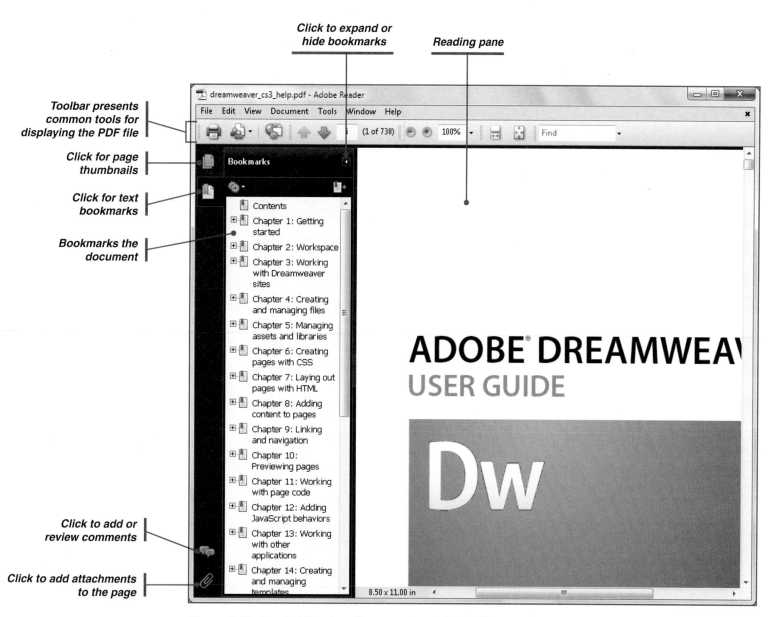

Figure 6-17: *Acrobat Reader allows you to read PDF files, a common file format.*

Callouts (clockwise from top):
- Click to expand or hide bookmarks
- Reading pane
- Toolbar presents common tools for displaying the PDF file
- Click for page thumbnails
- Click for text bookmarks
- Bookmarks the document
- Click to add or review comments
- Click to add attachments to the page

Within the application window:

dreamweaver_cs3_help.pdf - Adobe Reader

File   Edit   View   Document   Tools   Window   Help

(1 of 738)   100%   Find

Bookmarks

Contents
Chapter 1: Getting started
Chapter 2: Workspace
Chapter 3: Working with Dreamweaver sites
Chapter 4: Creating and managing files
Chapter 5: Managing assets and libraries
Chapter 6: Creating pages with CSS
Chapter 7: Laying out pages with HTML
Chapter 8: Adding content to pages
Chapter 9: Linking and navigation
Chapter 10: Previewing pages
Chapter 11: Working with page code
Chapter 12: Adding JavaScript behaviors
Chapter 13: Working with other applications
Chapter 14: Creating and managing templates

ADOBE® DREAMWEAV
USER GUIDE

Dw

8.50 × 11.00 in

Chapter 7
Stepping into Digital Photography

You've probably noticed that the corner drugstore is carrying a limited selection of roll film today and that you have to mail it somewhere to get the film developed and printed. And friends and family might be asking you when you're going to post last month's reunion pictures on your online gallery.

There are many reasons why today's photography is beckoning you to get your hands on an affordable digital camera! This chapter takes you through everything you need to know to take advantage of your digital camera—how to get your photos from your camera into your computer, how to perform minor retouching to pictures, and how to share your precious images with other members of the online photo community.

Get Pictures into Your Computer

Even after you've taken some terrific digital photos, you can't really use them until you get them into your computer. You can do it using Windows' default software that automatically downloads the pictures from the camera, or you can do it manually, using Windows Explorer.

Use AutoPlay to Get Your Pictures into the Computer

The common way to get your photos from your digital camera to your computer's hard disk is to plug the cable that came with your camera into your PC. Another way is to use either the PC's memory card reader or an external card reader. Here's how to transfer camera data to your computer:

1. Connect your camera or memory card to a computer:

    a. Plug the cable into your camera, and then into a USB or FireWire port on your PC (most cameras use USB connections). Make sure the camera is on; put the camera's memory card into the PC's memory card reader slot, if it has a slot, or into an external memory card reader that is attached to the computer.

    b. You may see a notification in the taskbar tray that the device has been recognized and any necessary drivers are being installed. Wait a moment or two for this process to finish.

    c. The AutoPlay dialog box appears and shows the options available to import, view, or manage the photos or videos. The options can be different, depending on which programs on your computer have an association with image files.

2. To use the Windows default program for importing photos and videos, click **Import Pictures And Videos Using Windows**. The Import Videos And Pictures dialog box appears and discovers items stored in the camera or on the memory card. If you have a lot of photos or videos, this might take a while.

AutoPlay

Canon PowerShot G5

☐ Always do this for this device:

Device options

Import pictures and videos
using Windows

Open device to view files
using Windows Explorer

EPSON SMART PANEL
using EPSON SMART PANEL

OmniPage SE 4
using OmniPage SE 4

View more AutoPlay options in Control Panel

3. Enter a new tag or choose an existing tag in the Tag These Pictures (Optional) drop-down list. Using default import settings, for example, entering Cats as the tag results in a folder named 2011-01-26 Cats in the My Pictures folder that contains the photos Cats001.jpg, Cats002 .jpg, and so on.

4. Click **Import**. Windows begins importing the photos. Leave the Erase After Importing check box unchecked.

5. Disconnect the camera from the computer, or remove the memory card from the reader when Windows has finished saving your files to disk. The Import Pictures And Videos dialog box automatically closes, and a Windows Explorer window opens that shows the folder where the pictures have been saved.

Download Photos Manually

Many photo management programs (including Windows) keep track of what images they have downloaded to your computer and won't import them a second time. This is to prevent duplicate images from filling up your hard disk. If, for any reason, you want to copy them to disk again, you can work around this restriction and copy them manually from the memory card to your hard disk.

Here's how to manually copy some of the memory card's photos to your hard disk:

1. Using Windows Explorer, navigate to where you want to save the photos. For example, if you want to save them in the My Pictures folder, click **Start**, click **Pictures**, and then click the **My Pictures** folder to select it.

2. To create a new folder, click **New Folder** on the toolbar; in the file list area of the window, a new entry is made (named New Folder) and is selected and open so you can type a different folder name. Enter any name you want for the folder, and leave the Explorer window open.

JACKIE ORGANIZES AND PRESENTS HER PHOTOS

I must have two dozen shoeboxes stuffed with family photos, and twice that in photo albums, but do you think I even take them out and look at them? This era of digital photography has been a boon to my family and me, because we actually look at the pictures my husband and I have taken…more than once!

When I'm teaching, with online galleries, I can upload pictures of my class' production of their junior high recital, and it encourages them to publicize events and other productions in a constructive and positive way. They learn that photography is a type of visual communication and not just snapping a picture with a mobile phone; galleries encourage a pride in authorship, and it's cultivating a respect for the work of others that restores some of what I feel the purpose of taking photos is all about.

Every picture tells a story. For a story to be told, though, you need an audience; this is what online photo galleries provide for my classes and my family. Photography is a personal way to share, and digital photography broadens the appeal and the value of the slices of life we capture.

Jackie S., New York

3. Plug the camera or memory card and reader in. When the AutoPlay dialog box appears, choose **Open Folder To View Files Using Windows Explorer**. A standard Windows Explorer window opens.

4. Your pictures might be stored in one or more subfolders; open any folders you see until you find your images.

5. Select the files you want to transfer. To copy all the files in a folder, press **CTRL+A**; to copy sequentially listed files, click to select the first file, then hold **SHIFT**, and click the last file in the list. To copy nonsequential files, press **CTRL** and then click the file name(s).

6. Drag the selected files into the folder on your hard disk that you created in step 1.

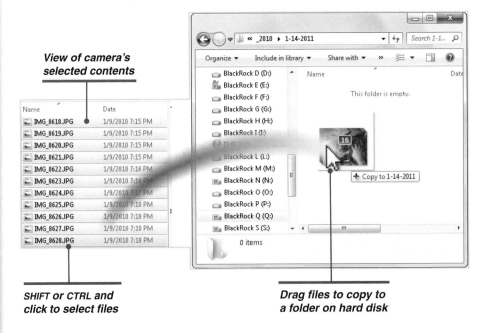

View of camera's selected contents

SHIFT or CTRL and click to select files

Drag files to copy to a folder on hard disk

View Pictures Using Windows Slide Show

You're understandably anxious to see what you and your camera captured; the sections to follow cover a range of options you have for viewing photographs on your desktop, from the native support

There is an extremely useful utility to view and rename photos. XnView (xnview.com/en/index .html) is free and can preview camera RAW images—which Windows cannot do. In addition to bulk renaming files, XnView can group images and then perform batch operations, like converting images from one file format to another, or resize them so they are suitable for posting in a web gallery.

XnView also has a shell extension version available on the XnView download page. If you install this utility, whenever you right-click an image file, the Windows context menu displays a large-sized thumbnail view of the image.

Windows offers, to free utilities that can not only display but also rename and create albums of your pictures.

Image thumbnails are terrific for organizing photos, but it's better still to watch and navigate a slide show of an entire folder of your pictures. Folders that have been optimized to show pictures, like the default My Pictures folder, have a built-in slide show feature. Here's how to run a slide show and how to work with the viewing options:

1. Click **Start**. Click **Pictures** if you want to see pictures that are stored in your My Pictures folder, or click **Computer** if they are stored elsewhere. Use the Explorer dialog box that opens to navigate to and open the folder that contains the pictures you want to view.

2. Click **Slide Show** on the toolbar. The screen dims and the first image in the folder appears in full-screen size. The slide show plays and automatically cycles through the pictures in the folder.

3. To manually go forward by one image, you can press **DOWN ARROW**, **RIGHT ARROW**, or **PAGE DOWN** or click anywhere in the window.

4. To go back one image in the slide show, press **UP ARROW**, **LEFT ARROW**, or **PAGE UP**.

5. To set other display options, right-click anywhere on the screen to open a context menu.

   - There you can choose to pause, or play (restart a paused show), or exit a show.

   - Choose **Loop** to make the slide show play continuously, and/or choose **Shuffle** to mix up the order in which they play.

   - Set the speed of the show by choosing **Slide Show Speed Slow**, **Slide Show Speed Medium**, or **Slide Show Speed Fast**.

6. To close a slide show, you can press **ESC**.

Figure 7-1 shows a full-screen image with the context menu displayed.

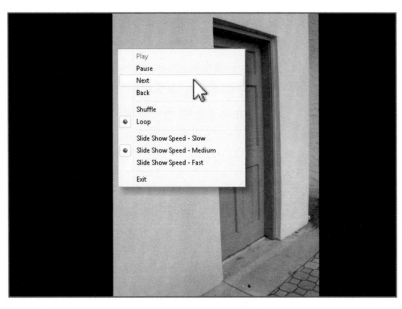

Figure 7-1: *You can control how your slide show is displayed in Windows Picture Viewer with a context menu.*

Perform Minor Retouching

If there's a small element that you don't like about a digital photo—but you really like the picture otherwise—you don't have to reach for Adobe Photoshop, the industry standard for professional image retouching, or pay a lot of money to hire a retoucher. "Free" is a price you can appreciate, and happily, the two basic photo-editing programs featured in the rest of this chapter are free for you to download and use.

The general concepts, methods, and tools used to fix simple problems or enhance photos are pretty much universal—so learning how to perform the fixes and enhancements in Photoscape, for example, will greatly shorten the learning curve if you eventually buy a different program to edit your photos.

Before you begin the steps in this section, download and install both Photoscape and Picasa so you can follow along. The links are listed in the sections to follow.

Evaluate Free Photo-Editing Programs

Photoscape and Picasa have in common these tools or features:

- Resizes and crops photos.
- Straightens the horizon in a photo.
- Clones or duplicates areas of a picture. (Using a Clone tool is covered in this chapter.)
- Rotates and/or flips an image.
- Offers Save As, so you're not overwriting valuable originals when you edit.

LOU UPDATES HIS PHOTO DARKROOM

I was hesitant about upgrading my camera gear to digital because I had invested so much in my lenses and darkroom equipment, but then a friend guided me at a Best Buy around the camera section and showed me that I could attach my old lenses to several popular brands of digital cameras. This got me to seriously consider what else I could now afford to update. There are free and shareware programs out there that easily replace my old darkroom stuff, some of which I gave up using anyway years ago. I can crop, straighten, and fix the exposure of pictures I just took without getting my hands messy with E3 kits, and inkjet paper costs less than the photographic paper I used to buy in small batches.

It's been a learning experience, and also a productive one, to "go digital." I feel as though I've discovered a lot more than I've given up, and I hardly notice or miss some of the old tricks I used to sweat through to get a print looking the way I want it to.

Lou F., 74, Florida

- Sharpens and improves the colors and brightness of a photo.
- Removes red eye from portraits of people.
- Adds text to a photo.

GET PHOTOSCAPE

Photoscape (photoscape.org) is used in several of the following procedures because it contains most of the basic features beginners need. Photoscape is actually a multifunction program: in addition to its Photo Editor module, you can print several photos to a single page at a specified size (such as wallet), you can batch together camera RAW files and convert them to JPEG, or you can rename a batch of files at once. It is a Windows desktop program that is free, but if you use it a lot, it is nice to make a donation to the software developer.

DOWNLOAD AND INSTALL PICASA

Picasa (picasa.google.com), from Google, serves several needs for people who love taking and sharing photos. In addition to a basic image editor, Picasa is a cataloger and an easy device for posting your photos in a web album you can share with the world or with only guests you invite. Cataloging and sharing is covered later in this chapter: as an image editor, Picasa offers basic features such as color and tone enhancement, special filters and effects, and image straightening.

Crop and Enhance with Photoscape

Once you have downloaded and installed Photoscape, you can break your project down into a series of processes. Using an ornamental scarecrow as an example, you can see how to perform color and exposure corrections, crop the photo to the desired size, and perhaps straighten the image's horizon.

Many free software programs, and Photoscape is one of them, earn programmers a little revenue when you agree to install toolbars and browsers sponsored by firms such as Google and Yahoo!. It's important that you read every screen when you install programs, and be sure to uncheck options you might not want. For example, Photoscape offers to install Google Toolbar, a web browser toolbar that will make Google always present as your default web browser. *Uncheck* these boxes as you proceed with the installation.

CROP, SCALE, AND STRAIGHTEN A PHOTO

If you have an image whose color isn't perfect and needs cropping, here's how to perform basic image corrections and enhancements:

1. Launch Photoscape from either the Windows Start menu or an icon on your desktop.

2. Click **Editor** (positioned at 12 o'clock) on Photoscape's opening screen. The Photoscape Editor window opens.

3. From the left pane, choose a hard disk location where you keep your photos. Beneath the folder list, thumbnails appear of images whose file types Photoscape recognizes.

4. Click the thumbnail whose image you want to work on. It appears in the main window.

5. If you're unfamiliar with zooming an image, making the photo look larger or smaller on screen is accomplished using the Zoom controls shown in Figure 7-2. From left to right, clicking the first zoom icon, **Zoom 1:1**, displays the actual size of an image. The next icon displays the entire image in the viewing window, called Window Fit. The next field offers preset viewing magnifications; clicking this area displays a pop-up list of zoom choices. Next is the Zoom In and Out button; clicking **Zoom In** increases the magnification to two times the current view. **Zoom Out** halves your current viewing resolution. Use the Zoom tool to work with small areas of an image with precision. For an invaluable navigational tool that you can use in an area at high magnification, click the **Tools** tab and click **Screen Scroll**—you can then push your way around the image view by clicking and dragging in the window. If you can't see the entire image right now, click the **Window Fit** icon.

6. Let's say the frame you want to use to print your image is 5 by 7 inches. Click the **Crop** tab, and then click **Crop Freely** to reveal the pop-up menu of predefined cropping sizes, shown here. Choose the size you want from the list (5:7 in our example), and then drag a rectangle in the image window. If you choose **Crop Freely**, you can drag a rectangle around a part of the photo, selecting the specific part you want to separate from the whole photo. Once a rectangle has

Figure 7-2: **The interface of Photoscape**

Selected hard disk folder

Selected image

Cropping

Color controls

Zoom controls

been created, it can be moved by dragging inside it. The preview crop rectangle can also be resized by dragging an edge away or toward the center of the crop rectangle.

7. When you're happy with your proposed crop, click **Crop** to make the change. If you want to cancel the operation, click outside of the preview rectangle. If you're unhappy with your crop and want to try again, click **Undo**, or press **CTRL+Z**, which is a common Windows command for Undo.

8. Also, when cropping, you have the option to crop to a lovely oval or circle shape, and Photoscape creates a matte background around the image to fill the rest of the rectangular dimensions. To make an oval crop, first select the **Crop Round Image** check box, and decide on a proportion for the crop exactly as you did in step 6, but then click the color swatch that appears only in Crop Round Image mode; doing this displays a color picker where you can choose the color background. Perform the crop as you did with the rectangular crop in step 6, and your image will look something like that in Figure 7-3.

9. Notice in Figure 7-3 that the scarecrow looks a little crooked in the picture, especially after it's been cropped. If a horizontal line such as the horizon of an ocean is crooked, click the clockwise arrow icon just above the Crop tab. This displays a pop-up window, where you drag the slider left or right until a horizontal area in the photo—the rope belt in Figure 7-4, for example—is level with the horizontal guides. Then click **OK** to apply the Level Off feature. Notice that this feature hides gaps around the edges of your photo by cropping inward just a little.

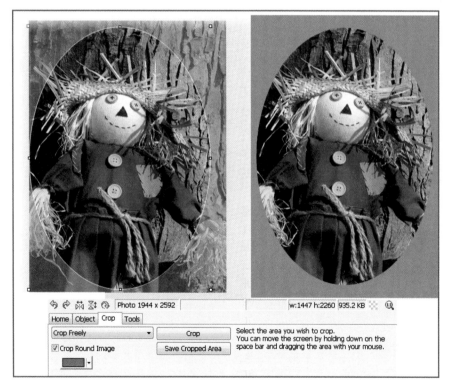

*Figure 7-3: **Create a "cameo" photo by using the Crop Round Image option.***

Figure 7-4: Use the Level Off feature to straighten a photo.

Clone Away Image Flaws

The term "cloning" is used in most image editors that support the feature to mean "sample an area, and then use this sample as a brush stroke." Photoscape has a Clone Stamp tool in the Tools tab section, and if there's an area where, for example, your subject has a blemish, or there's an unsightly telephone wire in an otherwise gorgeous sky, use the Clone Stamp tool to first sample a good area of the photo, and then stroke over the unwanted area to replace it. The Clone stamp has three brush sizes, indicated in Figure 7-5, and the following steps show how to use the tool, not for image correction, but instead for a little playful image enhancement. The scarecrow's shirt only has two buttons, but a third can be added easily. Here's how:

1. It's usually best to work at a 1:1 view so your retouching work is precise. Click the **Zoom 1:1** icon before proceeding.

2. Click **Tools**, click the **Clone Stamp** tool, and then click the brush size you want to use for both sampling and retouching.

3. Click a "good" area from which you want to sample. In this example, the top button on the shirt was clicked to set the sample point.

4. Move the cursor where you want the cloned image, and click and drag over the area into which you wish to clone. In this example, the area directly between the top and bottom shirt buttons is being stroked over. Figure 7-5 shows the work in progress. The sample point always travels parallel to the area you're cloning over. You'll see a faint inverted circle where you stroke, connected to a faint inverted circle of the area currently being sampled. At some point, you might want to redefine the sample point: right-click to break the link between the sample and clone locations, and then click to set a new sample point.

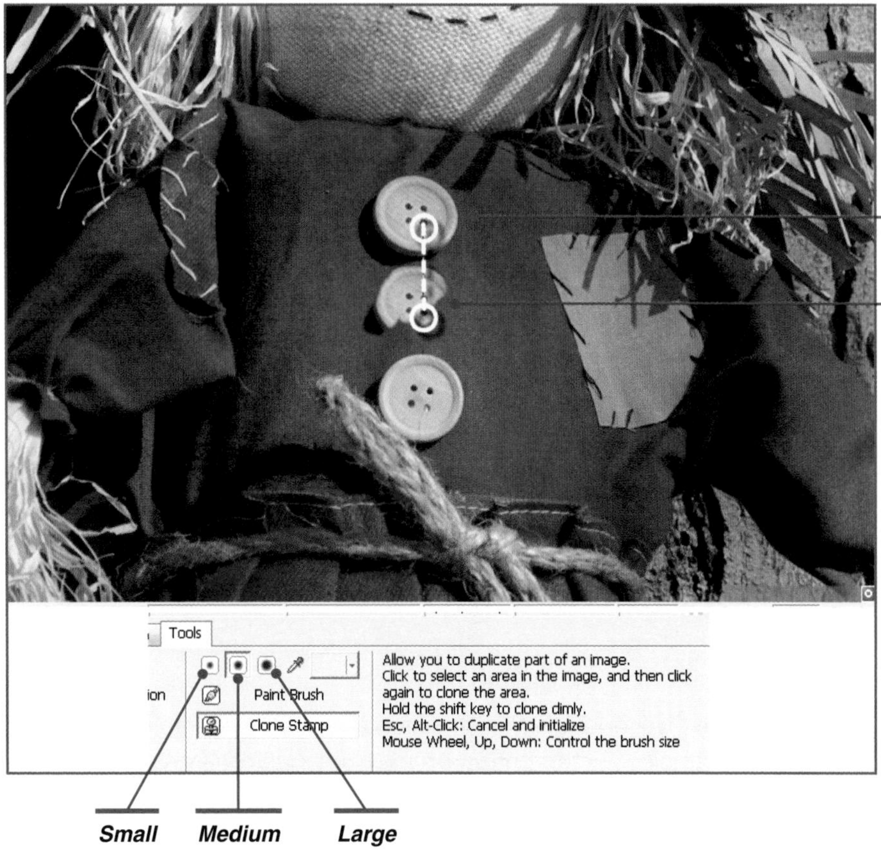

Figure 7-5: *Cloning is how professional retouchers create fancy illusions in cosmetics ads and magazine covers.*

TIP

You can change brush size on-the-fly, without leaving the area you're retouching, by using your mouse scroll wheel. Scroll toward yourself to make the tip smaller; scroll toward your monitor to make the tip larger.

Use Color Correction

Color—the quality in photos you perceive as predominant hues such as brilliant orange or deep blue—is tied to a photo's *tones*, the relative brightness values of colors from deepest to lightest, as they appear in the quiltwork of pixels that make up the digital images you see. The importance of this fact is often demonstrated by adjusting the brightness values in an image; when you add contrast by deepening all the colors and making the overall image brighter, you'll always see some sort of change in the colors in addition to the tones. This is why often by adjusting the tones in a photo, you make the colors brighter and more intense.

Photoscape has auto-correction features for photos, such as Auto Levels and Auto Contrast. However, a little understanding of what they do, what's wrong with a photo, and the correct command to make are in order here; no software program can intelligently discern what's wrong with a photo—every photo is unique—and fix it for you to your complete satisfaction. You can always click Undo if, for example, you applied Auto Levels and selected High; it doesn't hurt to give it a try if a photo looks washed out, and often Auto Levels will produce a richer, more colorful photograph.

Figure 7-6 shows a brief example of how playing detective, discovering what's wrong with a photo and then using the appropriate commands, can result in a much better photo, and one that clicking an auto-correction

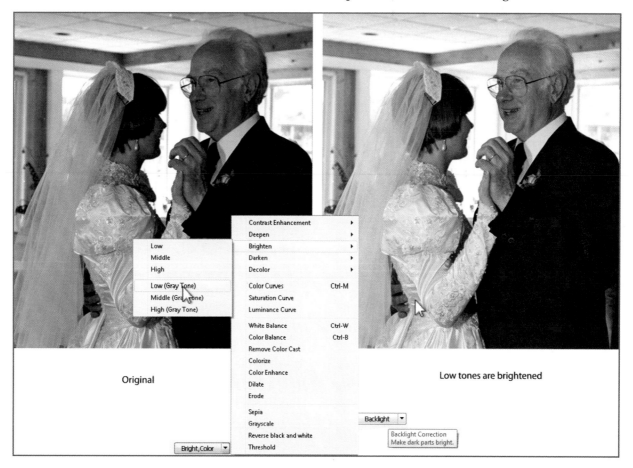

Figure 7-6: *Backlight and the Brighten menu are invaluable for restoring poorly lit photos.*

WALT CREATES NEW USES FOR DIGITAL CAMERAS

Although I've used a camera since I was in the Army, the concept of "taking pictures" has always seemed limited to me. I'm just as big a fan of "organization" as I am of fine photography, and buying my first digital camera satisfied both cravings. Not only can I document weddings and anniversaries, but I'm also documenting where we parked at the mall, what the contents of boxes are in our garage, and the serial numbers on mechanisms if and when I need to take them apart. I'm serious!

A digital camera can instantly take a photo of the contents in a storage box: I print a copy, and then we tape a copy to the top of the box after we seal it. This is much less of a hassle than typing out or hand-printing labels, and recently, my wife and I have adopted my strange use of the camera for finding our car at the local mall, too. We snap the section and aisle on those large colored signs, and hours later when it's time to leave, I just look in the preview screen after backing up to that image. Digital photography isn't just for taking pictures. It's also great and immediate for taking down *facts*.

Walter W., 55, Illinois

button won't provide. The figure shows a beautiful photo, but the flash didn't fire, and the room has strong lighting coming from behind the couple. The midtones are muddy in the faces of the subjects, which often mean that the highlight and midtone brightnesses are fine, but the shadow tones are too dark and need lightening. In the Home tab, click the **Bright, Color** down arrow for a pop-up menu. Point to **Brighten** for a submenu that offers low, medium, and high auto-corrections, but also low, middle, and high brightness corrections for gray tone. Used in this context, gray tone means "evaluate and correct shadow, middle, or high brightness areas based on equal presence of red, green, and blue primary colors." Tone is brightness without regard to the predominant hue of any pixel in the image. So, in this case, the low gray tones were brightened and then Backlight was used (you can click to apply Backlight more than once), which corrects for backlit subjects by deepening brighter colors and lightening up shadowy areas; see Figure 7-6.

When you adjust the relative brightness values in a photo—regardless of whether the program uses terms such as "tone," "luminance," or anything else, you are bound to improve the distinctness of color. Note that in the preceding picture, the father and daughter display richer skin tones, yet no specific color adjustment was applied. Many times, the secret to image enhancement is in the tones.

Use Picasa to Organize, Tag, and Share Your Photos

Before you know it, you're going to have dozens, possibly thousands, of outstanding personal photos you'll want to share with family and friends. The first move is to *organize* your collection of photos so they don't wind up like those in the 47 shoeboxes in your attic! Happily,

Google provides a desktop program that performs minor retouches, helps you sort through your photos and tag your favorite ones, and lets you upload your photos to a private or public gallery on the Web. And your Google email account, your web gallery, and Picasa software are free. The following sections describe how to catalog and publish your photography.

Install and Use Picasa

A lot of goodies are available for download when you have a Google account, and Picasa software—Google's image editor and organizer—is one of them. To sign up for Google, type google.com in your browser's URL address box, on the Google Home page click **Gmail** in the top link bar, and then click **Create An Account**.

Picasa can be downloaded at picasa.google.com. It takes only a moment to install, but as with all software, read the options boxes as you install. The last screen in Picasa offers to make Google your default search engine in Explorer. Uncheck this box, and then rest assured knowing that your personal hard drive data isn't being shared.

Once Picasa has been installed, it offers to run the program. Allow it, and then read on to see how Picasa can work for you in everyday image organization, editing, and sharing.

Explore Picasa by Task

Figure 7-7 shows the Picasa's interface; it changes when you select an individual photo to edit, but upon launch, Picasa features a drive directory at left called the Library, and your Pictures folder is always included here. Here is a list of easy navigation commands for Picasa, based on task. Before beginning, click the **Set View To Show Folder Tree Structure** button on the toolbar.

TIP

While installing Picasa, It's best to only allow Picasa to search your pictures and documents folders, and what might be on your desktop. Your other choice is to let it index your entire system, and it just takes too darned long!

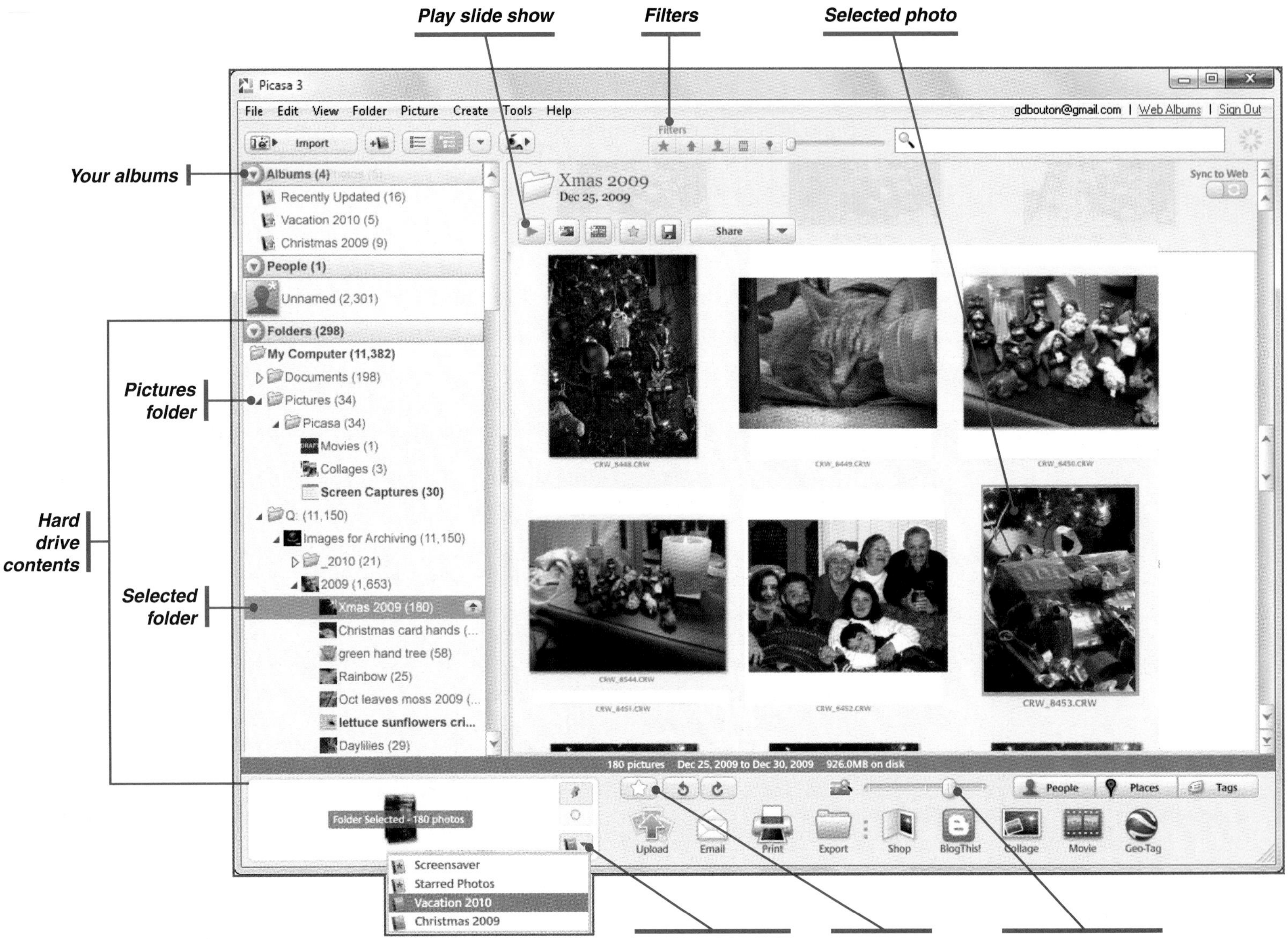

Play slide show

Filters

Selected photo

Your albums

Pictures folder

Hard drive contents

Selected folder

Add selected photos to album

Tag image with a star

Zoom thumbnails in window

Figure 7-7: Picasa's interface is simple, clean, and easy to use.

- **View a folder of images**   An entry on the Library list that has a triangle (Expand or Collapse) means it's a folder that contains subitems, either other folders or individual images or movies. Click the **Expand** down arrow to view the images in a folder. Individual images are listed in the Library, and a single-click displays them in the main window.

- **Open an image for editing**   Double-click an image in the main thumbnail viewing pane.

- **Return to Library view**   When you're in editing or another mode, Picasa displays a Back To Library button in the upper-left area that takes you back to the main view of your collection of images.

- **View slide show**   Click the green forward arrowhead above the thumbnail images to play all the images in the main thumbnail window as a slide show. However, move your cursor while in full-screen slide show mode to display the controls for slide show playback, including rotate image buttons, duration for each image, clever transition effects between images, and an Exit button (pressing **ESC** exits slide show mode as well).

- **Make an image a Favorite**   With an image selected in the main view, click the **Add/Remove Star** button in the top tray area. The star is nonprinting, and any editing you perform on images in Picasa has to be saved to become permanent. Tagging an image with a Favorites star lets you filter through a large collection of images to show only the ones you've tagged as such. Starred images can become nonstarred by selecting the image and then clicking the **Add/Remove Star** button again.

- **Make a new album**   By default, there's an area above the hard disk directory in Picasa named "Albums," and initially, it doesn't contain a user album. Click **Create A New Album** above the Albums directory. You're then prompted to name the album and provide optional information. Then, you'll see a new album in the Albums list.

- **Add an image to one of your albums**   Right-click an image in the main thumbnail window, choose **Add To Album**, then choose the album to which you want the photo added.

QUICKSTEPS

UPLOADING AND SHARING A PICASA WEB ALBUM

Although uploading a Web Album to Picasa's website—and then allowing people to visit your album—are two different processes, they've been combined in this procedure because both processes are simple and easy. Before you know it, you'll be sharing photos with family and friends.

1. In Picasa, create a new album by clicking **Add Selected Item To An Album**. Click **New Album**. In the Album Properties dialog box, type the album name, select a date and music if needed, and add the location and an optional description. Click **OK**.

2. To add photos to your album, first select all the images you want to include by pressing **CTRL** and clicking them. When the images are selected, click **Add Selected Item To An Album**, and then choose the name of the album. In the directory, right-click the album and then choose **Upload To Picasa Web Albums** from the pop-up menu.

Continued . . .

- **Make thumbnails larger or smaller** Drag the **Zoom** slider beneath the images to the left (makes images smaller) or to the right (makes images larger).

- **Show only Favorites** Click the **Star** button on the lower tray to display only images you've tagged with a star, making them Favorites. This is a terrific way to locate an image you know you designated as a Favorite a week or a month ago.

- **Find where an image is really located** Picasa doesn't move image files and it doesn't apply permanent edits. If you want to find where the original image is located, click the thumbnail and then press **CTRL+ENTER**, or right-click the thumbnail and then choose **Locate On Disk**. Doing this displays a folder window that contains your original photo.

Create an Online Gallery

A good way to share photos with loved ones across great distances is by uploading images to a Picasa Web Album, and you can upload more than one. The service is free; you're given 1GB of server space and can buy more at a future time. However, 1GB of free gallery space is quite a lot if you post images in JPEG file format: a 5-by-7 inch photo that has 300 dpi (dots per inch) resolution—suitable for printing—is typically saved as a JPEG file to about 1MB. There are 1,000 MBs in a gigabyte, so in reality, you could post almost 1,000 images to your Picasa Web Album for free.

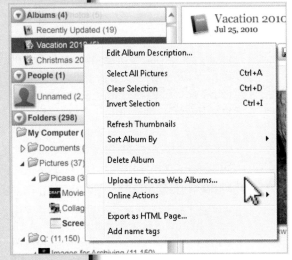

QUICKSTEPS

UPLOADING AND SHARING A PICASA WEB ALBUM *(Continued)*

3. In the Upload To Picasa Web Albums dialog box, there are two choices you need to make before clicking Upload.

- First, you might not want to share your album with everyone who has a Google account. Click the **Visibility To This Album** drop-down list, and choose your preference: Public means that anyone who performs a Web Album search can discover and view your album. Unlisted means that anyone who wants to see your album needs an authorization key (see the next Note); Sign-in Required To View specifies that only visitors who have a Google account and sign in can see your album's contents.

- To restrict viewing to names you determine, click **Share** and then choose **Create And Edit Groups**. In the next dialog box, click **Add** in the top left. On the right you can enter the name, email address, and other contact information about a friend you want to add to a list of people who are invited to see your Web Album. Click **Save** once you've completed the form; for security reasons, keep the contact information minimal.

4. Click **Upload**, and Picasa informs you when your album has been uploaded. Click **View Online** to see your album. Figure 7-8

Continued . . .

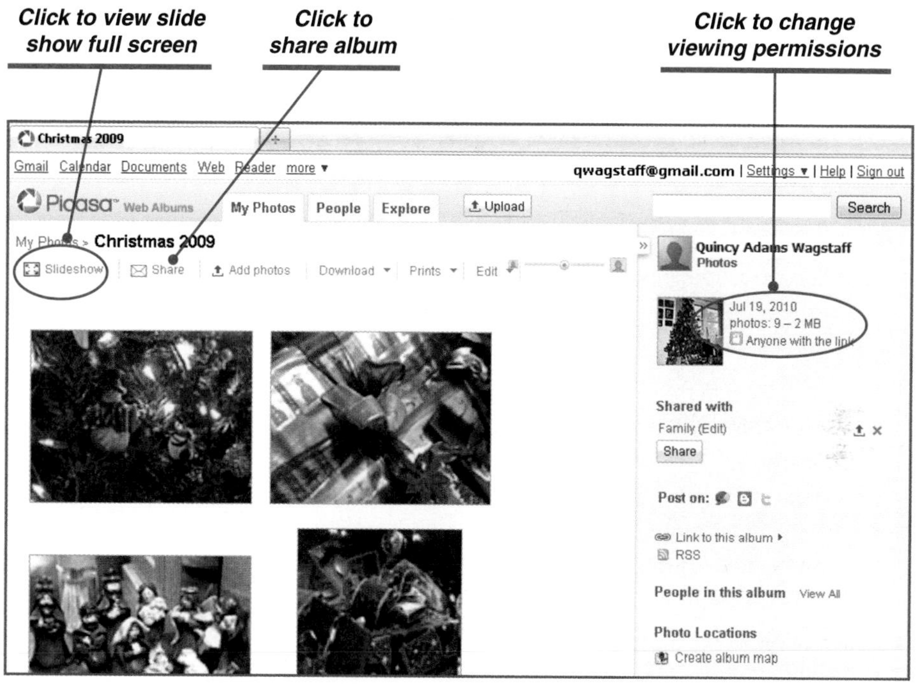

Figure 7-8: Share your photos with friends, family, and anyone you give permission to on Picasa Web Albums.

To create and upload a Picasa Web Album, see the "Uploading and Sharing a Picasa Web Album" QuickSteps.

Add Photo Captions

Any image—whether you're viewing it in Picasa or you have it in an album—can have a description you type.

1. Click an image to select it. You have two ways to add descriptions or captions. One applies to a whole album, the other to an individual image.

   a. Click the **Add A Description** text box above the image. A field then opens, and you can type away. If the image is part of an album, the description applies to the entire album.

**UPLOADING AND SHARING
A PICASA WEB ALBUM** *(Continued)*

shows a completed and posted Christmas album. Click **Slide Show** to view the album at full-screen size (controls appear below the picture for timing and exiting this viewing mode); you can share the album by clicking **Share** and filling in a recipient's email address; and you can change the privacy level of an album from this view.

5. At any time in the future, while you work in Picasa, you can see your Web Albums by clicking the **View Online** hyperlink to the right of the Share button. If you want to add photos to an online album in the future, you first add them to your album in Picasa, and then click **Sync To Web** on the upper right of the image area. Your online gallery is updated to reflect those images currently in your Web Album within your desktop copy of Picasa. An active Internet connection is necessary to keep your online Web Album up to date.

b. If you just want to type a description of a single photo, double-click the image in Picasa, and then click the **Make A Caption** text box beneath the image, and type.

It might be more fun on special occasions, however, to add text directly to a photo and make it a special "greeting card"; there is a text tool in Picasa that lets you do this (see "Make a Headline in Your Photo").

Make a Headline in Your Photo

Picasa offers many options for adding text to a photo, which is great for creating a caption, dating the photo for all to see, and making a picture into a greeting card. Text is not permanent in a Google composition until you choose to export a copy of it with the text, so you're not ruining your originals. Here's how to add text to a photo:

1. Select an image thumbnail, and then double-click it to display the editing features.

2. On the Basic Fixes tab, click **Text**. Sample text telling you how to add text is displayed above the chosen image, and when you click the image, this placeholder text vanishes and you can begin typing your custom headline. The Basic Fixes tab is replaced with Edit Text features.

3. Type something first in the image, just so you can see what typeface you desire. You can press **BACKSPACE** after typing a word or phrase to correct it at any time.

4. Click the **Font** down arrow, and point to the names of fonts. As you point, the text you've typed is immediately displayed in this font. Click to select one. Try something fancy but legible—Arial might be at the top of the list, but it's a fairly sterile, clinical font.

5. You can stack text on more than one line; press **ENTER** after a word to bump subsequent text down to its own line.

6. To align more than one line of text, click the **Left**, **Center**, or **Right** Alignment buttons.

7. To make text (or only a selected character or word) bold, italic, or underlined, click the appropriate Style buttons. Underlined text doesn't look particularly attractive, but you might want to use it for directions on a map image.

8. To move text, drag the round edged box outside of the text.

9. When you click the image, a circle with a small, red dot either inside or outside the circle will display. To increase the size of the text, drag the red dot to the right, toward the outside of the circle. Dragging right increases the text size; dragging left, toward the inside of the circle, decreases the size. If you want some text smaller or larger than the rest, highlight the text and then click the **Size** field, located to the left beneath Font.

10. To rotate text, drag the red dot up or down. You'll notice four points of "resistance" at 0, 90, 120, and 270 degrees. Stop dragging while you rotate text when you feel a slight resistance to align text perfectly with the edges of the photo.

11. To specify a color for the text, click the circle to the right of the leftmost "T" at the left to reveal a color picker.

12. To specify an outline color for text, click the circle to the right of the hollow "T" to reveal a color picker. The color pickers also have a "no color" swatch at the far left if you want a solid fill with no outline or outlined text with no fill.

13. To set the width of an outline around text, drag the **Width** slider left or right.

14. To make the text partially transparent, drag the **Transparency** slider left or right.

15. When you're happy with your text, click **Apply**. Figure 7-9 shows the features and an example image in the works.

UICKSTEPS

INVITING A FRIEND TO SEE YOUR PHOTOS

Regardless of the privacy settings you define for an album or your Picasa gallery, you can override any security setting when you choose to share images. To share an image or album and let your friends know about the image(s):

1. Go to your Picasa Web Albums online by clicking **View Online** to the right of the Share button.

2. If you do not see the album you want, click **My Photos**. Then click the album you want to share, and then click the **Share** button, the letter envelope icon.

3. Uncheck the **Let People I Share With Contribute Photos** check box to allow others to add to your Web Album if you have friends who are inclined to eat up your free available space online with uninteresting photos.

4. In the To field, type the name of the recipient.

5. In the Message field, type a brief explanation why your recipient is receiving this email.

6. Click **Send Email**.

TIP

See Chapter 4 for details on how to share your beautifully retouched photos as email attachments.

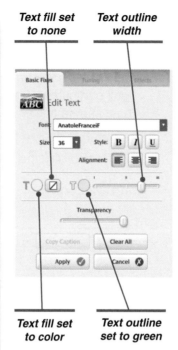

Figure 7-9: *Create text on your image in Picasa.*

Print Your Pictures

Naturally, your entire family, all your friends, and people you've just met cannot be expected to be web savvy or even have an email account. That's why today, it's easier and faster than ever to make a print of your photos or have a service print them for you. Your options for printing your photos are:

● Print pictures yourself if you own an inkjet printer. Windows itself can print a photo (details later in this chapter), and Picasa can print individual different-sized photos to a single page—covered next in this section.

DAVE BACKS UP HIS PHOTOS PAINLESSLY

I've taken a lot of photos in my life, and one of the perennial problems has been locating a photo I like, or at least the negative, so I can have a copy made. Since the world has gone digital with photography, I think we have killed two birds with one stone: first, there aren't any more negatives. If you have a file, you can make as many copies of it as you want. Second, I'm bowled over by the sheer amount of paper I've bought or had printed over the past 50 years, no less by the space it takes up. Actually, the second purchase I made was a new digital 12mp camera—the first was a multipurpose inkjet printer I picked up for about $200. It includes a scanner that has higher resolution than a lot of the snapshots I own, so I've faithfully scanned a handful of archive photos every day. Then I've sent relevant photos to the appropriate parties, and guess what? This is a real painless way to back up my photographs: they have a copy; I have a copy; end of the searching story.

Searching you do with Easter eggs once a year; if you have search for photos, you're either taking too many or you just haven't gotten into high tech yet!

Dave D., 67, Colorado

- Ask an online service to print your uploaded photos, bill you online, and then physically mail your prints. Snapfish (snapfish.com), Kodak (kodakgallery.com), Picasa, and other sites will be happy to mail you prints from galleries you've created at these web addresses. If you're unhappy with the prints you receive, it's about as easy to get a refund as it is to get a refund from any mail-order company, so be forewarned.

- Have prints made at a printing kiosk you can find at supermarkets and in malls. First, pick up literature that might be offered on the file formats these kiosks will accept. Second, make a CD you can take to the mall and put in one of these kiosk machines.

Print Your Photo to a Home Printer

Windows has a Print command when you right-click photo file types in folders. BMP, TIFF, PNG, and JPEG, among other formats, will prompt the Print command to appear on the context menu. Here's how to print one of those beautiful images you've worked on in this chapter:

1. With Windows Explorer open, right-click a photo you want to print, and then choose **Print** from the context menu.

2. Click the **Printer** down arrow, and choose your printer from the available list on the Printer drop-down menu.

3. Click the **Paper Size** down arrow, and choose the paper size. This is not the size of the photo, but instead the size of the photo paper you've loaded your inkjet printer with.

4. Click the **Quality** down arrow, and choose the quality you desire. This is a "generic" and fairly vague list of print quality; for the best print, click **Options**, and then click **Printer Properties** to access all the features available with your printer.

5. Choose the paper type that you've loaded your inkjet paper with. This is an important choice: if you choose, for example, plain paper when you have glossy paper loaded, your print will look dull. The paper type is well calibrated to match the inkjet pigment dispersion with the amount of absorption a specific type of paper best accepts.

If you're thinking of buying an inkjet printer in the near future, check out some of the home models that are called "multifunction." These models not only print pictures from your computer, they also have a scanner and a fax machine. A scanner is invaluable to anyone who has a collection of physical photos and even slides that are deteriorating through age. You read the documentation, Windows 7 is quite good at recognizing new devices correctly as you plug them into your computer, and you can complete your genealogy, your scrapbook, or any project that needs heirloom photos by adding digital scans to all the photos you've taken with your digital camera.

6. Choose a full-page photo print, a 4 by 6 inch, or another print size by clicking the corresponding icon in the right column. Doing this only sets the size of the printed photo; if you choose a small size but want multiple prints on the same page, read step 7.

7. If the print size is smaller than the paper size, you can set the number of copies per page by entering a value in the **Copies Of Each Picture** number field. For example, here you can see four photos per standard paper size because 3.5 by 5 inches was chosen as the image size. You can also check or uncheck the **Fit Picture To Frame** check box, which is useful if your photo doesn't exactly work out to a preset photo size and Windows' cropping is lopping off someone's head in the preview window.

8. Click **Print**, and in a moment or two you'll need to find a utility blade or a pair of scissors.

How to...

Chapter 8
Enjoying Digital Music, E-books, and Videos

It might be hard to imagine that your entertainment roster is incomplete with your TV set hooked up to 7,000 cable stations, but there's at least tenfold the amount of videos, music, and other types of media right on your computer. When you have Internet access and know how to find and play today's online digital media, you discover that "your favorite program" isn't on TV, but rather on one of the millions of websites and online stores that cater to special interests. This chapter takes you through viewing, acquiring, and playing back digital video, audio, e-books, and more.

8

Set Up Audio Hardware and Software

You might have purchased a new computer whose vendor makes the claim that it's ready to go, and all you have to do is switch it on and experience the multimedia event of your life. But it's a claim, and that's all. If you're not fairly experienced with computers, enjoying content from the Web is a three-part process:

- You need to *get* the media, which can be done by watching video and listening to audio as it streams off the Web, or you can purchase media—either digitally or physically on disk—and then play it.
- You need to ensure that your computer system's hardware is configured properly to play media.
- You might need to download and install software that can play or let you view digital media.

Let's tackle the show-stoppers first; in the sections to follow, you learn how to set up hardware and software to turn your computer into a media playing device and get the media files. It's not as daunting as it might sound; set aside about half an hour of quality time for the steps.

Get Digital Media in Two Formats

After having located the appropriate online music store, you have a choice whether to purchase your digital media on a CD or download it onto your computer. This second choice is faster, less expensive

QUICKFACTS

UNDERSTANDING DIGITAL MEDIA CONCEPTS *(Continued)*

because electrical signals on recording tape can drift, they acquire randomness with age (causing static and hiss), the voltage used to play analog media varies and causes visible changes, and the vinyl grooves on those precious 33 1/3 records eventually becomes worn away as a diamond needle reads the analog information.

Another benefit of digital media is its availability—you simply use an online browser (see Chapter 3) to search for a song or video. Many online stores with huge selections offer either CDs, DVDs, downloading a file onto your computer, or streaming a video onto your computer monitor or TV at your fingertips. See "Get Digital Media in Two Formats."

TIP

On the taskbar tray in Windows is a Speakers icon. This is a great shortcut to configuring your audio setup. If you hear no sound while playing music, right-click the icon and then choose **Playback Devices**, because it's possible that Windows is not correctly identifying the type of speakers you've installed. For example, if you have headphones plugged into your system and they don't seem to work, check the list of Sound devices. If, for example, Speakers is highlighted, click **Headphones**, then click **Set Default**, and then click **OK**.

because of tax and shipping, and easy to do. In either case, you'll need software to play the content—some comes with Windows, or you can download free or for-cost other software.

BUY A PHYSICAL ALBUM

1. You've found a physical album by conducting a search at, for example, Amazon.com.

2. If you don't have an account at Amazon, you'll need to create one.

3. Choose the album you want, add it to your shopping cart, proceed to checkout, and then choose the shipping method that fits the time you have to meet that deadline with the dance club and what you feel like spending for shipping.

DOWNLOAD MUSIC

1. You've found the album, or singles, for example, at Amazon.com.

2. Navigate Amazon's store to the MP3 downloads area, type in the search field for the genre of music you want, and then click the **Play** button to listen to a short snippet of a song that appeals to you before you buy. Music stores used to have listening rooms, and this is the digital equivalent. Alternatively, certain albums are offered as a digital download, so if the content of an entire album appeals to you, you add the album and not individual songs to your shopping cart.

3. Add the songs to your shopping cart, and then use an existing account (or create a new one) to buy the songs. Proceed to the checkout area, and when you've completed the transaction, Amazon sends you the MP3 digital files to your computer.

8

GORDON'S HEARING IMPROVES WITH MP3S

I've been collecting record albums almost all my life, replacing worn-out favorites with tapes, and then music CDs. Finally, I began buying replacement songs as MP3 downloads to my iPod a few years ago, and I couldn't believe my ears! I thought I'd been losing some of my hearing, but the problem proved to be old vinyl 33s and 45s. Digitally remastered recordings are restoring some of the quality in Beatles and Rolling Stones songs, and they're usually less than a dollar to download from the iTunes Store.

In the past few years, I've been able to reorganize my music collection like never before, arrange mixes of my all-time favorites, and put a collection on my iPod that would take an apple crate to store otherwise, no less play back. I think I might retire my record changer soon, not only because MP3s sound so much better than LPs, but because it's getting impossible to find replacement needles.

Gordon J., 56, Washington

4. Decide on the order of the songs you've purchased, and then use Windows (or other) software to burn a music CD for your dance club.

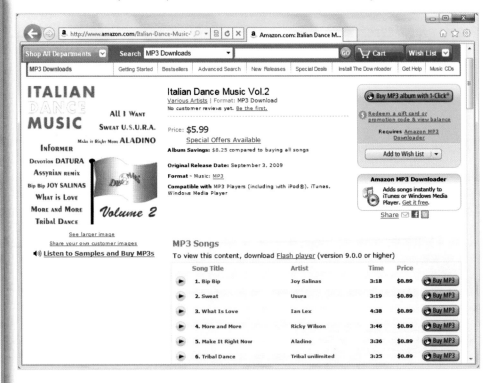

Set Up Audio on Your PC

You need a software player on your computer to listen to music, and happily, Windows comes with a utility called Windows Media Player, which plays video *and* music. Say you have a music CD you want to listen to on your computer: you push the button on the optical drive to open the tray, put a music CD in, and then close the tray. Your chances are good on a Windows PC that the AutoPlay dialog box opens automatically.

Figure 8-1: **The AutoPlay dialog box in Windows can be configured to automatically use specific software to play audio and video files, and to view photos and other digital content.**

The first time you use an optical or flash memory drive that contains digital media files, Windows displays the AutoPlay dialog box, which asks you to choose which software you want to use to play your media. These choices are specific to a kind of media (audio CD, DVD movies, pictures on a flash drive) and the physical drive or device. In this example, Figure 8-1 shows the AutoPlay options for what Windows recognizes as a music CD. Windows Media Player is offered as a possible playback software for the CD's music tracks, with alternative programs that can play digital music, if you have installed other programs. Some software is easier to use than Windows Media Player, while others offer more features.

CHOOSE AUTOPLAY SETTINGS FOR A SINGLE DRIVE

If you want to simply play a music CD using your favorite computer software and not be interrupted by the AutoPlay options all the time, here's how to configure AutoPlay to load your music CD in Windows Media Player every time you insert a music CD or plug a USB flash drive with digital music into your computer:

- On the AutoPlay dialog box, click to check or uncheck the **Always Do This For** check box. Leave this box unchecked if you want to choose each time you play a CD or DVD. Check the check box if you want the choice you make now to be the automatic choice—Windows will no longer ask you; it will just start playing the digital media using the player you choose in the dialog.

- Click the software or action of your choice in the Audio CD Options section. The dialog will close, and in a moment the selected player will open with your content loaded and playing.

- If you want to do something other than playing the files (such as copying them), click **View More AutoPlay Options In Control Panel** to open the AutoPlay Control Panel. In the Control Panel AutoPlay dialog box, for each media or device type, click the down arrow, and then click the option you want. For example, for the Audio CD, you might click **Play Audio CD Using Windows Media Player**.

LAUNCH AUTOPLAY MANUALLY

If you insert a disk and the AutoPlay dialog box doesn't appear *and* your media doesn't start to play in a few moments, this indicates that AutoPlay has been disabled. You can enable it on a one-time basis by following these steps:

1. Click **Start** to open the Start menu. Click **Computer** in the right pane of the Start menu.

2. Right-click the drive in the Devices With Removable Storage section of the Computer Explorer window containing the CD.

3. From the context menu, click **Open AutoPlay**. The AutoPlay dialog opens for that drive or device where you can make your choices.

Tour Windows Media Player

Windows Media Player is capable of playing not only a music CD, but also an MP3 file on your computer, a disk, or from an Internet site, in addition to videos. Let's take a look at the features and options of this free media player.

LEARN ABOUT VIEWS AND FEATURES IN MEDIA PLAYER

When your pointer is over the dialog box, the controls on the bottom of the Media Player look and work like your familiar home entertainment DVD players or an audio cassette player. The stop, play, next, and previous song buttons (with music CDs) are easy to discern. There are more features for enjoying your music albums;

TIP

To manually play a music CD when AutoPlay is disabled, click **Start**, choose **Computer**, and then double-click the letter of the drive containing the music CD. The player you've specified in the Control Panel's AutoPlay dialog box appears and plays your music CD.

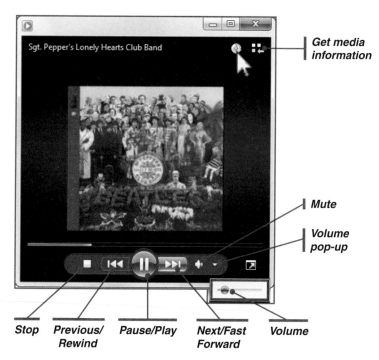

Get media information

Mute

Volume pop-up

Stop   Previous/Rewind   Pause/Play   Next/Fast Forward   Volume

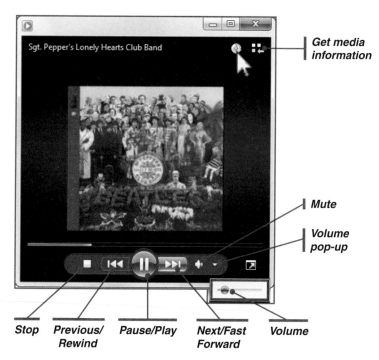

NOTE

The volume control in Windows Media Player applies only to the volume of the music you're currently playing. It doesn't affect system sounds or the general sound level of your computer. For global control over audio volume, click the **Speakers** icon on the taskbar's tray.

as you can see in this illustration, here are what the Player's elements do when in Now Playing mode.

- **Pause/Play** The single large button at bottom center switches the playback from pause to play.

- **Next/Forward** When you play a digital album, this button skips the album over to the next track. However, when you load a single digital song (such as an MP3 file), clicking and holding this button fast-forwards the song.

- **Previous/Rewind** This performs the opposite function of the Next/Forward button.

- **Stop** There's very little functional difference between Stop and Pause when music is playing. When you click **Stop**, however, it's easier to load a different song or go directly to a different track on a digital album.

- **Volume pop-up** Clicking this button causes the volume slider to appear.

- **Volume** Drag to the left to decrease the output; dragging right increases the volume.

- **Mute** Clicking this button mutes the sound but doesn't stop the music from playing. Clicking again restores the audio.

- **Rip CD** *Ripped* has become part of digital audio vernacular for "copy." You can copy the contents of a music CD to hard disk (it typically takes about 15 minutes), and then play back the music tracks from disk in any order, and even burn your mix of any music to a blank music CD.

- **Drag to fast forward and rewind** The blue strip below the album art is an interactive element. When a song is playing, drag left or right on it to move to any part of the song.

- **Switch to Library** By default, you use the Now Playing view of the Media Player. Clicking **Switch To Library** reveals a wealth of additional features for organizing collections of music and selecting from different media sources.

Work with Media Player's Library View

The Library view of Windows Media Player is where you can view all the tracks on a music CD album, identify songs if they are not labeled as data on the music CD (older CDs don't have this music track metadata), and perform other tasks. You can also make a collection of favorite songs and sync a collection or music CD with a portable device such as an MP3 player.

To make Media Player easier to use, reveal its menu—commands can be more easily accessed and Media Player's menu is hidden by default. Click **Organize**, click **Layout**, and then click **Show Menu Bar**.

Archive Your Music CDs

The easiest way to copy your music onto a portable digital device is to allow Windows Media Player to sync a device with Media Player's Library. Part of your collection, all of it, or just your favorites from a music CD can be duplicated to hard disk from an optical drive. Here's how to rip a music CD:

1. In the Library view, make sure any changes to the data you've applied (such as title and artist obtained from a Media Player search) is finalized. Choose **Tools** and then choose **Apply Media Information Changes**. (If your Tools menu doesn't show, click **Organize**, click **Layout**, and click **Show Menu Bar**.)

2. If there are songs you don't want ripped to your hard disk, clear the check box(es) next to the title(s). On the toolbar, click **Rip CD**. If the music CD has copy protection, you'll next see a dialog that you need to click a check box indicating that you understand the music is copy-protected. Then each checked song is copied to Windows Music Library in a compressed yet high-fidelity file format.

3. Wait until all the songs have a legend to their right that says "Ripped to Library."

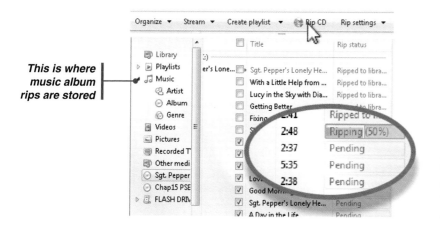

This is where music album rips are stored

At any time now, you can remove your music CD from the optical drive and put it back in its physical sleeve or jewel case. You're done and can listen to a copy of your album on your computer now.

Create a Playlist

If you have ripped music CDs (see "Archive Your Music CDs") you'll soon have several music CDs available on your Music Library on your hard disk. You're free to play any and all of your albums using Windows Media Player or other playback software, and can listen to an album in any order of songs, skip songs entirely, or add songs from other albums to a *playlist*. Your playlist can have as many or as few songs as you like. Here's how to create a playlist:

1. In the Library view of Windows Media Player, click **Create Playlist**, and an entry called "Untitled Playlist" appears below Playlists in the left column of the Library view. Immediately type a name in the field that's open for editing, because if this field is deselected, the temporary entry will disappear and you'll have to click **Create Playlist** again. Double-click the name of your new playlist in the left column to open a new, blank area at right where you can drag music files. Alternatively, click **Clear List** (right column, menu item toward the top) if you want to clear any unsaved playlists in the right column. The right column then displays the text "Drag items here to create a playlist."

2. Double-click to open your music library, as shown in Figure 8-2: doing this reveals thumbnails of album covers in the center pane, along with individual tracks listed to their right. You can sort large collections by clicking **Artist**, **Album**, or **Genre**, but only if the albums in your library have labels.

3. To add a track to your playlist, drag the track's title to the playlist area. To copy an entire album, drag the album thumbnail into the playlist area.

Your computer music

Save list after making all edits and entries

Create a new playlist

Type the name of your playlist

Displays all your ripped music

Shuffle

Repeat

Drag a track to add it to your playlist

Figure 8-2: *Create a playlist for burning to a blank CD, and then add songs to your playlist.*

4. If there's a song you don't want in your playlist, after it's copied to the playlist from the entire album, right-click the title and choose **Remove From List**.

5. If you have a song on your hard drive that's not in your Media Player Library, locate it on your hard disk first. Then choose **File**, choose **Manage Libraries**, and choose **Music** (if your File menu doesn't show, click **Organize**, click **Layout**, and then **Show Menu Bar**). In the Music Libraries Locations dialog box, click **Add**, and then navigate to the hard disk folder that contains the song(s). Click the folder name, and then click **Include Folder**. Click **OK** to change the library's contents. To see the new contents, click the music item in the left column, scroll down to the bottom of the center pane, and view the contents of that folder. Drag the title of the song to your playlist.

6. You can right-click the playlist and use the context menu to move the order of a song up or down, but it might be easier to use the mouse to drag a song up or down on the list.

7. After adding the songs you want to make up your playlist—you can make up a playlist for any occasion, so be choosy about any particular playlist mix—click **Save List** to finalize the playlist.

Burn and Sync a Playlist

You can make mixes of different songs and burn them to a blank CD or copy them to a memory card for playback on mobile devices. The term *sync* means to first duplicate files—in this case, music files—to a different device. Then, as you change and update your music collection, the device to which you sync updates your playlists every time you plug the device into a computer port.

Much of the digital commercial music today permits copies of music on a limited number of devices, so you're within the license agreement to sync music files. Copying songs for friends, however, is *not* part of a license agreement, so steer clear of this act!

You might want to mix up a music CD with tunes you've bought online, digital music that was given away for free (Amazon frequently offers free Christmas music), and selected cuts from the music CDs you've ripped to your Windows Music collection. Let's say you have several music CDs successfully ripped to your computer, you have a few MP3 files, and you want to put a collection together on CD.

1. If you want to make a music CD with a playlist on it, a music CD is capable of holding about 76 minutes of music. A favorite playlist of yours might exceed 76 minutes—approximately 24 three- to four-minute songs will fit on a CD. You can copy *some* of a saved playlist to a new playlist, however, without a lot of fuss. First, choose **Create Playlist** on the Windows Media Player toolbar, and then give the playlist a unique name such as <u>For the car</u>.

2. Press **CTRL** and click individual songs to select them from an existing playlist open in the right pane.

3. Drag the selected files to on top of the new playlist title in the left pane, as shown in Figure 8-3.

4. Click the name of the playlist in the left pane and then look at the contents of the playlist in the right pane. You can see how many minutes the playlist runs to the right of Disk 1. If it's less than 78 minutes, you're good to go.

5. Put a blank CD in the optical drive, and then close the door.

6. Click **Start Burn**. The process takes about ten minutes.

Play length   Drag into new playlist

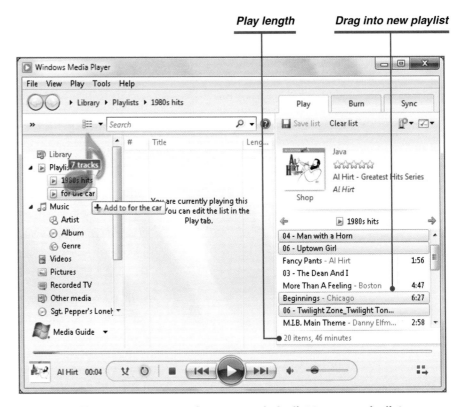

Figure 8-3: *You can copy songs from a saved playlist to a new playlist.*

LORI DELIGHTS IN DIGITAL MUSIC

I don't have the time to get out to one of the music or electronics stores to buy an album I enjoy or I've heard on the radio and would like to hear more of. I was happy to discover that music CDs aren't the only way to buy new or older music; Amazon offers an extensive collection of pop and classical music, and it's right there at my fingertips. A friend had told me that Amazon wasn't just for buying books, and that prompted me to check out all the different departments on their website.

What a pleasant surprise! Not only is a lot of the music cheaper than buying a music CD at the store, but I can listen to what I've purchased in only a minute or two.

I found I was also able to send an MP3 album as a gift when I ordered online. I took my son completely by surprise when I gifted him with an album by one of his favorite groups for his birthday. He says he prefers digital downloads anyway, because all he does is sync his music to his mobile player from his computer and he's good to go.

Lori H., Pennsylvania

7. Media Player signals you when the burn is done and that the disk was successfully written. Try playing the disk in your computer now to make sure it plays correctly instead of going on a trip and discovering the CD won't play in your car.

Broaden Your Multimedia Experience

Your computer didn't come with every piece of software on Earth, nor did it come with utilities, plug-ins, or all the helper applications you might want, so you can browse the Web for interesting videos, podcasts, and other media. There are two categories of programs you'll want to investigate:

- **Media players**   These applications download and install various media types to your computer system; they enable you to play media that can't be accessed using the "base set" of tools that came with your operating system. For example, Windows does not support Apple QuickTime movies; you can download a QuickTime player from Apple, however, that works within Windows.

- **Web browser plug-ins**   These small applications work with your web browser to provide online content that cannot be displayed without a little help. No web browser comes complete with every plug-in to, for example, play flash videos or read an Acrobat PDF document online.

Choose Which Programs to Install

Bulk installation services offer many different kinds of programs that can be included in the install bundle. The following list is made up of digital- and multimedia-related programs you might want to download and install, with a brief explanation why you'd like them. If you choose not to use a bulk installer, you can go to the software

QUICKSTEPS

ADDING A PLAYLIST TO A MOBILE DEVICE

Suppose your grandchildren chipped in for your birthday and bought you a flash USB MP3 player. And they're snickering because they presume you'll need their help loading it up with your favorite tunes. Boy, are they in for a surprise after you follow these steps.

1. Insert the USB plug on the MP3 player into an available USB port on your computer. It might take Windows a moment to recognize the device, but you'll eventually see a message icon in the taskbar tray reporting that a USB device has been found.

2. In Media Player, click the playlist you want to sync with the MP3 device.

3. Click the **Sync** tab. The device is listed, and you can see how much space is available on the flash USB device. Flash USB MP3 players come in different capacities; a 4GB model, for example, can hold approximately 500 songs, probably enough space to copy your entire library to your player.

4. Click the **Sync** tab, and in a very short time, Media Player signals that the music files are synced. You can remove the device from the USB port, turn it on, put your headphones on, and enjoy your music anywhere for hours.

company's site and then download and install the software manually. Here are the current addresses where software can be obtained:

- **Mozilla Firefox**, a web browser that takes advantage of many advanced features that web developers like to use on their sites. *mozilla.com*

- **Apple iTunes (and QuickTime)**, useful for subscribing and listening to podcasts; necessary for managing media used with an iPod, iTouch, iPhone; and a gateway to the iTunes store. QuickTime is also installed when you choose to download iTunes. *apple.com/quicktime/download*

- **VLC**, a free, open-source media player, this can be used to play just about everything, from DVDs, to music CDs, streaming media, and flash videos. *videolan.org*

- **Google Picasa** is a desktop-based photo editing and album software that makes it easy to optionally upload photos for sharing to your personal 1GB of free storage space on Picasa Web Albums. *picasa.google.com*

- **Evernote** clips images and text, similar to a screen capture utility, but it can store your visual and text data in the "cloud" and also on your computer. Easy to use, Evernote comes in both a free and a paid version. This is a terrific utility for capturing online recipes, news stories, and anything that is displayed on your computer screen from files on your hard disk. *evernote.com*

- **CutePDF** is a free program that installs as if it were a physical printer attached to your computer. When you "print" to CutePDF from any Windows application, an electronic document in PDF format is created that can be read by Acrobat Reader and other applications. Essentially, CutePDF is an alternative to buying Adobe's Acrobat Pro. *cutepdf.com/products/CutePDF/writer.asp*

- **Assorted runtimes** are categories of software that allow you to view online videos, play games, and do things like view interactive photo galleries. They're also called plug-ins, and as mentioned earlier, they're usually web browser plug-ins that help the browser of your choice to play media that's not directly supported by it.

- **Flash**, which is available for both Internet Explorer and other browsers, lets you watch videos. Other online video parlors use flash video encoding as well, and you can't watch the media online without this web browser plug-in. *get.adobe.com/flashplayer*

- **Microsoft Silverlight** is Microsoft's answer to Adobe's Flash format. You'll increasingly see Silverlight media on the Web in the years to come, so you need this plug-in to watch Silverlight media. *microsoft.com/getsilverlight*

- **Java** and Flash are both used to build small programs that can run from your desktop or online. You need the Java engine in order to make any of these programs "play." *java.com*

Install Many Media Player Files

Ninite is an online service that makes collecting additional applications for enjoying all sorts of digital content painless and fast. Ninite ensures that the appropriate version of the software for your computer and operating system is installed. It *only* installs the software you picked, and not any third-party toolbars or other junk.

1. With an open Internet connection, use your Internet browser to go to ninite.com.

2. Based on the information in the Choosing Which Programs To Install section, click to put a check next to the programs you want to install. Don't click **Get Installer** until you've completed all your choices.

3. Click **Get Installer** now. You're redirected to a page where the icons for the programs you've chosen are listed at the top. Click the hyperlink **Click Here To Download Your Installer** to proceed.

4. You have a choice to run the installers or to save the installation programs to hard disk. Because these free programs are updating

TIP

If you own an iPod or other mobile Apple device, the simplest way to sync MP3 files on your computer to your mobile device is with iTunes, a free desktop player and organizer for the Mac and Windows available at apple.com.

all the time, you probably don't need to save the installers, so if you have about 15 minutes to dedicate to installing the programs now, click **Run**. You are prompted for installation locations and preferences, and when the installations are finished, you'll have new program file listings on the Start menu and the installation files are usually deleted from the temporary location on your hard disk.

Tune into Podcasts

A *podcast* is an ongoing collection of digital media files available much like TV or radio episodes and often downloaded through web syndication. A podcast can also be delivered as online streaming media. You do not have to own an Apple iPod to enjoy podcasts.

In the following steps, let's assume that you downloaded and installed the iTunes player and that you have an interest in some of the ongoing music features on National Public Radio online. The steps will walk you through how to locate the series—which in this case is a podcast—how to subscribe to it, and then how to play your episodes at your convenience using iTunes.

1. Using the search engine you favor (Google, Bing, and so on) in your web browser, type <u>npr podcasts</u> into the Search text box. When the results are displayed, click the **NPR Podcast Directory** link.

2. For this example, pretend you're interested in listening to all types of music: scroll down the page and then under **More Podcasts**, click **NPR Music Podcasts**, and then click **All Songs Considered**.

3. The All Songs Considered link takes you to a page where you decide which software plays the podcast. Let's choose iTunes in this example, but note that Microsoft's Zune is also offered for podcast playback, and you can even download a podcast as an MP3 file and then play it using Media Player. Click the **iTunes** button.

TIP

It's more of a chore to subscribe to podcasts manually than to use a "podcatcher" setup such as the one iTunes provides, but you are not *obligated* to use iTunes or a special online utility such as a personal start page to enjoy podcasts. Using Windows Internet Explorer, if you land on a page that offers podcasts, the RSS button on the toolbar will become active, and clicking the button displays a dialog box. In the Subscribe To This Feed dialog box, you check **Add To Favorites Bar**, and Internet Explorer now features a button on the Favorites bar you can use to access the podcast series you chose.

4. In the Launch Application dialog, click **iTunes**, and then click **OK**.

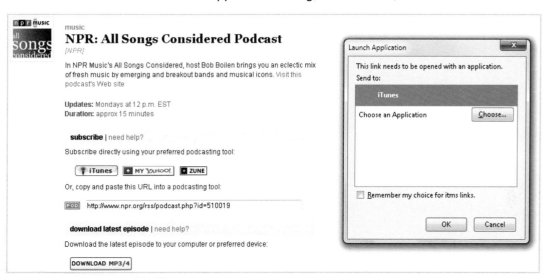

5. In a few moments you'll see the entire series listed in iTunes. At the left, you can see that the collection is listed in the iTunes Store and not under "podcasts." However, iTunes' Store carries free and retail items; you can clearly see here that the subscription is free, so go ahead and click **Subscribe Free**.

6. Click the podcast entry on the left column, and then double-click the thumbnail image to see and listen to all the episodes within "All Songs Considered."

Congratulations! You've just learned to tune into one of the largest media libraries in the world.

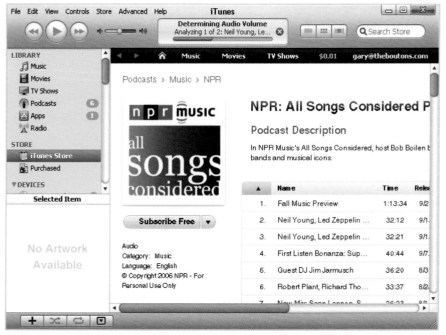

Listen to Online Music Stations

If you care to listen to a wide selection of music, or only classical or blues, "web radio" is your ticket to playing music from your computer, music you might not own. There are at least two ways to find a web audio station to suit your tastes.

- Browse available stations using Apple's iTunes. This is by far the easiest solution to getting your style of music playing all day. Click **Radio** in the Library area to reveal music styles organized by general category. Then click the triangle at the left of a music style to expand the list, and finally, double-click the station to begin playing music. Figure 8-4 shows iTunes playing music from Adagio FM. The quality you hear on web radio depends only on the quality of your system's speakers.

- Use your web browser to conduct a search for your style of music played on web radio stations. For example, if you're into classical music, go to classicalwebcast.com/usa.htm, which is an excellent index of classical stations in North America alone. Some stations use flash as a web device for playing content, while others use Windows Media Player.

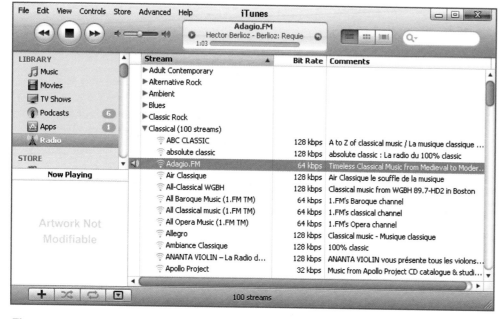

Figure 8-4: *Play your desktop iTunes application like you would a traditional radio.*

Regardless of how you choose to play online radio stations, the media is *streaming* (broadcast live, not permanently downloaded to your computer), so you cannot save or pause the music to your computer.

Watch Video on Your Computer

Watching video on your computer can be essential when you want to learn something and instructions are only available as video content. As with digital audio, video can come to your desktop in two different ways.

- You can put a commercial DVD into your computer's optical drive, and Windows Media Player and third-party players such as FLV Player will play the DVD. Although it's not quite as comfortable gathering around your PC to watch a movie as it is in the family room on your TV set, the video (and lots of times the audio) is of a much better fidelity than when playing media on a TV set's DVD player.
- You can surf the Web for online videos.

The approach of watching a commercial movie with your computer's DVD optical drive really requires no further explanation beyond "it can be done." Let's move on to watching videos online in the following section.

Find and Watch a YouTube Video

YouTube, which is owned by the search engine giant Google, is the repository of everything from soft-core video clips and commercial television shows, to educational video how-to's, to independent small movie makes, to just plain silly home movies of pet tricks and outrageous home accidents.

Let's suppose that you've heard of the famous photographer Ron Roesler and that he has a video of his photography work on YouTube. Here's how to search for any of Ron's work and to watch the video:

1. In your Internet browser, type youtube.com in the URL field, and then press **ENTER** to go to YouTube's website.

> **NOTE**
>
> YouTube is moving toward converting posted videos to MPEG-4 file format, but there are easily millions of older video posts that are displayed in Adobe's Flash format. Flash files will not play on Apple mobile devices such as the iPad, and they will fail to display on computer screens unless your web browser has Adobe's Flash plug-in. The plug-in is free and takes a mere second or two to download and install.

2. In the Search field, type <u>Ron Roesler</u> in this example, and then press **ENTER** or click **Search**. A list of videos credited to Ron Roesler are listed. Click the thumbnail you want to watch.

3. In the viewing area of YouTube, there are several features and controls. Figure 8-5 displays the specific controls explained next. Some of the controls may seem dim until you place your pointer over them.

   - **Play/Pause**   Use this on-screen control to play or pause a playing video, much like you play and pause Windows Media Player.

   - **Volume flyout**   Click this on-screen element to reveal the volume slider.

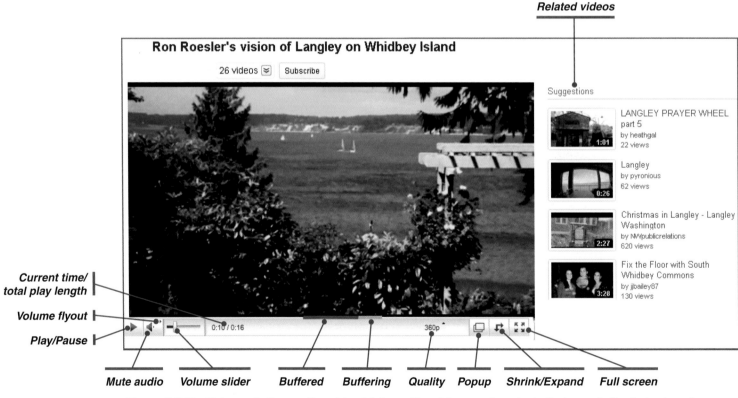

Figure 8-5: *YouTube and other online video bistros offer videos and controls that are similar in look and function to a TV set DVD player.*

- **Mute audio**   Click once to mute the playing video; click a second time to hear the video's audio track. Some videos on YouTube do not have an audio track.

- **Volume slider**   Controls the *local* volume of YouTube videos, but has nothing to do with your computer's speaker volume setting. If the audio is too faint, even at full volume on YouTube, try increasing Windows speaker volume.

- **Current time/total play length**   This area below the video tells you first how far you are into the video and then how long the total play length is.

- **Buffered**   The red line below the video tells you how much of the total video is buffered to your computer system. Because playing videos is processor-intensive, videos on YouTube and other video bistros are presented as streaming media, and the amount of buffered data tells you when in the video and how much of the video is in your system in a temporary file.

- **Buffering**   The lighter red line to the right of the buffered line tells you how much video is *in the process* of being buffered. If there is no light red line, pause the video and wait until more buffering indicator shows. If after 30 seconds there is still no buffering indication, this is probably because too many users are online watching video and YouTube's streaming media server is overtaxed. The solution is to bookmark the video in your browser and visit it later.

- **Quality**   You Tube offers different quality/sizes of the same video. Click this area, for example, if 360p looks too coarse; try 420p or higher if offered. If you're watching a video on a mobile device and the video halts or stutters, try the 240p setting for a smaller video dimension that streams faster.

- **Popup**   Clicking this button forces the video to play in its own browser window instead of from the website's page.

- **Shrink/Expand**   Click this button to expand the playback window and get rid of the related videos list at the right of the page.

- **Full screen**   Click this button to expand the video to fill your monitor.

- **Related videos**   This column contains thumbnails you can click to play that are compiled by a YouTube server, based on your search criteria.

JOHN WATCHES OLD TV RERUNS

Frankly, the television shows I used to watch in the 1960s weren't all that good in the first place. I won't name names, but you know: all the cowboy series, and the dumber-than-dumb family who was supposed to be your next-door neighbors. But recently, I became a little nostalgic for the reruns, especially since television seems to be getting worse and not better. I learned that a lot of the old TV shows were free to watch online, while other shows I could buy as a boxed set…I can even do some comparison pricing online.

To come clean, there are some shows I've seen you couldn't pay me to watch a second time, while others I still get a charge out of. The nice thing is that the programs are still mostly free when you watch them on the Web, and some places offer links to other shows, so it's not hard to get your fill of television watching with only a few clicks.

I can still wait for some of the better, current programs to come around to free broadcast on the Web, because a friend of mine told me he'd found a whole bunch of recent shows on a Torrent site. He made the mistake of trying to download the pirated shows, and not only did he not get to see them, he had to take his PC in to get viruses removed from it. Web television is great, like all things, in moderation.

John K. 76, New York

Other video bistros you can try include Vimeo, Flickr, and Metacafe—if you conduct a web browser search with the keyword "online videos," you'll surely hit pay dirt.

Watch a TV Program Online

TV programs that were aired last night, as well as episodes originally broadcast 50 years ago, are all out there, and your success in locating them all depends on what keywords you use in searching with your web browser.

There are a few different types of "web TV":

- **News broadcasts**   Occasionally, you can watch a live television broadcast, but for the most part, news videos are "canned." CNN (cnn.com) carries a combination of new stories in text and videos, and the news is usually up-to-the-minute. Other sites that carry a combination of news, special interest stories, and politics are MSNBC (MSNBC.com), Yahoo! News (news.yahoo.com), and for international news, there's BBC.com, to name but a few. On historic events, such as the last presidential inauguration, you'll often find the coverage live on sites such as NYT.com, the online version of the *New York Times*.

- **Last night's TV**   You can watch last night's episode of Jon Stewart and Steve Colbert at thedailyshow.com. You can also watch highlights of "The Tonight Show," "Charlie Rose," and snippets of other television broadcasts, but you may find that the owners of this video content limit your entertainment to five to ten minutes of what the programmers believe are the best segments. You need to just search for the official sites and try it.

- **Television classics**   You can watch online classic episodes of *The Twilight Zone*, *Rawhide*, and other adventures and sitcoms from generations ago. Some past TV programs were never specifically copyrighted for digital broadcast, and users who have taped and digitized these shows legally post them on private websites and occasionally on YouTube. Websites such as Hulu.com, a joint venture among television broadcasters, offer some free content, but increasingly are charging a subscription fee for more recent televised programs. There are also licensed distributors of past television shows. AOL TV (television.aol.com), a subsidiary of Time-Warner, has a huge playlist of past television shows, for example. The media is streaming exactly like YouTube, and the playlist is amortized by advertisements, much like broadcast television. AOL TV has a daughter website, Slashcontrol.com, that features complete seasons from 1960s shows, including every episode of *Gilligan's Island* if you'd like to take more than a three-hour tour.

Access Online Books and Publications

There's a lot of free text content on the Web if you prefer the printed word over moving pictures and talking heads. Authors and columnists are still cranking out virtual pages of manuscripts, and you can find anything from recipes to government forms you can download when you have the appropriate reading software.

Use E-books

Electronic books come in different file formats and require different reading programs. After much disagreement between content distributors and providers, the electronic document arena has shaken down to three major players—ePub, Kindle, and Adobe PDF—with several others withering and likely destined eventually to disappear.

FIND ePUB DOCUMENTS

ePub, used for mobile devices, can be found in several locations. One of the largest open-source initiatives is the ePub standard. Project Gutenberg (gutenberg.org/wiki/Main_Page) offers more than 32,000 free books in several different file formats, and one of

QUICKSTEPS

SETTING UP FIREFOX TO DISPLAY ePUB

Think about electronic books and how convenient they can be; there's no trip to the public library on a rainy day, the environment is spared trees used to process paper, and your family bookshelf never needs dusting. Here is a way to download some ePub books using Firefox.

1. Install Firefox as an additional web browser to Internet Explorer, launch Firefox, and then type addons.mozilla.org/en-US/firefox/addon/45281/ in the address bar; press **ENTER**.

2. Click **Add To Firefox**, and then click **Install Now** in the Software Installation dialog box.

3. In a moment, the Add-ons dialog box appears. Click **Restart Firefox** to launch Firefox again, this time with the add-on (plug-in) activated. When Firefox is restarted, you may be offered an opportunity to find updates. Click **Find Updates** to do this.

Continued . . .

them is ePub. See "Setting Up Firefox to Display ePub" QuickSteps to read or retrieve a copy of a document from gutenberg.org, using Mozilla Firefox to load an ePub reader as a plug-in. Another source is ePub Books (epubbooks.com/ebook-readers). This website offers free ePub-formatted books that are in the public domain, copyright free, or the author has given permission for the e-books to be available.

USE ADOBE DIGITAL EDITIONS READER

The Adobe Digital Editions is a desktop application—it's designed around the Flash engine, so many mobile devices cannot use the program. Reading an ePub you've saved in Adobe Digital Editions is as hard as dragging the ePub's file icon into the reading program. Adobe Digital Editions has controls for increasing text size and moving between pages and chapters just like Firefox's add-on for ePub reading, and if you want to copy a passage from a book, highlight text with your cursor, press **CTRL+C**, and then in a document using Microsoft Word or a text editor, press **CTRL+V** and you have your copied text.

GET KINDLE SOFTWARE FROM AMAZON

Kindle electronic books are part of the Kindle Reader offering by Amazon; the books are electronic, many can be ordered online at Amazon.com, and many electronic books are free to download. The Kindle Reader, like several other handheld devices, is proprietary. It's not a true computer in the sense that you can't run all commercial applications such as Microsoft Excel. Kindle Reader was designed to do two things: download books you've ordered and display them. Although the Kindle electronic book file format is proprietary and not open-source, you *don't* have to own a Kindle Reader to read Kindle books.

Suppose you're into mystery novels: Arthur Conan Doyle and his Sherlock Holmes novels would probably be at the top of your list.

![clock icon] **QUICKSTEPS**

SETTING UP FIREFOX TO DISPLAY ePUB *(Continued)*

4. To try out the new ePub reader feature, type gutenberg.org/wiki/Main_Page in the address bar and then press **ENTER** to see the main directory of books in ePub and other file formats you can read. To test how this works, type United States Constitution in the Title Words search field and press **ENTER**.

5. Scroll down the list; toward the bottom you'll see a text link "The United States Constitution." Click this link.

   You'll see many different file formats for this document, but what you seek is the EPUB link. Click it, and you'll see in the left pane an index to the document and the document itself in the right pane.

6. Click **File** and click **Save** to save the ePub document to your hard drive. When you do this, you don't have to connect to the Internet the next time you want to read the publication. Adobe Systems offers a free offline reader that can handle the ePub file format: go to adobe.com/products/digitaleditions.

The *Adventures of Sherlock Holmes* is available for free to download at Amazon.com. At Amazon, you can find and install a Kindle Reader software program for your computer, your Blackberry mobile device, the Apple iPad, or Google's Android. If you'd like to tuck into a spell-binding mystery in the next ten minutes, follow these next steps to install a Kindle Reader for your computer and download a book:

1. If you have not done so already, open an account with Amazon.

2. In your web browser, type Amazon.com into the address bar. Beneath the Shop All Departments area, choose **Kindle** and then choose **Free Kindle Reading Apps**.

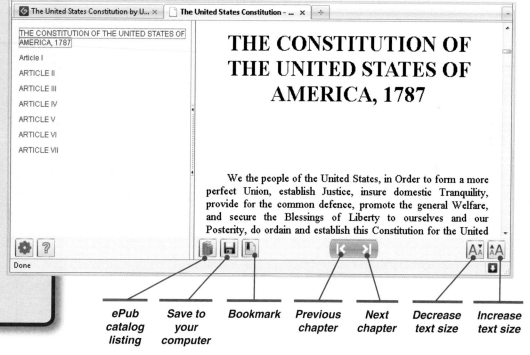

ePub catalog listing | Save to your computer | Bookmark | Previous chapter | Next chapter | Decrease text size | Increase text size

3. Click your device type. You can choose a mobile device or a Mac or PC. For purposes of this illustration, we are using a Windows PC. If your computer firewall is working properly, you need to click over the faint yellow bar (which then turns blue) and then click **Download Now**.

4. In the next dialog box, click **Save** to save a binary file. A Downloads dialog box will appear. Double-click the name of the download, in our illustration, KindleForPC-Installer.exe. Once it's been downloaded, double-click the EXE file to install the Kindle Reader application.

5. When installation is finished, a registration box appears, and you need to fill in your account number at Amazon along with your password. Click **Register**. If you don't already have an Amazon account—which is good for *all* merchandise and not just books—click the **Create One Now** hyperlink text in the registration box.

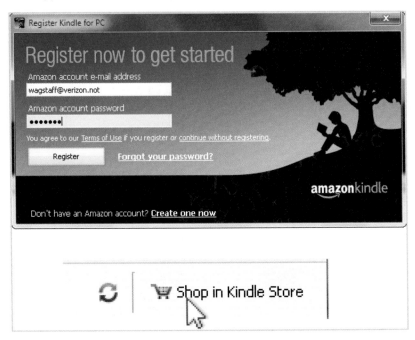

6. You can now browse for a retail or a free Kindle book. Click the **Shop In Kindle Store** link at top right.

7. The easiest way to browse the free Kindle books is by typing <u>free Kindle book list</u> in the search field. Click **Go**, and a list of free downloads appears.

8. Select a title by clicking the book thumbnail—which takes you to a page where you can download your electronic merchandise—and then click **Buy Now With 1-Click**, as shown in Figure 8-6. Don't worry; you're not "buying" anything because clearly the amount value for the book is $0.00. One-click ordering saves you the time of going through credit card validation for a free item.

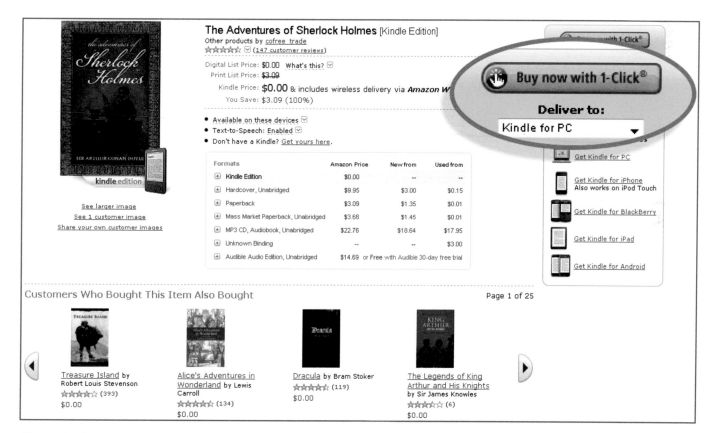

Figure 8-6: **You are downloading free content from Amazon, although the button mentions "buy."**

9. Once you've clicked the one-click button, you'll get a thank-you screen. Click **Go To Kindle For PC** to launch your Kindle software on your computer and display the book you've downloaded.

10. In the Kindle For PC Reader, your book is listed on a reading pane. Double-click the book icon to load the book in the Kindle Reader. After you have downloaded other books, click **Home** and then press **F5** to refresh your list.

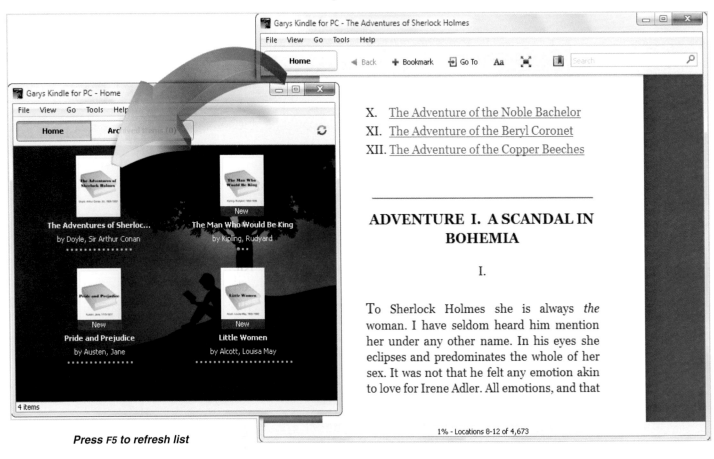

Press F5 to refresh list

FIND KINDLE E-BOOKS ON YOUR PC

The books you download from Amazon are stored in a folder on your computer. To find them in Windows 7, click **Start**, choose **Documents**, choose **My Documents**, choose **My Kindle Content**, and there they are. Clicking one of these documents will launch the Kindle Reader.

Share Books Between Devices

A copy of your own book is also online at Amazon, and this leads to some wonderful reading possibilities. It is retained in its current status, including bookmarks, highlighting and notes, and pages read. Both free and purchased Kindle e-books can be read and shared between any or all of the following devices:

- Any computer running Windows XP or newer
- Any computer running Mac OS 10.5 or newer
- Any iPhone, iPod Touch, or iPad
- Many Blackberry and Android smartphone models
- The Kindle wireless reading device

When you launch the Kindle Reader on your chosen device and have an open Internet connection, the software automatically logs you into your Kindle account. All your devices have immediate access to the exact same books, and each device knows exactly which book you were last reading and where you left off. Here's how to sync a copy of your favorite book you haven't finished reading on your desktop computer but you want to continue reading on a mobile device while on a trip:

1. Open the Kindle for PC Reader. After using the reader once, you do not see the Archived Items tab, so click **Home**.
2. Click the **Archived Items** tab to view the books you already own.

NOTE

Adobe PDF file format is often used for creating short books and other documents. See Chapter 6 for details on how to download the Acrobat Reader.

3. Click one of the books to download it to your device so that you can access and read the book even if you no longer have an active Internet connection.

4. If you were reading this same book on another one of your devices and were farther along, a dialog box would open, asking you if you want go to the farthest read page (on any device). Click **Yes** to pick up your story where you left off. If you've used the Kindle Reader previously on this device, it will automatically open and display the last book you were reading.

5. If you want to read a different book than the currently displayed one, click **Go To** and then **Home** beneath the menu bar, or press **CTRL+ALT+H**, and click the book you want to read.

Like any piece of technology, digital media has a learning curve, but it's a small one—in a single chapter, you've just learned how to access video, music, and electronic publications.

Chapter 9
Working with Your Finances Online

For many of us, working with our finances means finding the check register and matching register entries to the paper statement sent by our bank. Or, the process may involve recording transactions from the statement sent by our investment broker to pages in a three-ring notebook. To pay bills, we locate the checkbook, get out the envelopes and stamps, and turn on the calculator. Then, we sit down to write the checks, put in the written checks, address and stamp the envelopes, and file the paid bills. The next step is driving to the post office to actually mail the bills. The entire process is time-consuming.

After many years of this routine every month, you might consider using the services provided by your bank or credit union and completing the tasks through your computer.

Online banking is the shorthand term for using a computer and the information available on a financial institution's database to pay bills, record deposits, reconcile an account, or transfer money from one account to another account.

Why Use Online Banking?

Working with your financial data over an Internet connection provides many benefits. Once you understand how to use your computer to complete chores you've previously done by hand, you will discover online banking is a safe, time-saving, and convenient alternative in financial management.

Understand Online Banking

Banking online may mean something as simple as having your monthly retirement check deposited directly to your bank account or checking your credit card online for unauthorized activity. It can also mean paying your bills online, purchasing a new stock using your broker's Internet site, transferring money from your checking account to your savings account, and much more. Some institutions even offer a higher savings account interest rate to their online customers.

Today, most financial institutions offer some type of online financial service. This saves them money and offers consumers a valuable tool. All such online services require an Internet connection. Some institutions charge a fee for these services, although many do not. Over time, your costs may be less than working with paper statements, paying bills by check, mailing payments, and buying stamps. Check with your institution to determine the costs for the services they provide. Table 9-1 explains these services.

1
2
3
4
5
6
7
8
9
10

SERVICE	DESCRIPTION
Online Account Access	This service allows you to look at your account through the financial institution's website. You can see which checks or deposits have been posted and any fees charged to your account. Many institutions allow you to transfer money between accounts. Some also allow you to transfer funds from your banking account to your credit card account to pay your bill.
	This type of access is now available through many types of companies. Firms as diverse as insurance, utility, telephone, and even gasoline companies are beginning to offer forms of online account access.
Online Bill Payment	With this service, your bank or credit union pays your bills from your existing account. Working with information you give them, the institution will either electronically transfer money from your account to your payee's account or actually prepare a check they send to your payee. Not all institutions support this service, but you can also subscribe to bill-paying services through financial management programs.
Transaction Download	With this service, you can **download** (copy from the bank's computer to a financial management or spreadsheet program) all of your account activity. There are three ways to download transactions. Which type you use will depend on your financial institution:
	• **Web Connect** This service requires that you log on to the institution's website, enter your identifying information, and indicate which items you want downloaded. With this method, you can usually specify a date range for the download.
	• **Express Web Connect** With this method, you can access all of the institution's services directly from within your financial management program (such as Quicken) and there is no need to log on to the institution's website.
	• **Direct Connect** If your institution offers this service, you can create two-way communication with your financial institution instead of the one-way communication available with Express Web Connect. You can transfer funds between accounts from within a financial management program such as Quicken and use the institution's online bill-paying services if they are available. Unlike the other two methods, some institutions charge a fee for some services when using the Direct Connect method.

*Table 9-1: **Online Services Offered by Many Financial Institutions***

Working online can save you time and money, but as more financial institutions are going online, their security procedures are becoming more stringent. Many institutions discuss these procedures on their websites, and others provide brochures about maintaining security online. You can help by ensuring that you keep your password and PIN (personal identification number) in a secure place, by keeping your antivirus program up to date, and by using a good firewall. When using any online service, remember that with any benefit comes some risk. Refer to the discussion of and steps to implement various security procedures in Chapter 3, in particular, how to create strong passwords.

Deposit Funds to an Account

Many of us are familiar with "direct deposits." Funds are sent electronically from your employer, the Social Security Administration, or other entity directly to your account at the financial institution you specify. This means you do not have to take a paper check to the bank to deposit or cash it. Usually, you will have instant access to the funds rather than having to wait for a check to clear. Since you don't receive a paper check, the deposit cannot be lost or destroyed. The process is safer for the payer, the payee (you!), and the financial institution.

In many cases, you can designate that the funds be put into more than one account. In most cases, you sign up for direct deposit as follows:

1. Notify the institution that will be sending you the funds that you want your money via "direct deposit." Make sure you have the bank name, address, and bank account number where you want the funds sent. Some institutions will also ask for your Social Security number to set up a direct deposit order.

   a. Go to your employer's payroll or human resources department and request direct deposit of your pay.

   b. Go online to socialsecurity.gov/deposit. Click **Start Or Change Direct Deposit Online** to obtain a password and to sign up for direct deposit as shown in Figure 9-1, or call Social Security's toll-free number, 1-800-772-1213 (TTY 1-800-325-0778). If you call Social Security, you'll need to identity yourself by answering a few questions. You'll also need your banking information (account and routing numbers) and your Social Security number.

   c. Go to the financial institution where you have an account and sign up there for direct deposit of any funds sent by the government, including Social Security and SSI.

Figure 9-1: *Direct deposit of your funds is safer and more convenient than receiving checks in the mail.*

d. Go to your broker, insurance company, or other institution from which you receive periodic payments and ask to sign up for direct deposit of your funds.

2. Complete and sign any online or paper forms that are required.

After you have completed the procedures required by the entities that send you funds, they will change their records to start sending those funds to the account or accounts you designated. Depending on the day you request the change and the time before the next funds are due, it can take one pay cycle to have the funds deposited electronically.

TRANSFER FUNDS ELECTRONICALLY

Most financial institutions will allow you to set up an automatic transfer of funds on a certain day from one account to another. Some examples are:

- Automatic transfer from a checking to a savings or money market account or vice versa
- Automatic payments to a credit card account
- Automatic withdrawals of mortgage or insurance payments
- Automatic transfers to or from an investment account

You will usually need to set up these transfers in writing, although some institutions will allow you to create the transfer authorization online on their secure website.

QUICK**FACTS**

USING QUICKEN BILL PAY

If your financial institution does not supply online bill-paying services, or if you choose not to use them, you can use the service that comes with financial management programs such as Quicken. Quicken Bill Pay is available for all U.S. customers with an Internet connection. You can use it to pay bills to any United States vendor from anywhere in the world.

These services are especially useful if you have a small business or travel extensively. The service allows you to choose the account from which to pay, how much to pay, when to pay, and to schedule recurring payments. The cost for these online services may be offset by postage, time in check preparation, and ease in handling this task.

Quicken Bill Pay

All-in-one bill pay from within Quicken

Get started ◯

Pay Bills Electronically

Since paying bills manually can often be the most time-consuming, the ability to pay your bills using your home computer is a good alternative. You can do this in several ways:

- Pay the bill directly from the company's website. An example is shown in Figure 9-2.
- Pay each bill from your bank's website.
- Use a financial management program such as Quicken on your home computer.
- Use an online bill-paying service.

Each method has its advantages and disadvantages. See "Work with Online Bill Paying" later in this chapter.

Figure 9-2: **Many companies accept online payments.**

Consider the Pros and Cons of Online Banking

There are a number of advantages to handling your financial dealings online. However, there are some disadvantages as well. Consider both before you make your decision.

Recognize the Advantages of Banking Online

There are a number of benefits to handling your finances online. Working with your bank accounts and investments online can:

- **Save time**   You will not need to write as many checks each month. Bills can be paid at your convenience from your home.

- **Eliminate late payments**   You can instruct your financial institution to pay bills on a specific date each month and never be late again.

- **Convenience**   Your accounts can be accessed from any location in the world. With a wireless Internet connection, you can transfer funds and pay bills from a hotel, your home, a motor home, a cruise ship, or your grandchild's soccer game.

- **Earn more interest**   Your financial institution may be one that offers a higher interest rate on online accounts.

- **Save money and gas**   You can eliminate trips to the post office, the bank, and your creditors' stores by paying online. Buy the stamps online that you do need for greeting cards and postal correspondence as well, as shown in Figure 9-3.

- **Simplify your life**   You have one less chore to perform and more time to indulge in your favorite pastime!

Acknowledge the Disadvantages of Banking Online

Although for many people today, the advantages of banking online far outweigh the disadvantages, it is important that you understand

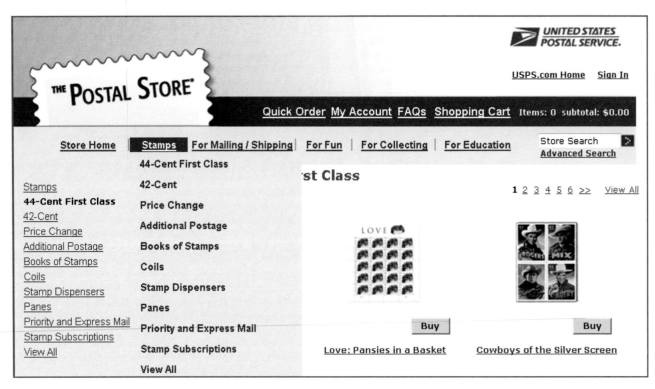

Figure 9-3: *Even the United States Post Office sells products online.*

and accept the "downside" of using financial services online. Consider the following before you make the move:

- **Trust**   Because we are used to receiving paper receipts for our deposits, we may be concerned about the success of our transaction. To solve this problem, print a copy of every transaction until you can verify that it has gone through. You can verify the transaction has been posted by viewing the account online or waiting for the paper statement to arrive.

- **Computer comfort**   If your idea of a mouse is something that taunts the cat, online banking may not be the answer for you. You should

CAUTION

Do not rely on public computers or wireless computer cafes for your Internet banking. Your information is too easily accessible to hackers when using public computers.

QUICKFACTS

USING ONLINE OR "VIRTUAL" BANKS

When we discuss online banking in this chapter, we are generally referring to the services offered by your neighborhood or national bank that has a building or office near you. There are also banks that are totally online, with no local office or personnel available for personal visits. Traditionally, these banks offer high interest rates, low minimum balance requirements, and low fees. Although these institutions are attractive to many, consider the following:

- Virtual banks do not have tellers or drive-in lobbies.
- Customer service may be slow or nonexistent.
- If you have to mail deposits to the online bank, you might have to wait for the mail to arrive at the virtual bank to start earning interest.
- Checks can take longer to clear.
- You may have to pay "nonmember bank" fees at ATM machines.

have basic computer skills and be at ease using the machine. See the first two chapters of this book and "Review Your Computer Skills" later in this chapter for more information.

- **Security** Your computer must be protected by a good antivirus program as well as a security firewall. Most banks today have several layers of security and encryption, so the most likely unsecure spot is your computer. See Chapter 3's discussion on computer security for more information on ensuring the security of your financial records.
- **Internet access** You must have access to the Internet from an Internet service provider to take advantage of all that online banking can provide (see Chapter 2).
- **Start-up time** When signing up for online services, some institutions require more paperwork than others. Some may require photo identification, signatures from all persons on the account, or that other forms are completed first. While this does take time, in the long run, the time you save by banking online is usually worth the time and trouble to set up the account.
- **Learning the systems** Each bank has its own process and set of procedures. Some offer tutorials or even online support, but many do not. After you have learned the system of your institution you will save time, but some systems are more difficult than others.

As with any new skill, working with your financial institutions may take some time to master, but for many people today, the time saved, as well as the knowledge that they can do their banking at any time, in any location with Internet access, is well worth the effort. Many people are even banking online with their smart cell phones!

What You Need to Bank Online

In making the decision whether to use online banking services, there are a few considerations. You need basic computer skills, access to the Internet, and an understanding of Internet security.

Review Your Computer Skills

As you have been working with your computer, you probably are beginning to feel comfortable with typing—even if you type with only two fingers! However, there are some basic skills you may need when banking online (also see Chapter 1).

- **Highlight or select**   To *highlight* or select an area, such as an account number or user name:

  a. Position your mouse to the left or right of the item you want to select.

  b. Hold down your left mouse key and drag the mouse across the area you want to select. The darkened area you have just selected is now highlighted, as seen in the illustration.

- **Copy and paste**   You can copy a selection (or highlighted area) from one place to another. For example, you can copy an account number from a location on your computer to the account number field on your bank's website. To copy and paste:

  a. After you have highlighted (selected) the item you want to copy, hold down the **CTRL** key on your keyboard and press the **C** key.

  b. Let go of both keys. You will not see anything on your computer screen, but the selected area has been saved in a special location on your computer called the "Clipboard."

  c. Click in the area you want the selected item to appear. Hold down the **CTRL** key and press the **V** key and release both keys. The item you selected is now *pasted* to the new location.

- **Save your files**   Most websites and all programs have tools that help you save what you have just accomplished. Here is one way some sites allow you to save your work:

  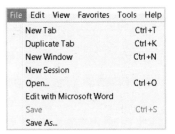

  a. Locate the toolbar and click **File**.

DIANA RELIES ON ONLINE BANKING

In these days of equality of the sexes and women's liberation in the workplace, in many families, the one who earns the most money makes the most important decisions. My husband had a white collar job and was responsible for the "big" bills such as the mortgage, taxes, automobiles, insurance, and pensions. I ran the household, managed our three children, and managed the remaining bills. However, when my husband had a severe stroke, I found myself responsible for all of the bills. And I floundered.

One of the methods that I've increasingly relied on to get on top of my bills is online banking. The websites are secure, and there is a record of every transaction, often archived for at least three years. Online banking allows me to check my balance and financial transactions as often as I want. Most importantly, I have set up a budget so that all of our important bills get paid first and the total budget is tallied up front. I begin by entering the big bills such as the mortgage and the date that I want them paid, then any credit cards or loans, and finally my household bills.

Diana C., 59, Washington

b. Click **Save As**. The Save As dialog box will appear. Choose the file into which you want this information saved.

c. Create a new file if needed and provide a name for it.

d. Click **Save**.

Prepare for Online Services

It is worthwhile to do a bit of preparation before using an online service to make sure it goes smoothly.

1. Reconcile all bank account and investment statements before you start online services.

2. Understand the fees you may be paying. Some financial institutions charge a fee for their online services, as seen in Figure 9-4. Compute the cost of doing it yourself (postage, gas to go to the post office, envelopes, and so on). Compare those costs to the fees charged by your financial institution or other bill-paying service.

3. Have a clear understanding of the service and how to use it. Do this by looking at any tutorials that are on the website, reading any literature that is online or printed, and, if it is available, having a customer service person in your local branch office go over the steps with you.

Cost	**Most of our customers qualify for FREE Bill Pay**[1]Learn How There's no monthly service charge when you have an eligible checking account or keep a combined minimum balance of $5,000 in qualifying accounts at all times. **Try it for two months** Even if you're not eligible for free Bill Pay, new customers can still try Bill Pay for free for the first two months. After that, the cost is $6.95 a month.
How to sign up	Once you have a Wells Fargo checking account: • Sign up for Wells Fargo Online® and Bill Pay. • Already have a password? Sign on and click the Bill Pay tab to add Bill Pay.
Stay on top of your bills - get Bill Pay today!	

Figure 9-4: **Fets for online bill-paying services vary by account and financial institution.**

9

Get Started with Online Banking

Once you have decided to use an online banking service, you need to get started. Consider your needs. Do you want to have funds from your employer, your retirement account, or Social Security deposited directly into the bank? Do you want to pay bills from your bank's website? After you have carefully considered what you want to accomplish online, it's time to start talking to your bank.

Ask the Right Questions

Each bank, whether a "brick and mortar" bank in your hometown or a virtual bank headquartered in another part of the country, has various types of accounts and services available. If your bank or credit union does *not* offer online banking, you might have to change banks to get the services you want. If your current institution offers online benefits, consider asking the following:

- What services do you offer for me online?
- What type of transactions are not available online?
- What are the fees for the various services available?
- Is there a tutorial for me to practice with on your website (see Figure 9-5)?
- Are there real people available for me to talk to 24 hours a day, 365 days a year? If not, when is no one available?
- Are those people local or at least in the United States?
- Is there a local or free long-distance telephone number to contact you?
- How are problems resolved?
- What problems have other customers had with online banking?
- Will I get a receipt for my transactions?
- How long does it take to have a deposit posted to my account?

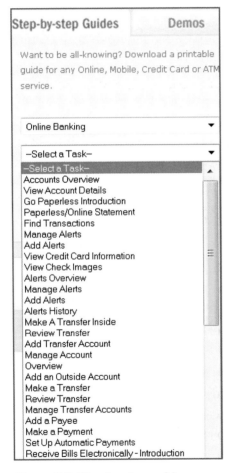

Figure 9-5: **Step-by-step guides, demonstrations, and tutorials are available on many bank websites.**

Begin the Process

The first step is to apply for online banking services. Most banks have similar procedures; however, check with each institution, as they may vary from company to company. To sign up for online banking using your computer:

1. Locate your account number and/or bank ATM card so that you can enter it when requested.

2. Go to your bank's website. If you don't know the address, use any search engine and type in the name of your bank. Usually, your bank's website will be one of the first "hits" shown.

3. Find the "Enroll in Personal Banking" icon or link and start the sign-up process. Some institutions require that you print out a form, fill it out by hand, sign it, and return the form to the bank. Others allow you to fill out all the information on a secure online form. You may be asked the following:

   a. Account name(s) and account number(s)

   b. The mailing address currently shown on these accounts

   c. Telephone numbers, including home, work, and cell

   d. Email address (this is often a requirement!)

   e. The Social Security number of the primary account holder, as well as that person's mother's maiden name (or other identifying information for that person)

   f. Which of the available services you want to use

   g. Additional information as required

4. If your financial institution allows you to submit the form via the Internet, complete the questions and click **Submit** at the last screen. You may be asked to save or print the application for your records. If so, print the application.

5. Your financial institution will then mail the PIN (*personal identification number*) for the account via U.S. Postal Service. In a separate mailing,

QUICK**QUOTES**

LINDA USES ID VAULT TO PROTECT HER PASSWORD

I do almost all my banking online. I have ID Vault, which gives me some security in knowing that I am not always entering my ID and password to get to the banking site. ID Vault does it for me (and at other shopping websites too) with just one password.

I do all my bills online. I keep a list of payees, with the needed information. One day, I could not find my list of payees when I went online! I decided to call for help from my bank and discovered I had two passwords for the same account and two different IDs! My payee list was with one ID and not the other, and I somehow managed to use the "other" ID to access my account. Everything was correct, except there were no payees for bill paying! Fortunately, it was corrected.

I have also accidently paid the wrong payee. Make sure you make a payee list with a nickname that indicates who you will be paying when you click it. I made a call to the payee in error, and they sent the money on to the correct payee who was in the same company. So even if you make a mistake, it can often be corrected.

Linda S., 66, Washington

you may receive other instructions on how to access your account. Normally, you will receive two mailings: one that includes your account information and instructions on using online banking and the other with your PIN included. This is the most time-consuming part of the process, as you have to wait for the bank to set up your account and then wait for the mail. The entire procedure may take as long as five to ten days.

Access Your Accounts

Once you have received the information from the financial institution, you have several ways to implement the online service.

1. Open your Internet browser (see Chapter 2). Click in the address bar of the browser, and type the Internet address for your bank. Examples are "usbank.com," either "bankofamerica.com" or "bofa.com," "wellsfargo.com," and "chase.com."

2. Press **ENTER**. Using the user name you selected (or the one assigned to you by your bank), sign in.

3. If requested, enter your PIN sent by the institution.

4. Enter a password and answer your "secret question" if required by your institution.

Keep Your Information Secure

We have discussed computer and Internet security earlier in this book. However, when you are working online with financial information, there are several other issues to address.

- Keep your financial passwords protected and in a safe location.

- Never reveal your password, user name, or PIN to anyone. If your institution allows it, create your own password and/or PIN.

NOTE

Most financial institutions *encrypt* their information. This means that the information stored in the institution's database is converted into a format only your computer can read.

VIEWING SECURE WEBSITES

When you access a financial website, you may notice that the company's address on the browser's address bar is preceded by the letters "http://". On a secure website, such as those of most financial institutions, the main webpage may include an "s" after the letters (https://). Some browsers may also display a locked padlock icon in the address bar or elsewhere on the page. You may also see privacy seals displayed on the pages. These seals are issued by Internet trust organizations that verify a company's privacy policies. You may also see the https:// on Internet auction sites or sites offering merchandise or services for sale.

Never enter any personal information on a website that does not have the https:// included in their address.

https://www4.usbank.com/internetBanking

- Always verify that you are on a secure site. To do so, look at the address bar of your browser to ensure that the address starts with https:// (note the "s," which means "secure") and that in the lower right of the browser page there is a padlock icon. See the QuickFacts "Viewing Secure Websites" for more information.

- *Never, under any circumstances*, give your personal information, including your ID, PIN, or password, to anyone on the telephone, even if they say they are from your bank and are trying to help you. Many people have been victimized by revealing account numbers, passwords, Social Security numbers, and the like to "that friendly girl from the bank who called." Your bank already has that information and would never call you on the telephone to verify it.

- In the same way, no bank will ever email you for personal information. If you receive an email purporting to be from your bank, it is probably a scam of some kind. Forward the email to your bank, and delete it from your computer.

- Consider having your paper statements and other correspondence sent to a post office box instead of your on-street mailbox. Identity thieves often obtain information from stolen checks, bank and/or credit card statements, or even letters from the bank.

- If you still write checks for some payments, take the payment to the post office rather than leaving it in your mailbox to prevent theft.

- Look at your mail before you throw it away to ensure that no one can find personal information if they rummage through your garbage can. One friend shreds each piece of mail and then uses it as compost.

Use Additional Online Banking Services

After you have been working with your financial institution's online banking services, you may consider paying your bills online, asking your bank to alert you when a credit card payment is due, or

9

10

downloading your transactions directly into a financial management program you have installed on your computer. Be sure to verify any fees charged by your institution before you sign up for the services.

Work with Online Bill Paying

As discussed earlier in the chapter, there are several ways you can pay your bills electronically. Each method has some advantages and disadvantages.

PAY BILLS DIRECTLY FROM A COMPANY'S WEBSITE

You can pay many bills by going to the company's website. Most companies, including utility, telephone, and insurance, have an option on their websites to directly receive payments. To pay the bill from a company's website, the procedure is usually something like the following:

1. Click an "Enroll" or "Signup" button on the company's website.
2. Enter your name, address, email address, and account number as required.
3. Create a password and/or user name, as shown in Figure 9-6.
4. Indicate how you will be paying the bill. Some firms require payment be made by credit card; with others, you can designate a bank account from which the funds will be withdrawn. If you use a bank account, you will be prompted to include the routing number and account number of that account.
5. Enter the date on which the funds are to be charged to your credit card or withdrawn from your bank account.
6. Print a copy of the confirmation for your records, and enter the transaction into your check register.

This method works well if you have only one or two bills to pay. However, going to a number of websites each month does take time. You have more passwords to remember, and you must still enter the transactions into your check register.

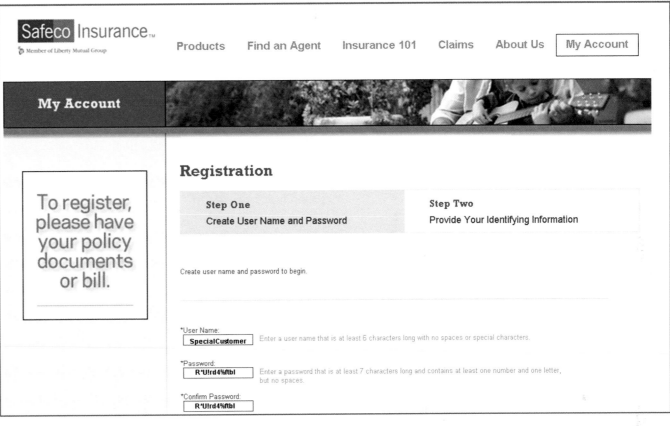

Safeco Insurance™
Member of Liberty Mutual Group

Products   Find an Agent   Insurance 101   Claims   About Us   My Account

My Account

To register, please have your policy documents or bill.

Registration

Step One
Create User Name and Password

Step Two
Provide Your Identifying Information

Create user name and password to begin.

*User Name:
SpecialCustomer   Enter a user name that is at least 6 characters long with no spaces or special characters.

*Password:
R*U!rd4%ftbl   Enter a password that is at least 7 characters long and contains at least one number and one letter, but no spaces.

*Confirm Password:
R*U!rd4%ftbl

Figure 9-6: *Many companies make it easy to pay your bill online.*

PAY BILLS FROM YOUR BANK'S WEBSITE

Most financial institutions have some form of bill-paying services. Some banks charge for this service; others do not. Still others have free bill-paying services as long as there is a minimum balance in your account. To pay bills directly from your bank's website, you must usually:

1. Click an "Enroll" or "Signup" button on the bank's website.

2. Enter your name, account number, and other information.

3. Create a password and/or user name.

4. Many institutions also require at least one secret question for which you enter an answer, and some have images or audio verification items from which you must choose. These images or audio clues must appear when you log into the bank's website; if they do not, you are directed to close the page and sign in again. These extra steps are to ensure your privacy.

5. Once the bill-paying account has been established, each time you want to pay a bill, you must enter the name, address, and account number of the company you want to pay. Some banks allow you to create a list of payees or select from an established list so that you do not have to enter the information more than once or even at all. Others require you to enter the information each time you pay a bill to that company.

6. Enter the date on which the funds are to be withdrawn from your bank account.

7. Print a copy of the confirmation for your records, and enter the transaction into your check register.

8. The financial institution then will do one of the following:

   ● Mail a check via the U.S. Postal Service on the day you have indicated and withdraw the funds from your account.

   ● Transmit the funds electronically if the company you are paying can receive payments in that manner.

If your bank charges for paying bills online, you must determine if the fees make up for the time you save.

PAY BILLS FROM A FINANCIAL MANAGEMENT PROGRAM ON YOUR COMPUTER

There are several financial management programs you can purchase and install on your computer. The best known is Quicken from Intuit, although there are others. Many offer online bill-paying services; however, some require monthly fees after a trial period. See the

QUICKFACTS

UNDERSTANDING CATEGORIES

A *category* is a description or label for an expense or a source of income. For example, payments to your telephone company might use the Telephone category. You can create subcategories for each category. For example, your trash pickup service might be a subcategory of Utilities. There are two types of categories: Income and Expense. As you set up your accounts and prepare to enter transactions, it is a good idea to set up categories at the same time. The purpose of categories is to allow you to compare how you are spending money with how you have budgeted your money. It is a management tool to better control your finances.

Financial management software such as Quicken supplies a number of preset categories for you to use. It also remembers the category you assign for each payee. You can add new categories and delete many of the preset categories that do not apply to you.

QuickFacts "Using Quicken Bill Pay" earlier in this chapter for more information. Each program has its own procedure, but most include the following:

1. Open the financial program and go to the account from which you want to pay the bill and select **Bill Pay** or the equivalent term.

2. Enter the name, address, and account number of the entity you are paying. In most programs, you need do this only once and the program will remember the information.

3. Enter the amount you are paying.

4. Indicate whether the payment is to be made electronically or by printed check.

5. Click **OK** or some similar command. If you are paying electronically, the transaction is sent over your Internet connection.

6. If you are printing a check, put a blank check into your printer, and click **Print**. Sign and mail the check.

When using a financial management program, you need enter the information only once, and the program enters the information into the proper category in the check register. However, if you have chosen to print a check, you must still sign the check, put it into an envelope, address and stamp the envelope, and take it to the post office.

The disadvantages of using a financial management program are the cost of the program itself as well as the learning curve involved in using the program. Paying bills online from such a program may cost more than the Bill Pay program from your bank.

PAY BILLS USING AN ONLINE SERVICE

If your bank does not offer online bill payment and you choose not to purchase a financial management program, you can still pay your

SHARIE WAS SAVED BY ONLINE BANKING WHILE TRAVELING

I love online banking. Last year, we had an unexpected trip out of town, where we had six hours to leave, which left most everything undone. Oops—what about the expected automatic deposit and the drafts that were coming out of our checking account? What about getting money for the trip? Not a problem. When we arrived at our destination and things settled down, I borrowed a family member's computer and simply went online to my bank and made sure the deposit had been made and paid a few bills that needed to be taken care of. I was also able to transfer funds to our checking account so we were able to use the funds for the trip.

Sharie M., 64, Washington

bills online. There are several online bill payment services, but before you subscribe, consider the following:

- **What bills do you want to pay online?** If the companies you want to pay are not normally paid online, you will need to find a service that can send payments by the U.S. Postal Service.

- **How does the bill-paying service get your money?** If the funds are transferred to the bill-paying service by credit card, which cards does the service accept?

- **How do you notify the service which bills to pay?** Must the bills be submitted electronically, or can you email the service and have them pay from that email?

- **What type of acknowledgment or receipt does the bill-paying service provide?**

- **How quickly does a bill get paid?** Is it done electronically, or by mail?

- **How much does the service cost?** You may find it is cheaper in the long run to buy a financial management program for your computer.

Use Financial Management Programs

There are a number of financial management programs on the market. The most widely used is Quicken by Intuit; however, there are many more. The programs vary in what you can do with them, but nearly all offer check registers, the ability to download data from a participating financial institution, a way to categorize and track your expenditures and income, the ability to print reports, and easy reconciliation of bank accounts. Many offer budgeting, financial calculators, tax, and investing sections.

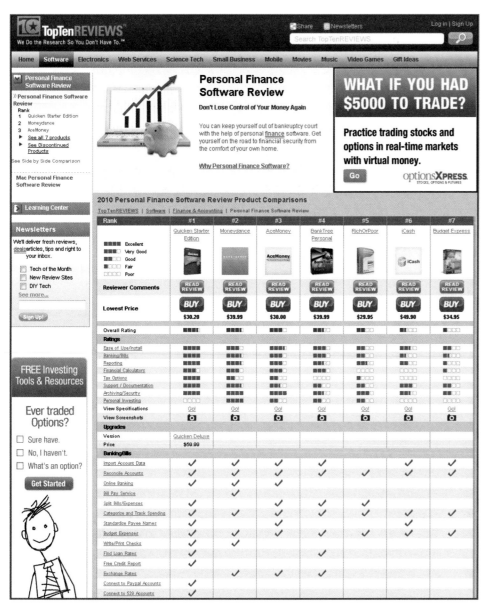

*Figure 9-7: **Searching the Web for comparisons and reviews can be worthwhile.***

Use Financial Management Programs on Your Computer

Most financial management programs have several versions. For example, Quicken comes in several versions. The version you select will depend on the tasks you want the program to perform. When you choose financial management programs that you run on your computer, costs include the one-time cost of the program itself, which is often around $50.00, as well as any monthly fees for services provided by your financial institution. See *Quicken 2011 QuickSteps* (McGraw-Hill Professional, 2010) for more information about using this product.

In addition to recording income and tracking your expenditures, financial management software programs can help you budget, track your investments, prepare for taxes, record loans, and help you manage your assets and liabilities. Many programs are available for both Windows and Mac computers. A great website for comparison purposes is found at personal-finance-software-review .toptenreviews.com (see Figure 9-7).

Use Financial Management Software Online

As you become more comfortable with your computer, you may want to consider using one of the several financial management programs available online (that you go on the Internet to use, called "cloud computing"). Many of these programs are free, while others require a monthly subscription payment. The most popular of these programs is Mint.com, a free program that simply tracks your spending and income directly from your bank's information. Since you do not enter personal information, your data is not linked with you personally. This program is also owned by Intuit, the Quicken folks, and has many of the same capabilities as far as categorization and great reporting, as seen in Figure 9-8. See the features at Mint.com.

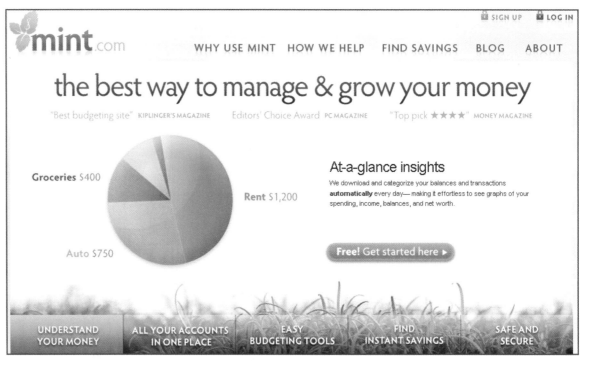

*Figure 9-8: **Online financial management programs, such as Mint.com, can help you organize your finances.***

The main advantages of online programs are accessibility from any computer and, in most cases, better security, as you cannot pay bills or move funds from within the programs. They are simply record-keeping aids. However, most of the online programs, such as Mint, offer budgeting tools and savings suggestions.

Use Other Online Financial Services

There are a number of other financial services available online in addition to those that relate to your banking accounts. Among these are investment services offered both by brokerages and independent investment services, insurance planning and tracking, and financial planning and budgeting tools.

Manage Your Investments Online

Most brokerage firms now have extensive online capabilities. You can download transactions, purchase and sell shares online, do research and analyze stock performance, and track purchases for tax purposes. Although each firm is slightly different, signing up for online services usually is similar to the following:

1. Locate your account number from the latest paper statement you have received, or open a new account.

2. Go online to your broker's website (see Figure 9-9). You can usually find the address on your latest statement or do an Internet search on the brokerage name.

3. Locate the sign-in or register link, and start the sign-up process. You may be asked the following:

   - Account name(s) and account number(s). Be sure to enter your name, date of birth, and other information in the same way as you did on the original application to your broker. For example, if your name shows on your paper statement as Charles N. Customer, don't use C. N. Customer to enroll.

TIP

There is a lot of variability in the offerings of online brokerages, both in the prices they charge and in the services offered. Do an Internet search on "ranking of online brokers" and look in particular at an annual Barrons' article in March on the best online brokers. Pay particular attention to fees, both commissions and "platform" fees, for the use of the online service and its software. Understand what you get for what you pay and the total cost of trading with a particular broker. Finally, consider the type of trading you will be doing. If you are or will be a frequent trader, low commissions are important, platform fees not so much. For the infrequent trader, the opposite is true.

Figure 9-9: *Almost all brokerages offer a wide range of services over the Internet.*

- The mailing address currently shown on these accounts
- Telephone numbers, including home, work, and cell
- Email address (this is often required)
- Your Social Security number and, perhaps, date of birth so that your information can be verified against what is shown on your account
- Additional information as required

For most brokers, filling out the form is all that is needed to access your account. You can now start to view the activity on your accounts, see detailed lists of your holdings and their current value, make trades, analyze your holdings, get copies of 1099s, and many other investment services.

Create an Online Portfolio

Should you choose not to access your broker's page, or if you just want to watch one or more stocks before you purchase, you can create an online portfolio. Go to a web finance page, such as yahoofinance.com or aaii.com and create a new portfolio. Yahoo! Finance is used in this example.

1. Type in the web finance page's address in your browser's address bar, and press **ENTER**.

2. Create a new account or sign in with your user name and password. At the Yahoo! Finance page, click the **My Portfolios** tab, and choose **New Portfolio** from the drop-down list.

3. Choose **Track A Symbol Watch List** to create your portfolio.

4. Enter a name in the Portfolio Name field.

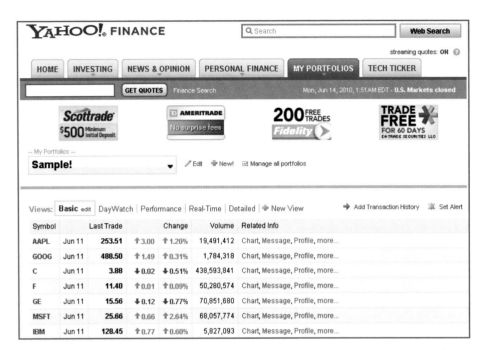

Figure 9-10: *You can create free online portfolios to watch the performance of selected stocks without using a broker.*

5. U.S. Dollar is the default currency. You may choose another currency by clicking the downward arrow in the currency field.

6. Enter the symbols for the stocks or mutual funds you want to track. Click **Look Up Symbol** to find the symbol from the name of the stock or mutual fund. Alternatively, click **Alphabetical Listing** for a list of stocks and funds.

7. Click the **Sort Symbols Alphabetically** check box if you want to see your list in alphabetic order rather than the way in which you entered the information.

8. Click **Finished** when you have entered all the stocks you want to watch.

9. You may view your new portfolio in several views, as seen in Figure 9-10. On your portfolio page, click **Edit** in the Views field to change what is displayed on your portfolio.

Build a Budget with Computer Tools

A budget is simply a formal spending plan. Whether you scribble it on the back of an envelope or create color-coded charts and graphs, a budget helps you plan where your money comes from and where it goes. There are tools on the Internet that will help you if you choose not to use financial software such as Quicken. Some are even free! Others offer a free trial period before you must purchase the software.

There are a few rules to keep in mind about budgeting.

- **A budget must be written.** Deciding on the 28th of the month that "next month we're not going to spend so much on eating out" is a great decision, but unless you create a budget that plans that, you are usually going to eat out just as much next month as you did this month.

- **A budget should be created *before* the month in which you are tracking your spending.** Make estimates based on what you have spent before. Average costs over at least the last three months and averaging how much you spend for a year is even better.

- **A budget should not be unilateral.** Unless you live alone, creating a spending plan for the future does not work if you are the only one in the household thinking about it. Work with your housemate and create a workable spending plan for everyone in the house!

- **A budget should include "mad money" to the extent your family can afford it.** Make a decision about pocket money for each person in the household for which they need not account.

Budgets are designed to be used. Review your budget each month with all of your family members to see what to adjust for the next month.

Produce Your Budget

A number of tools are available to you to create a budget. One of the easiest ways is to use a template. Two examples of this are using a Google Docs template and using an Excel template.

BUDGET WITH A GOOGLE DOCS TEMPLATE

A free template can be found on the Google Docs site.

1. Open your Internet browser, type google.com in the address bar, and press **ENTER**.

2. On the Google page, click **More** at the top of the page, and choose **Documents** from the drop-down list.

3. Either sign in with your Gmail account user name and password, or click **Create An Account** and create a new Google account.

4. Once you are on the Google Docs page, click **Browse Template Gallery**.

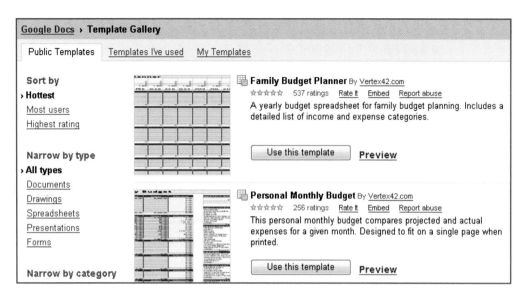

Google Docs › **Template Gallery**

Public Templates   Templates I've used   My Templates

Sort by
› **Hottest**
Most users
Highest rating

Narrow by type
› **All types**
Documents
Drawings
Spreadsheets
Presentations
Forms

Narrow by category

Family Budget Planner By Vertex42.com
☆☆☆☆☆ 537 ratings   Rate It   Embed   Report abuse
A yearly budget spreadsheet for family budget planning. Includes a detailed list of income and expense categories.

[Use this template]   **Preview**

Personal Monthly Budget By Vertex42.com
☆☆☆☆☆ 256 ratings   Rate It   Embed   Report abuse
This personal monthly budget compares projected and actual expenses for a given month. Designed to fit on a single page when printed.

[Use this template]   **Preview**

Figure 9-11: **There are many sites on the Internet where you can obtain budgeting templates.**

5. Choose either **Family Budget Planner** or **Personal Monthly Budget** to begin. Click **Use This Template** by your choice, as seen in Figure 9-11.

6. Follow the on-screen directions. Click **Help** for more information.

7. After you have created your budget, you can download it to the hard drive on your computer or save it until you return to Google Docs.

8. To leave the page, click **Sign Out**.

BUDGET WITH AN EXCEL TEMPLATE

If you have the Microsoft Office Suite installed on either a PC or a Mac, you can use Excel's excellent templates to create your budget as we've done here.

1. In Microsoft Office Excel 2007, click the **Office Button**, and click **New**. In Excel 2010, click the **File** tab, and click **New**.

2. In Excel 2007, click **Installed Templates**, and click **Personal Monthly Budget**. In Excel 2010 under Office.com Templates click **Budgets**, and then double-click **Personal Monthly Budget**.

3. In the monthly budget that opens (see Figure 9-12), enter the income amount in both the Projected and Actual Monthly Income fields for a given month.

4. Work through the Projected and Actual costs for each item in the Expense sections.

Excel computes any differences between what you projected and what you actually spent.

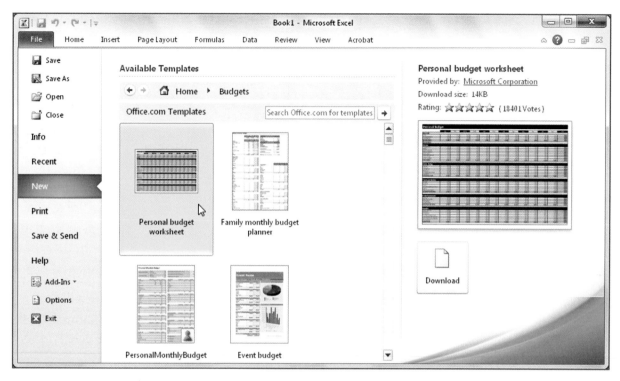

Figure 9-12: *You may have powerful financial management tools already available with your existing software.*

Review Quicken's Possibilities

Throughout this chapter, we've referred to Quicken from Intuit. This program helps you set up your checking, savings, investment, and credit card accounts; enter transactions into those accounts; balance or reconcile the accounts to the institution's records; print checks; create reports; design and print graphs; manage your debt; and see tips to help save your hard-earned dollars. If you are connected to the Internet, you can download information from your bank, investment house, and credit card company. Quicken also makes it quick and easy to transfer your data to TurboTax at year-end to make tax preparation less stressful.

Most financial institutions in the United States offering online services include Quicken's format as an option. That means you have the ability to create a check register and, with an Internet connection and a few clicks, download all the transactions from your bank directly into the register. Using Quicken makes online financial transactions an easy process.

UNDERSTAND QUICKEN VERSIONS

Quicken has several versions. For most users, Quicken Deluxe may be the most useful. This version gives you the ability to track both banking and investment accounts, as well as plan for life-changing events. Quicken Premier gives the user all of the usefulness of the Deluxe version, plus more in-depth investment capabilities and the ability to print income tax Schedules A, B, and D.

DISCOVER QUICKEN TASKS

Practically all of your financial matters can be handled from within Quicken. You can:

- Track your checking and savings accounts

- Track your cash

- Record your home and other real estate and track its worth

- Watch your loan balances and discover how much interest you are paying

- Adjust any credit card, loan, or mortgage balance if values or rates change

PLAN FOR YOUR FUTURE

In both the Quicken Deluxe and Premier versions, you can create spending and savings plans, create a roadmap for your retirement, and devise a workable budget. These planning tools are easy to use and allow you create "what-if" scenarios. Both versions also include a tax planner.

How to...

- *Explore Genealogical Records*
- *Using Foreign Census Records*
- *Begin Your Journey*
- *Set Up Your Records*
- *Organize Your Records*
- *Discover the Tools*
- *Learn Online*
- *Using Computer Software*
- *Give Credit When Due*
- *Join a Group*
- *Preserve the Now*
- *Saving Your History*

Chapter 10
Exploring Genealogy

Have you ever wondered how your ancestors came to this country? Do you know what your mother's grandfather did for a living? Your computer is a wonderful tool to help you answer these and many more questions about your family. It can also help you to preserve today's memories for your great-great-granddaughter in the year 2090. Using many free online resources, you can search databases in the United States, and for small fees, search those of other countries as well. With a small digital recorder, you can tape Uncle Bill's memories of the cold winters when he had to walk through the snow to school, "uphill both ways." Or with a digital video camera, record Great-Aunt Susan's apple pie recipe while she is showing you how she does it and revealing the *real* secret ingredient! You can even create a free family website to display your research and make it available for every member of your family. Genealogy is the basis for the history of *your* family.

Become the explorer and record the information, which may well unite you and your family for years to come.

Start a Genealogical Search

People start genealogy projects for a variety of reasons. Perhaps you want to find out why your newest grandson has red hair and blue eyes, and you vaguely remember your grandfather talking about his father's red hair and freckles. Or, you might want to discover if anyone in your family fought in the Civil War and on which side. Whatever your reasons, once you decide to start looking, you may be hooked. The search can be time-consuming but highly rewarding.

Explore Genealogical Records

From U.S. Census records to old love letters, from marriage announcements to photographs, all can provide information for you as you re-create your family history. You can find information in federal and state census records, cemetery lists, vital statistics databases, passenger lists, alumni notices in college yearbooks or online at the school's website, military records, and the like. Many of these databases have been published and can be found at your library as well as on the Internet. There are so many websites about genealogy that a recent Yahoo! search for "genealogy research" resulted in 12,700,031 results. You can also find books, articles, and other writings at your local library.

As you start looking for information, consider these possibilities as starting points:

- Postmark dates on letters
- Newspaper clippings found in boxes of photographs or inside books
- Birth announcements
- Wedding invitations

QUICK**FACTS**

USING FOREIGN CENSUS RECORDS

Most nations in the world today take some sort of a census. While not all are a matter of public record, most are available online in some form. Release dates of individual information vary among countries. For example, Canada releases individual information 92 years after the information was gathered, while the United Kingdom holds the records for 100 years. Canada's first census was in 1666 when it was considered New France. You can access census information about many nations at En.wikipedia .org/wiki/Census.

Some of the most accessible census records come from the United Kingdom. The United Kingdom has taken some form of a census since the seventh century. Since 1801, a census is taken every 10 years. However, the 1841 census was the first in which names were recorded. Beginning in 1851, the records include the name, age, place of birth (usually but not always accurate), and relationship to the head of the household. As with the United States census records, some of the information contained in the records is neither complete nor precise. Currently, one can access the records from 1841 through 1911. The current website for these records is Nationalarchives.gov.uk/ records/census-records.htm. You can look at the records for free, but according to the website seen in Figure 10-2, there is a small fee for downloading the information.

- Property tax records or even old, cancelled checks showing payment of property taxes
- Pictures and snapshots
- Funeral cards and announcements
- Programs from graduations or other formal ceremonies
- Family names that repeat in several generations
- Old income tax records, both state and federal

UNDERSTAND THE UNITED STATES CENSUS

The United States Constitution directs that a census be taken every ten years. Starting in 1790, census workers went door to door, recording the name of the head of the household and the number of people in the home, sorted by age groups. Then, beginning with the 1850 census, census takers attempted to identify each member of the household by name. While not everyone was counted in every census, the 1850 census is the first that included those designated as "slaves" or indentured servants. It was not until 1860 that Native Americans were counted, and even then, not all were included. However, some records exist for individual tribal census records. You can find them at Censusfinder.com. Click **Native American Census Records** to see a list. An example of what was included in the 1860 census is shown in Figure 10-1.

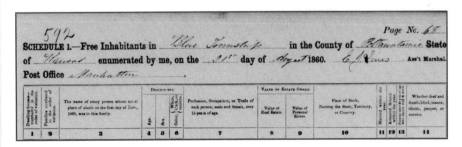

Figure 10-1: The 1860 census recorded the name of each person in the household, the value of the property owned by the head of the household, each person's place of birth, and other information.

Figure 10-2: The National Archives in the United Kingdom offers 1,000 years of UK government records.

QUICK QUOTES

ANNE USES A PROGRAM, SUPPORT GROUP, AND BOOKS

I have been pondering my family history ever since my mother handed me a thick packet of papers sent by my cousin. "This is about your father's family," she said. "It's time you found out more about them." She often dropped names of family ancestors she thought might be interesting, but she wanted me to do the grunt work. Back then, during my working years, genealogy consisted of sorting masses of papers without the help of a computer. Most of my searching was put on hold.

Now, in my retirement years, I have more time and a computer. Other than a love of history and geography, three things make my search for family minutiae possible: a computer genealogy program—the data entry is still tedious—a support group who know a lot more than I do, and several genealogy books.

The computer program is essential, because it gives me an organizing tool. My genealogy books are full of labeled Post-It Notes for those times when my computer is turned off and I want to review forms or sources. The support group pull the whole thing together with their help and encouragement.

Ann H., 66, Washington

The United States Code requires that individual answers to each census be withheld from publication for 72 years to protect each person's privacy. That means the "newest" census for which we can gain information about individuals is the 1930 census. The 1940 census will be released April 1, 2012. The current 72-year delay may be adjusted as life expectancy in the United States increases.

Begin Your Journey

The best way to start with your family history is with yourself. Create a list that includes as much of the following information as you know:

- Your father's first, middle, and last name; his date of birth; and where he was born.
- Your mother's first, middle, and maiden name; her date of birth; and where she was born.
- Where and when your parents were married.
- Names and dates of birth of each of your siblings.
- List all of your aunts and uncles by name and whether they were your mother's or your father's sibling. Include all the information you can remember about when and where they were born.
- Include the names of the spouses and children and as much information as you know of dates of birth, locations, and so on.
- List the names of your parents' parents, including your grandmothers' maiden names. Include as much information as you know about where and when they were born.

If you need an example of a format for the information, there are many templates online for you to download to your computer. Figure 10-3 shows an example of one available from Microsoft.

START TALKING

One of the best ways to gather information is from your own family members. If you don't have all the information you need to complete the lists provided earlier, call your aunt or visit your uncles. Send an e-mail to family members to see if anyone else has already done some research. Many families have one or more members who are seeking information. First, fill in information about your generation and then your parents'. Find out as much as you can about each person, including the following:

- Dates and places of birth.
- Middle names.
- Where they grew up and any other towns in which they lived.
- Verify how names were spelled and any variations that the person might know.
- Other names that might have been used. For example, many people changed their name when coming to this country to make it easier to spell in English. I have a relative named Johan who sometime in the 1840s changed his name to John.

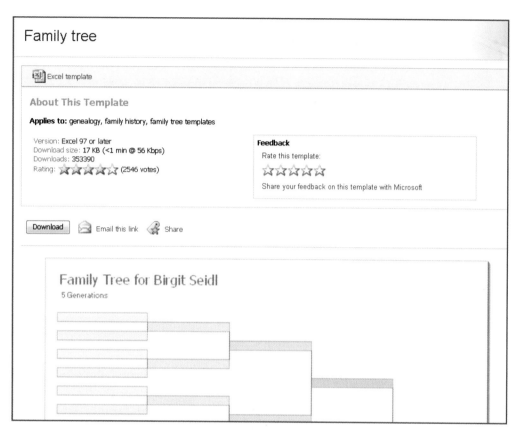

Figure 10-3: *Family tree templates can help you organize your information.*

TIP

To use the template shown in Figure 10-3, open Excel as explained in Chapter 6, click **File** and click **New**. In the Search text box opposite Office.com Templates, type <u>family tree</u>, and then click **Download**.

- Maiden names for all married women.
- When and where relatives were married.
- Common family names, especially those that have been used for both men and women.
- When family members died and when and where they were buried.
- When and where family members were divorced or marriages annulled.

Ask for old family bibles, scrapbooks, pictures, newspaper clippings, or any other mementos they have that they might share with you. If your relative has a scanner and a computer, have them scan the item and save the file to a flash drive or e-mail it to you. When you go to meet with any family member, take a notebook and perhaps a digital recorder, or digital still or video camera with you. See "Preserve the Now" later in this chapter for additional information.

Organize Your Project

You may find that you are putting family pictures in your desk and sticking other mementos, such as birth announcements, in the top drawer of your dresser for "safe keeping" until you have the time to put them into a scrapbook. This may not be the most efficient way of preserving precious memories.

Set Up Your Records

As you begin to build a file of information, you might want to start organizing it. You can use a three-ring notebook, file boxes, or a computer program. When I first started keeping records, I kept a three-ring notebook with a page for each person. I used a manila envelope after each person's page to keep clippings, pictures, and other tangible memorabilia. Today, there are many free forms you can obtain on the Internet. Here are several for you to download for your own use:

- **Familysearch.org/eng/Search/Rg/frameset_rhelps.asp?Page=./research/type/Form.asp&ActiveTab=Type** has a list of forms from which you can choose to begin your search. It is worth typing the full, long URL to get to these forms.

- **Colorado-cemeteries.com/support-files/familygroupform.pdf** provides an excellent two-page form for collecting all the information for an individual family member.

- **Genealogysearch.org/free/forms.html** has a form that allows you to create a blank census worksheet for every United States census from 1790 through 1920. That way, you can simply cut and paste information into the blank sheet.

Whether you create your records online or on paper, make sure to keep copies. See the "Saving Your History" QuickSteps later in this chapter to learn how to back up the information in your computer. If you are using paper, use the local copy store or invest in a small home copy machine (many personal computer printers can function as a copier). Keep one copy of all of your work in another location to protect it.

Organize Your Records

If you are storing images, database information, downloaded records or certificates, scanned documents, or other items on your computer, you may want to create folders and subfolders to organize your data. We will look at two different systems here. You may find others that better suit you. Depending on your computer system and the way you work, use the system that best fits your needs. You may also want to start a journal or loose-leaf notebook as a log of what you have found, where and when you found it, and the name of the folder on your computer where you saved the information.

ORGANIZE BY ITEM TYPE OR NAME

This process separates each type of document into a type. You create a folder for each type and then subfolders by family group or surname. You can also reverse this and have primary folders by name and subfolders by document type.

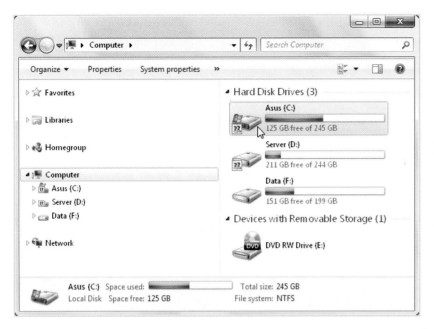

1. Create your folders. In Windows 7, right-click the **Start** button, and click **Open Windows Explorer**.

2. From the window that appears, in the right column, double-click (or single-click in the left column) the letter of the hard drive on which you want to create your folder. In most cases, that will be the "C" drive.

3. Click **New Folder** and a New Folder box appears on the right side of the window. Type the name of your new folder; for example, if you are creating a folder for photographs, you might call it "Genealogy Photos." Press **ENTER** to save your folder's name.

4. To create a subfolder in your new folder, double-click the new folder, and click **New Folder** again.

5. Type the name of your new subfolder, and press **ENTER** to save the folder's name.

You have now created a subfolder in your Genealogy Photos file for one of your families. Follow the same steps for each family name.

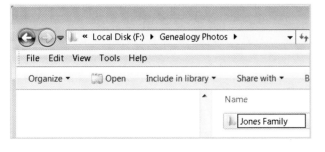

Create a new folder for each type of file you want to save. Consider using a folder for certificates, census records, tax rolls, and so on. Use whatever names make the most sense to you and the way you file.

DOREEN FINDS ONLINE DATABASES A GREAT RESOURCE

The computer and the Internet have been a huge boon to genealogists, who can now keep track of their research using databases, which simplify the task enormously. With the Internet, the number of original records available online continues to increase almost daily. While many sites are free, some require a membership fee.

One of the newest free sites features information from original records held at the Family History Library in Salt Lake City. This is the world's biggest and most comprehensive genealogy library. I've found records on this site that were not found when I paid state or county officials to look them up in their official records.

Also with computer databases, the Internet, and email you can easily share your data, pictures, and documents.

The negative aspects of genealogical data on the Internet is that anyone can put virtually anything out there—be it well researched and sourced or not. Caution is called for when using online genealogical data. Good data should always be sourced to records that you can trace.

Doreen J., 64, Washington

No person files in the same way. Create folders on your computer that match the way you would file papers in a file cabinet.

FIND YOUR DOCUMENTS

After you have created your folders and subfolders, start checking your computer for files that may belong in one of your new folders. The following folders may contain files you want to organize:

- **The Pictures** (or My Pictures in prior versions of Windows) folder can be used for documents you've scanned in as well or digital copies of items found online. Figure 10-4 shows Windows 7 Libraries in which you may have stored your files.

- **The Documents** (or My Documents) folder can contain items you've downloaded as well as any files that have the .txt, .doc, .docx, .odt, or

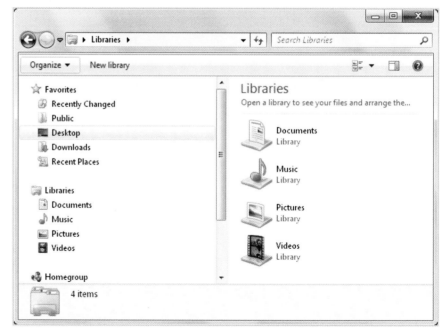

Figure 10-4: Look in the folder in your Libraries for files you may have saved.

other word processing file extensions. If you have received letters as attachments to email, you may have put them into this folder.

- **The desktop** is an easy place to save a file for retrieval at a later time. Check to ensure you've not left any important genealogy information there.

- **The Downloads** folder is often automatically used to store downloaded items.

- **Your computer genealogy program** folder, often found in the Program Files (or Program Files (x86)) folder, is sometimes automatically used by the program to store reports it has created or information downloaded by the program.

- **Email folders** are automatically used to save an email, which can be forgotten. It is smart to save a copy of your genealogy-related email with your other genealogy records.

Utilize the Internet

One of the most useful sources may be as near as your computer desk. With a myriad of programs, databases, references, and family webpages, information about your great-great-grandfather may be as near as a mouse click (or two).

Discover the Tools

There are many tools to help you in your search for your family's past, as shown in Table 10-1. Although some charge subscription or membership fees, many are free. These tools should help you get started in discovering facts about your family. This list is by no means a complete one. There are millions of sites available, and throughout this chapter we've listed several more.

WEBSITE ADDRESS (URL)	PURPOSE	COST
Usgenweb.org	This page provides links to all the free websites for each state in the United States.	Free; however, some states charge for downloading information or providing copies.
Archives.gov/genealogy	A research site provided by the National Archives. The site provides links to census, military, land, immigration, and naturalization records. Although most items are not online, you can find tips on how to locate the various types of records. One of the databases that is available online through this site is a group of names from a list of naturalization records for selected geographic areas in the United States.	Free.
Catalog.loc.gov	This is the gateway to the United States Library of Congress. The library has links for dozens of databases; information about thousands of books, periodicals, photographs; and other data.	Free.
Worldvitalrecords.com	This site provides links to vital statistic records, such as birth, marriage, and death certificates. It also has some census and voter records, some land and probate information, and many other sets of data. Through its World Collection it offers some of the same for other nations.	Membership required; however, some library systems offer access to this site with your library card.
Ancestry.com	This site bills itself as "the world's largest online resource for family history documents." It offers other services too, such as books, maps, gifts, and scrapbooks. It is the owner of Family Tree Maker computer software for genealogy. When you do a search for genealogy sites, many of the responses are linked to this site.	Subscription fee for both U.S. and international memberships.
Ngsgenealogy.org	National Genealogical Society's page. This site provides courses and videos, sponsors conferences, and provides members with many resources not available elsewhere.	Annual membership fee.
Geneasearch.com/tools.htm	Lists of free research tools and great tips.	Tool list is free, but the site GeneaSearch.org charges for search results.
Familysearch.org	This site is a free service of The Church of Jesus Christ of Latter-Day Saints (LDS). It provides free classes, tutorials, forms, and a free software program for recording your family history. It also has one of the largest online databases available.	Free registration.
Genealogytoday.com	A great resource for getting started on your research.	Offers both free and fee-based databases.
Genealogy.com	This site has information on getting started in genealogy, classes, access to the Social Security Death Index and other databases.	Annual membership fee.
Ancestorhunt.com	This site lists dozens of free searchable databases.	Free.
Publicdomaingenealogy.com	This site explains the differences between public and copyrighted genealogical material and provides some links to free sites.	Free.

Table 10-1: Websites Devoted to Family History

Once you have started collecting information, you may encounter new acronyms and references with which you are not familiar. The following list explains some of them. Additional terms can be found at Cyndislist.com/diction.htm and Tarver-genealogy.net/aids/abbreviations.html.

- **GEDCOM**   This stands for Genealogical Data Communication. Developed in 1985 by the Church of Jesus Christ of Latter-Day Saints, GEDCOM is a format for the exchange of information among genealogists. GEDCOM data can be downloaded into nearly all genealogy programs. By itself, it doesn't make much sense, but each genealogy program interprets the information for you.

```
0 @I1@ INDI
1 NAME John /Doe/
1 BIRT
2 DATE 10 JAN 1800
2 SOUR @S1@
3 DATA
4 TEXT Transcription from birth certificate would go here
3 NOTE This birth record is preferred because it comes from the birth certificate
3 QUAY 2
1 BIRT
2 DATE 11 JAN 1800
2 SOUR @S2@
3 DATA
4 TEXT Transcription from death certificate would go here
3 QUAY 2
```

- **RootsWeb**   Rootsweb.com provides a connection point for genealogy researchers. It has a list of more than 1 million surnames, many lists that have been contributed by other researchers, and is part of the World Connect Project, which is a database of family trees. You can join mailing lists, post messages on a message board, and find the tools to build and register a website. Many local genealogical societies have websites connected to this site. It is a part of Ancestry.com.

- **NARA** The National Archives and Records Administration. This storehouse of records has millions of records available for U.S. searches. Many of the records can only be accessed on-site; however, their website offers information about finding some of the information online. An example of the site is shown in Figure 10-5.

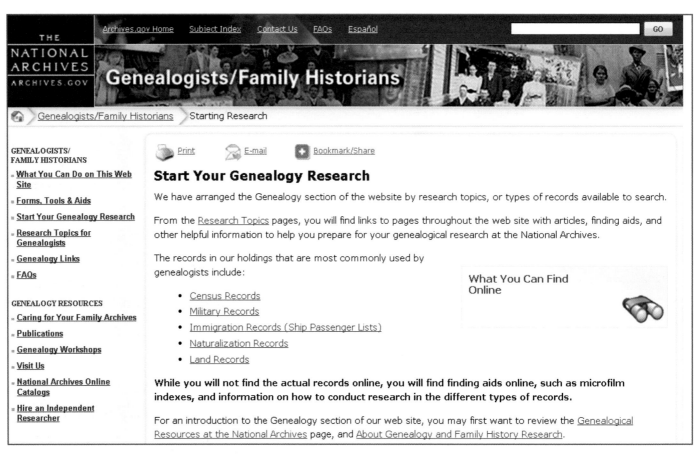

Figure 10-5: The National Archives Genealogists' page offers many tips to start your research.

Alabama
Alaska
Arizona
Arkansas
California
Colorado
Connecticut
Delaware
District of Columbia
Florida
Georgia
Hawaii
Idaho
Illinois
Indiana
Iowa

Figure 10-6: The USGenWeb project is designed to make genealogical research accessible to everyone with a computer.

- **GenWeb**   The GenWeb project was started in Kentucky and now includes all 50 states. It provides Internet access to data within each county or parish within the state. While not all information is yet available for all states as the project is run by volunteers, it is a good starting place. Go to Usgenweb.org to begin a search, as seen in Figure 10-6.

Learn Online

After you have talked to your family, searched some databases, and organized your records, where do you go next? Several websites offer free tutorials and classes on all phases of genealogical research.

USING COMPUTER SOFTWARE

There are a number of software programs for your use. Some are free for downloading; others vary in price. Most packages offer both chart and text forms for you to enter information. Some software includes membership in various database sites. When contemplating the use of software for your research, consider the following:

- Computer requirements (PC or Mac or both)
- User-friendliness and ease of installation and setup
- Organization of the program
- Documentation and available help
- Additional features available, such as membership in genealogical sites

Some of the most well-known software packages are:

- **Family Tree Maker** is found at Familytreemaker .com. It is owned by Ancestry.com. There is both a Windows and a Mac version.

- **Legacy** is found at Legacyfamilytree .com and offers a basic package that you can download for free. This program is for Windows.

Free PAF Family History Software

Personal Ancestral File (PAF) is a free genealogy and family history program. PAF allows you to quickly and easily collect, organize and share your family history and genealogy information.

→ Download PAF

Free Color Charts with PAF Companion

Print your family tree in colorful ancestor and descendant charts. PAF Companion is easy and fully compatible with PAF.

→ Download PAF Companion Basic

→ Download or Order Other Products

Continued . . .

One of the best is the Family Search website. This site offers classes, as well as tips, suggestions, and articles about research. The site even has classes on doing research in England, Ireland, Italy, and Russia. Many of the classes are video classes you can watch on your computer screen on your own schedule.

Use The Learning Center on the Ancestry.com site for free videos and tutorials, as well as suggestions for other genealogy projects. Other free courses can be found at:

- Genealogy.about.com/library/lessons/blintro.htm
- Genealogy.com/university.html
- Archives.gov/research/start/
- Learnwebskills.com/family/intro.html (for a complete course)

Give Credit When Due

As you find more and more information, it is important to consider how reliable your sources are and how someone else could check this or find more information. You are documenting information and need to reference just where you found it. The *source* of your information is the place where you found it. It might be a letter from Great-Aunt Sally to her cousin who homesteaded in Kansas, or it might be the 1880 census. The location of the information should be recorded somehow in your records. Most software programs have a place for this.

To properly note where you got the information, include the following:

- Author name
- Name of the article or publication
- Place published

- Year published
- Publisher name
- Page number or numbers if applicable

Most of the citation forms can be found online at such sites as Mla.org or Chicagomanualofstyle.org/tools_citationguide.html. You should include information gained from every source, including newspaper clippings, official records, oral stories, and photographs. This is information *you* have found, not data found by others, and you are responsible for reporting correctly.

Join a Group

There are many genealogical groups, clubs, and societies, both within the United States and throughout the world. You can meet others working on their histories, take classes, attend programs, and participate in field trips. Many groups sponsor trips for research, and some have lending libraries of research material just for members. These groups are a great way to learn or perfect your research skills, evaluate sources, learn new techniques and options for your research, and make connections with others who share your interests.

Consider joining a group in an area you're researching. Dues are usually modest, and even though you're not there physically, with the Internet, you can still participate and you might find a member in the far-away area that is working on a branch of your own family. Most societies have newsletters or other publications that include searches being done by their members. Still others volunteer for tasks such as digitizing local records. That information might be just what you need to complete the information about your father's grandmother.

QUICKQUOTES

JERRY USES GENEALOGICAL DNA TO RESEARCH ANCESTRY

One of the most recent tools that has been provided to genealogists is the availability of specialized genealogical DNA laboratories. Numerous surname projects have been established to collect and merge data on particular surnames. I joined such a surname project provided by FamilyTreeDNA and, within a few months, discovered the existence of several individuals related to me in the Carolinas.

DNA testing serves two purposes: it validates (or disproves) previous research and establishes previously unknown familial relationships. For example, as a result of the surname project, I am corresponding with a family researcher in Arizona who is doing research on her husband's family. So far, we have been unable to document the relationship, but we know that her husband and I have a common ancestor prior to 1800, as he and I match on 65 out of 67 genetic markers. It is only a matter of time until documentation is discovered. Though documentation of relationships is still required, the DNA information assures us that we are on the right track.

Jerry C., 73, Washington

You can find groups listed on Cyndi's List (cyndislist.com; see "Societies"), Ancestry.com, and at fgs.org, the website of the Federation of Genealogical Societies in the United States. You can also go to any search engine and type genealogical society and the name of your location to find local groups, as you can see in Figure 10-7.

Make Use of Your Findings

Genealogy is not just searching for old records or discovering that your grandfather's mother wanted to be a doctor. It offers you a chance to save today's memories for your descendants. You can create sounds, pictures, and written records to tell your future grandchildren's children what it was like to live in the beginning of the 21st century.

Preserve the Now

Do you remember your grandmother's voice? How about those awful puns Uncle Robert used to tell? Think about being able to hear their voices again. Today, we have the inexpensive technology that allows us to record voices telling the family stories as well as capture images of all the cousins catching fireflies in Aunt Helen's backyard.

USE DIGITAL VOICE RECORDERS

Digital voice recorders work much like tape recorders, except instead of recording sound onto a tape, the sound is converted into digital signals. Most are small enough to carry in your pocket and connect to a Universal Serial Bus (USB) port on your computer. Some come with cords that connect the recorder to the USB port. You can save the digital file, copy it onto CDs or DVDs, or include it as narration in a video. Not only do these recorders work for a face-to-face interview, you also could record your granddaughter's first piano recital (if the venue allows it), the surprise party for Aunt Rhonda

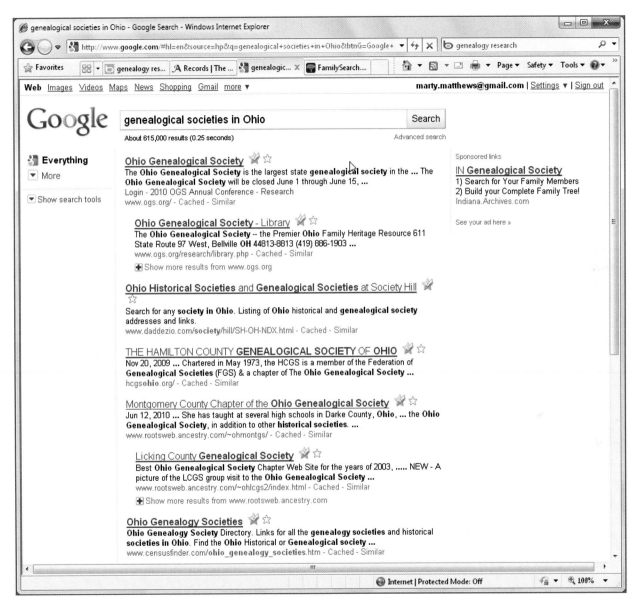

Figure 10-7: *Joining a genealogical group or society can be helpful when you reach a seeming dead end.*

SAVING YOUR HISTORY

One of the most frightening thoughts a genealogist can have is the idea that all of their hard work might be lost. If you are keeping your data on your computer, do regular backups or subscribe to an online backup service. You can use several different types of media to copy or back up your records. You can burn your data to a CD or DVD, copy it to an external hard drive, copy it to a flash drive, or copy it to an online storage site, such as Microsoft's free skydrive.com.

Both Apple and Windows have built-in backup systems with step-by-step instructions. You can purchase backup software or even download free programs from the Internet. Each program operates a little differently, so whichever program you choose, allow for a short learning curve.

Another option for saving your data is to use an online service. For a small fee, these services back up your data over the Internet. Should something happen to your computer, you need only connect to the service to restore the files.

It does not matter which method you use to make copies of your data, just that you do it on a regular basis. Consider copying all of your data at least monthly and running an "incremental" backup weekly. An "incremental" backs up only the files that have been changed since your last complete backup.

and Uncle Joe's 47th anniversary, or the conversation around the table at Thanksgiving.

Recorders range from small, pocket-size recorders on which you can record your grocery list to large, professional units that allow you to save documents, images, and other items in addition to the audio file. Digital voice recorders have a wide variety of features, so before you buy, think about which features you will need. Some of these considerations are:

- **Recording time and quality**   The maximum recording time, and therefore the size of the file that is created, varies among voice recorders. Some recorders have the capability of recording at several quality levels. In most cases, the higher the quality, the shorter amount of time you can record.

- **Size**   Some recorders are small enough to fit in a shirt pocket, while others are more substantial. If you are planning on carrying your recorder to a family reunion or all-day event, size may be an issue.

- **Storage media**   How does the recorder store the digital recording? Some recorders have memory cards, similar to those of digital cameras, on which they save the data. Others simply store it internally, and the oldest ones still use tape. Separate memory cards are the most flexible, especially if they are the same type of card as you use in your digital camera.

- **Connectivity**   How do you get the recording off the recorder and on to your computer? If it has a memory card and you have a memory card reader on your computer, that is a good solution. Another is to connect to a USB port on your computer either directly by plugging the recorder in or by using a cable.

- **Microphone quality**   Some recorders have stereo mikes so that you can record both sides of a conversation. Also, be sure to consider the distance at which your recorder can catch the sound, especially if you're going to be recording more than one person's voice.

Whatever recorder you choose, when you do a recording, be sure to include complete details about it, such as the person's name, the date on which you recorded the file, and any other pertinent data. Save the digital file in the appropriate folder on your computer and, if you are keeping a log, include a notation there as well.

CAPTURE DIGITAL IMAGES

If you have been using your digital camera as discussed earlier in this book, you know how easy it is to capture moments and edit your images. However, in addition to your digital still and video camera images, you can easily preserve old, deteriorating photos and create long-lasting digital images with a digital scanner. Many "all-in-one" printers have the capability of scanning, and stand-alone units are usually reasonable in cost. I recently scanned an image of my mother at age three and combined it with a picture of my granddaughter at the same age just to show my daughter-in-law how much they look alike.

With a scanner, you can digitize photographs; diplomas; and birth, wedding, and death certificates—almost any flat document. With a flatbed scanner, you can scan an image from a high school yearbook or pages from your Girl Scout scrapbook. Scanners work in much the same way as photocopying machines, except the result is not a paper copy but a digitized record.

When considering a scanner, look for the following:

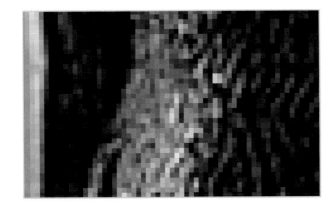

- **Resolution**   The more resolution, which is measured in pixels across by pixels down, the clearer the scanned image will be. A *pixel* is short for "picture element." A pixel is the smallest unit in a digital picture. (The German word is "bildpunkt" for which the literal translation is "picture point.") If you've ever seen a digital picture blown up or expanded so that you can see small squares, those squares are the pixels. Of course, the higher the resolution at which you scan, the larger the digital file will be. This illustration shows the "pixels" in a highly enlarged image.

- **Connectivity**   How does the scanner connect to your computer? Usually, this will be a cable to a USB port on your computer.

- **Control**   What changes or adjustments can you make to the output of the scanned image? Most scanners let you adjust brightness and contrast, while others allow for more advanced adjustments, such as enlarging, removing red eye, or heightening the original's colors.

- **Compatibility**   Will the scanner work with your operating system, for example, Windows 7 or OS X Leopard?

- **Type of scanner**   Flatbed scanners allow you to scan both flat images as well as pages from a scrapbook. Some all-in-one printers require that you feed pages in one at a time around a drum to scan the item.

- **OCR** (Optical Character Recognition)   This capability scans documents so that you can later edit the result with word-processing software. These programs work the best with large-print items; however, some scanners allow you to enlarge or "zoom in" the items being scanned. If you just want a copy of Grandma's marriage certificate, you are better off scanning it as a photograph.

- **Speed**   Depending on the resolution you choose, the speed of the scanning process can make a difference. If you are scanning in all those photos you found in Grandma Carmen's attic, you might consider a scanner with a faster-than-normal speed. Also, an automatic feeder can be handy for scanning a lot of documents.

- **Scanning software**   Most scanners and many all-in-one printers come with photo-editing software. If you have a preference or want more than basic features, consider purchasing a program with more advanced capabilities (see Chapter 7's discussion of photo-editing software; you often can use the same software).

Some scanners advertise the ability to scan film strips or slides. Be sure to read the reviews carefully before you invest in this type of scanner. Often, good film or slide scanners are more expensive than the normal consumer flatbed scanner.

E

e-books
  ePub documents, 227–228
  Kindle Reader, 228–233
  sharing between devices, 233–234
eHarmony dating service, 148–150
elections, following, 57
email. *See also* messages; Messenger;
  Windows Live Mail
  attaching files to, 112
  copying text from, 48
  creating, 102–104
  deleting, 105
  explained, 98
  filtering, 107–110
  receiving, 104–105
  responding to, 105–107
  sending, 102–104
email account, establishing, 101–102
email address, adding to Contacts
  list, 107
ePub documents, using, 227–229
events, adding to Calendar, 114–115
Excel program, using, 172–173, 270
Excel ribbon, using, 171
Excel template, creating budget
  from, 262
Excel Web App. *See also* Web Apps
  choosing chart types, 173–174
  editing workbooks in, 169–170
Excel worksheets, using, 170–172
Explorer. *See* Windows Explorer
external disk drive bay, 6

F

Facebook, using, 125–132. *See also*
  social networking
family history. *See* genealogical
  searches
Family Search website, 280
Family Tree Maker, 280
family tree templates, using, 270
familysearch.org, 276
FarmVille game, playing, 131–132
Favorites
  adding sites to, 43
  deleting items from, 49
  opening, 43
file sharing, setting up, 77–82
files
  attaching to email, 112
  contents of, 26

copying in folders, 184
deleting, 35–36
dragging to messages, 114
hiding, 83
locating, 31–33
protecting folders, 83
renaming, 35
restoring to view, 83
finance.yahoo.com, 264
financial advice, finding online, 264
financial information, finding
  online, 264
financial institutions, online
  services, 237
financial management programs
  categories, 252
  on computers, 255
  online, 256
  paying bills from, 252–253
financial services. *See* online financial
  services
Firefox web browser, 218, 228–229
firewall, setting up, 78–79
flash drives, backing up information
  to, 84–87
Flash files, playing, 223
Flash plug-in, 219
floating windows. *See also* windows
  aligning, 22
  maximizing, 22
folder sharing, setting up, 77–82
folders
  contents of, 26–27
  copying files in, 184
  creating, 36
  deleting, 35–36
  deleting in SkyDrive, 158
  displaying list of, 35
  hiding, 83
  locating, 31–33
  navigating, 33–36
  in navigation pane, 34
  protecting folders, 83
  renaming, 35
  restoring to view, 83
  selecting and opening, 32–33
  system-related, 10, 12
  user-related, 10–11
fonts, choosing for photos, 200
forum, explained, 98
funds, depositing to accounts,
  238–239

G

games, accessing, 27
genealogical group, joining,
  281–282
genealogical searches
  backing up information, 284
  capturing digital images,
    285–286
  consulting relatives, 269–270
  digital voice recorders, 282,
    284–285
  DNA testing, 282
  documenting, 280–281
  Family Search, 280
  Family Tree Maker, 280
  family tree templates, 270
  finding documents, 274–275
  foreign census records, 267–268
  learning online, 279–280
  Legacy software, 280
  organizing records, 272–275
  PAF software, 281
  Reunion software, 281
  RootsMagic software, 281
  saving data, 284
  setting up records, 271–272
  starting, 266–267, 269
  U.S. Census, 266–267, 269
  using scanners, 285–286
genealogy forms, downloading,
  271–272
genealogy websites, 276–279
genealogy.com, 276
genealogytoday.com, 276
geneasearch.com, 276
GenWeb genealogy website, 279
Google Directions, 59
Google search, 42, 54
google.com, 51
government agencies, accessing,
  56–57
grammar, checking in Word Web
  App, 166

H

hard disk, 5
hardware devices, changing
  settings, 13
Help And Support Center, 13, 26
hiding files and folders, 83
home page, changing, changing,
  44–45

homegroups
  explained, 81
  sharing libraries in, 81–82
hotmail, signing up for, 113–114
HTML formatting, using with
  messages, 111
https:// security, use in online
  banking, 249

I

IM (instant messaging). *See* Messenger
images. *See also* photos; Picasa; pictures
  printing, 203–204
  protecting in AutoPlay, 183
  zooming in Photoscape, 188
information. *See also* backing up files
  getting from Internet, 50
  saving to cloud, 87
inkjet printers, buying, 204
InPrivate feature, using in Internet
  Explorer, 96
instant messaging (IM). *See* Messenger
integrated computers, features of, 4
Internet
  Bing search engine, 43
  browser navigation, 41–42
  browsing, 40–42
  getting information, 50–51
  Google search, 42
  links, 41
  menus, 41
  opening recent pages visited, 42
  search sites, 42
  searching recipes on, 51–53
  shopping for airline tickets,
    61–65
  shopping for digital cameras,
    60–61
  site navigation, 40–41
Internet audio files, playing, 49
Internet connections
  requirements for, 38
  researching, 38
  setting up, 38–40
Internet Explorer
  adding sites to Favorites, 43
  adding sites to Favorites bar, 48
  browsing and viewing sites, 96
  categorizing websites, 93–94
  closing tabs, 45
  copying pictures from Internet,
    47–48

online financial services
 building budgets, 260–261
 investments, 257–258
 portfolios, 259–260
 producing budgets, 261–262
online identity, protecting, 132–133.
 See also social networking
online investing, 259
online portfolio, creating, 259–260
online programs, advantages of, 257
online services, preparing for, 245
optical disc drives, 3–4, 6

P

PAF genealogy software, 281
pages
 copying from Internet, 48–49
 copying text from, 48
 opening in tabs, 44
Paint program, using, 176
panes, turning on and off, 16
paper type, choosing for photos, 203
paragraphs, formatting in Word Web
 App, 168
Parental Controls
 Content Advisor, 96
 setting, 75–76, 95
password-protecting computers, 90
passwords, managing, 71–73, 132
PDF format
 reading documents in, 176–179
 saving documents in, 168
photo file types, 203
photo-editing programs, 186–187
photos. *See also* images; Picasa;
 pictures
 downloading manually, 183–184
 importing, 182
 printing, 202–204
Photoscape
 adjusting tone, 194
 auto-correction features, 192
 Backlight option, 194
 Brighten option, 194
 changing brush size, 192
 Clone Stamp tool, 191–192
 color correction, 192–194
 correcting lighting, 193
 cropping photos with, 188–190
 features of, 186–187
 getting, 187–188

scaling photos with, 188–191
 straightening photos with,
  188–190
 zooming images, 188
Picasa. *See also* images; photos
 adding photo captions, 199–200
 adding photos to albums,
  196–198
 adding text to photos, 200–202
 albums, 196
 assigning stars to images,
  196–197
 creating albums, 198
 creating online galleries, 198–199
 downloading, 187
 favorites, 197
 features of, 186–187, 197, 218
 filters, 196
 galleries vs. albums, 197
 hard drive contents, 196
 installing, 187, 195
 Library view, 197
 locating images, 198
 making headlines in photos,
  200–202
 opening images for editing, 197
 Pictures folder, 196
 resizing thumbnails, 198
 saving copies of photos, 197
 selected folder, 196
 selected photo, 196
 sharing albums, 198–200, 202
 sharing images, 202
 showing favorites, 198
 slide shows, 196–197
 tagging images, 196–197
 uploading albums, 198–200
 viewing Web Albums, 200
 Web Album privacy, 201
 zooming thumbnails, 196
pictures. *See also* images; photos
 copying from Internet, 47–48
 printing, 202–204
 selecting in Word Web App, 165
 viewing in slide shows, 184–185
plane tickets, shopping online, 61–65
playlists
 adding to mobile devices, 218
 burning, 215–217
 creating in Media Player,
  213–215
 playing back, 215
 syncing, 215–217

plug-ins, 219
podcasts, accessing, 220–221
pointing devices, 3–4
portfolios, creating online, 259–260
priceline.com, shopping on, 65
Print command, displaying, 203
printers
 changing settings, 13
 connecting, 6
 multifunction, 204
printing
 documents in Web App, 169–170
 images, 203–204
 pictures, 202–204
privileges, displaying for accounts, 71
programs. *See also* Web Apps
 associating with file types, 13
 bulk installation of, 217–219
 Calculator, 175–176
 Character Map, 176
 choosing for installation,
  217–219
 Notepad, 176
 Paint, 176–177
 running, 175
 starting, 8, 12
Project Gutenberg, 227–228

Q

Quick Access toolbar, 102
Quicken, versions of, 263–264
Quicken Bill Pay, using, 240
QuickTime, features of, 218

R

recipes, searching on Internet, 51–53
recovering files and folders, 36
Recycle Bin in Windows 7, 7
 deleting files to, 35–36
 deleting folders to, 35–36
renaming files and folders, 35
reset disk, creating and using, 73, 75
Restart option, 25
Restore option, using, 36
restoring maximized windows, 22
Reunion genealogy software, 281
ribbon, features of, 102, 165
routing numbers, finding, 250
runtimes, features of, 218–219

S

Save button, using with Word Web
 App, 166
saving
 documents in PDF format, 168
 documents in Word Web App, 166
 information to cloud service, 87
scanners, considering, 285–286
Scottrade.com, 259
screen tips, appearance of, 13
screens, features of, 3–4, 8
search boxes, 50
search engines, changing, 43
search sites, 50
searches, performing on Internet, 50–53
security. *See also* backing up files;
 UAC (User Account Control)
 activity reporting, 76
 creating reset disks, 73
 file sharing, 77–82
 folder sharing, 77–82
 locking computers, 90
 Parental Controls, 95
 protecting files, 83
 protecting folders, 83
 resetting passwords, 72–73
 setting Parental Controls, 75–76
 setting passwords, 71–72
 setting up users, 68–72
 switching among users, 74
 using reset disks, 73
 Web filtering, 76
security programs. *See also* Internet
 threats
 AVG Antivirus Free Edition,
  92–93
 AVG Internet Security, 92
 BitDefender Internet Security, 92
 Microsoft Security Essentials, 92
 using, using, 92
semicolon (;), using with
 addressees, 103
servers. *See* cloud computing
session-end choices, 10
shopping on Internet
 for airline tickets, 61–65
 for digital cameras, 60–61
shortcut keys. *See* keyboard shortcuts
Shut Down option
 clicking, 24
 explained, 25
 vs. Sleep, 25

signatures, attaching to messages, 111–112
Silverlight plug-in, 219
Simmel, George, 123
site navigation, using, 40–41
sites. *See* websites
SkyDrive cloud service, 87–89
    adding files to, 157–158
    deleting folders, 158
    folder types, 158
    logging onto, 156
    setting privacy options, 156–157
    using, 155
Sleep option, 25
slide shows, running, 185–186
Small Icon view, 68
social networking. *See also* Facebook; LinkedIn; online identity; Twitter
    among seniors, 124
    beginning of, 123–124
    "A Small Experiment," 124
Social Security Administration, contacting, 56, 238
songs
    adding to playlists, 213–214
    downloading, 207–208
southwest.com, shopping on, 65
spam, dealing with, 107–110
Speakers icon
    locating in Windows, 207
    in Windows Media Player, 211
spelling, checking in Word Web App, 166
spyware, definition and solution, 91
Standard User account, setting up, 70–72
Start button, 6–7
Start menu, 10–13
Sticky Notes, using, 176
Stop button, 6
storage devices, identifying, 31–32
styles, applying in Word Web App, 166–167
surfing the Internet, 40
Switch User option, 25
system-related folders, opening, 12

T

tabs
    closing, 45
    opening in Internet Explorer, 44
    switching among, 45–46
    using in Word Web App, 162

taskbar in Windows 7, 7, 9
taskbar previews, 18, 23
text
    adding to photos, 200–202
    copying in Word Web App, 164–165
    entering in Word Web App, 162
    moving in Word Web App, 164–165
    pasting in Word Web App, 164–165
    selecting in Word Web App, 163
text directions, changing in Word Web App, 168
Thestreet.com, 264
toptenreviews.com, 92
transaction download
    Direct Connect, 237
    Express Web Connect, 237
    Web Connect, 237
Trojan horses, defined, 91
Tudor, Mary, 50–51
TV programs
    classics, 226–227
    last night's TV, 226
    news broadcasts, 226
    pirate sites, 227
    watching online, 226–227
Twitter, using, 132–138. *See also* social networking

U

UAC (User Account Control), 68, 70. *See also* security
underline keyboard shortcut, 168
updates, downloading and installing, 24
U.S. Census, using in genealogy, 266–267, 269
USB connectors, 6
USB drives, backing up information to, 84–87
user access, controlling, 76–82
User Accounts option, accessing, 69
user accounts, setting up, 70–72
users
    changing accounts, 70
    logging on as administrator, 69
    setting up, 69
    switching among, 74
usgenweb.org, 276

V

video connector, 6
video files
    importing, 182
    playing from Internet, 49
video formats, 223
videos, YouTube, 223–226
views, changing in Control Panel, 68
viruses, definition and solution, 91
VLC media player, features of, 218

W

Wall Street Journal, 54
Web Apps. *See also* Excel Web App; programs; Word Web App
    creating documents, 159–161
    features of, 154
    printing documents in, 169–170
    using, 159–161
    Word, 159–161
Web browser plug-ins, features of, 217
Web Connect service, 237
Web filtering, accessing, 76
Web History, using in Internet Explorer, 45–46
web mail, 113
web TV. *See* TV programs
webpages
    copying from Internet, 48–49
    copying text from, 48
    opening in tabs, 44
websites
    adding to Favorites, 43
    entering directly, 40
white bean soup, searching recipe for, 51–53
window features
    address bar, 13–14
    border, 14–15
    Close button, 14–15
    details pane, 14–15
    Maximize button, 14
    Minimize button, 14
    navigation pane, 14–15
    opening, 13
    preview pane, 14–15
    scroll arrows, 14–15
    scroll bar, 14–15
    scroll button, 14–15
    sizing handle, 14–15
    subject pane, 14–15

title bar, 13–14
toolbar, 13–14
window layout, changing, 16
windows. *See also* floating windows
    closing, 24
    distinguishing from dialog boxes, 16
    maximizing, 14–15
    minimizing, 14–15, 20
    restoring, 23
Windows 7, 6
    Control Panel, 12
    controlling access to, 76–82
    desktop, 7–9
    desktop icons, 7–9
    editions, 11
    games, 27
    Help feature, 26
    mouse, 8
    mouse pointer, 7–9
    notification area, 7–8, 10
    Recycle Bin, 7
    screen, 8
    session-end choices, 10
    Start button, 7–8
    Start menu, 10–13
    starting, 7
    taskbar, 7–9
    user-related folders, 11
Windows desktop. *See* desktop
Windows Explorer
    adding playlists to mobile devices, 218
    address bar, 28
    Back button, 28
    Change Your Views, 30
    customizing, 29–31
    details pane, 28
    display options, 27
    Folder Details view, 31
    Forward button, 28
    identifying storage devices, 31–33
    Libraries folder, 33–35
    locating files, 31–33
    locating folders, 31–33
    navigating disks, 33–36
    navigating folders, 33–36
    navigation pane, 28
    opening, 29
    opening drives, 32–33
    opening folders, 32–33
    Organize menu, 30
    preview pane, 28